# THE IMPLICATIONS OF CAPITAL GAINS TAX RATE PREFERENCES

JOHN MINAS



OXFORD
UNIVERSITY PRESS
AUSTRALIA & NEW ZEALAND

OXFORD
UNIVERSITY PRESS

Oxford University Press is a department of the University of Oxford.

It furthers the University's objective of excellence in research, scholarship, and education by publishing worldwide. Oxford is a registered trademark of Oxford University Press in the UK and in certain other countries.

Published in Australia by
Oxford University Press
Level 8, 737 Bourke Street, Docklands, Victoria 3008, Australia.



Cover image by Shutterstock

Text design by Sardine Design

Printed and bound in Australia by Ligare Book Printers, Pty Ltd

# ABSTRACT

This book examines key aspects of one of the more controversial questions in tax policy: what is the appropriate way to tax capital gains? The focus of the book is the capital gains tax (CGT) rate and rate preferences. The research is by way of a review of the relevant tax literature on capital gains, followed by qualitative and quantitative studies and recommendations and conclusions. The literature review identifies an absence of empirical evidence on how Australian personal taxpayers respond to CGT rate changes. This significant gap in the knowledge is the primary motivation for this book. The qualitative study presents findings from in-depth interviews conducted with 24 CGT experts in Australia, Canada and the United States on issues related to the taxation of capital gains. In particular, it explores the role of CGT preferences. The interview data are compared with relevant tax literature as well as current practices in the three jurisdictions in taxing capital gains. The study establishes that most interviewees do not support CGT rate preferences. Armed with this background, the quantitative study uses regression analysis to estimate the capital gains realisations response in Australia, with the tax rate change of interest being the enactment of the 50% CGT discount in 1999 for personal taxpayers. The elasticity point estimates from the quantitative study support the primary hypothesis that the 50% CGT discount has caused a decrease in CGT revenue. This raises questions about the central rationale for the introduction of the CGT discount—the forecast increase in CGT revenue. The qualitative and quantitative results are drawn on to recommend a tax policy reform to improve the operation of the CGT regime in Australia: specifically, reinstating taxation of personal capital gains at marginal rates and introducing an annual exempt amount for net capital gains.

# ACKNOWLEDGMENTS

I am indebted to my PhD supervisors, Professor Chris Evans and Dr Youngdeok Lim, who provided invaluable advice and feedback over the six (part-time) years that it took to complete the thesis on which this book is based. I am grateful that my supervisors insisted on my completing the research and writing the thesis to a high standard. Their patience afforded me the opportunity to improve (and, in some cases, discard) previous drafts. Obviously, any errors or omissions that remain in the finished work are my own.

The time that I spent working on my PhD thesis coincided with the early years of my academic career. I acknowledge that the quality of the supervision of Professor Evans and Dr Lim has greatly influenced my development as a tax researcher, as has our collaboration on several conference papers and journal articles. The papers that I published as a sole author also benefited from helpful comments and advice from my supervisors.

My sincere thanks to the interviewees (who are not identified by name in this book) who agreed to participate in the qualitative study that is the subject of Chapter 4 and to the University of Tasmania for making the in-person interviews possible through the funding provided to support the project. Thanks also to the anonymous reviewers who provided useful feedback on papers related to the book that I authored or co-authored and to the editors of the journals in which those articles were published.

My thanks to all members of my PhD Annual Progress Reviews at the University of New South Wales in the years 2013 to 2016: Binh Tran-Nam, Dale Boccabella, Gordon MacKenzie, Kalmen Datt, Michael Walpole, Neil Warren and Pamela Hanrahan.

# TABLE OF CONTENTS

# LIST OF TABLES

# LIST OF FIGURES

# PUBLICATIONS

This book draws upon various publications I have authored or co-authored. These publications are as follows:

(1) Evans, C., Minas, J., & Lim, Y. (2015). Taxing personal capital gains in Australia: An alternative way forward. *Australian Tax Forum, 30*(4), 735–61.

(2) Minas, J. (2014). Data choice in capital gains realisation response studies – a review. *Journal of the Australasian Tax Teachers Association, 9*(1), 157–79.

(3) Minas, J. & Lim, Y. (2013). Taxing capital gains – views from Australia, Canada and the United States. *e-Journal of Tax Research, 11*(2), 191–215.

(4) Minas, J. (2011). Taxing personal capital gains in Australia – is the discount ready for reform? *Journal of the Australasian Tax Teachers Association, 6*(1), 59–67.

(5) Minas, J., Lim, Y., & Evans, C. (2018). The impact of tax rate changes on capital gains realisations: evidence from Australia. *Australian Tax Forum, 33*(4), 635–66.

# LIST OF ACRONYMS AND ABBREVIATIONS

| | |
|---|---|
| **ABS** | Australian Bureau of Statistics |
| **AEA** | Annual exempt amount |
| **AGI** | Adjusted gross income |
| **ATO** | Australian Taxation Office |
| **CBO** | Congressional Budget Office (United States of America) |
| **CGT** | Capital gains tax |
| **GFC** | Global financial crisis |
| ***ITAA1936*** | *Income Tax Assessment Act 1936* (Cth) |
| ***ITAA1997*** | *Income Tax Assessment Act 1997* (Cth) |
| **IV** | Instrumental variables |
| **JCT** | Joint Committee of Taxation (United States of America) |
| **OLS** | Ordinary least squares |
| **Ralph Review** | Ralph Review of Business Taxation |
| ***TRA86*** | *Tax Reform Act of 1986* (United States of America) |
| ***TRA97*** | *Taxpayer Relief Act of 1997* (United States of America) |
| **U.K.** | United Kingdom |
| **U.S.** | United States of America |

# CHAPTER 1

# Introduction

## 1.1 OVERVIEW

The definition of capital gains and losses and their treatment for tax purposes are two of the most controversial policy issues that confront every income tax system (Avi-Yonah, Sartori & Marian, 2011). An equally controversial issue, which has received surprisingly little attention outside of the United States, is the responsiveness of capital gains realisations to changes in the tax rate. Although previous research has referred to an inverse relationship between tax rates and realisations, there has been some debate over the degree to which tax rates affect the level of realisations. The appeal of a large realisations response for policy makers is that it implies a capital gains tax (CGT[1]) rate cut that is self-financing. Conversely, a CGT rate cut where there is only a moderate realisations response can lose tax revenue. While it is accepted that raising revenue is not the only purpose of a CGT regime, all governments need to be mindful of the revenue implications that can eventuate when CGT rates are changed, particularly in times of economic austerity (Evans, 2002).

This book is concerned with the taxation of capital gains and the responsiveness of personal taxpayers in Australia to changes in the CGT rate.

The rationale for taxing capital gains rests principally in one of two modern economic approaches to taxation. The first approach is the Schanz-Haig-Simons concept of comprehensive income, under which income is the 'algebraic sum of (1) the market value of rights exercised in consumption and (2) the change in the value of the store of property rights between the beginning and end of the period in question' (Simons, 1938, p. 50). Under this approach, the taxation of capital gains is in the same manner, and at the same rate, as any other form of income.

The second approach, optimal tax theory, holds, in some instances, that no capital income taxation is appropriate (Chamley, 1986; Judd, 1985). Evans, Minas and Lim (2015)

1 In many jurisdictions, capital gains are not taxed under a separate tax—rather they are taxed under the income tax provisions. Nonetheless, capital gains tax—or CGT—is used as a convenient shorthand throughout this book to refer to the taxation of capital gains, whether under a separate tax or as part of the income tax.

noted that some proponents of this approach appear to accept that it may be appropriate to tax capital income, albeit at lower rates than those applicable to ordinary income.[2]

The definition of a capital gain is a pivotal issue in taxation. Depending on the type of tax system in operation, the definitional boundary between income and capital gains can have implications for the ability of the tax system to meet its revenue raising objectives. There is an incentive for taxpayers to receive more of their income in the form of capital gains where these are subject to preferential tax treatment.[3] Furthermore, there is an added incentive to re-characterise what would otherwise be ordinary income as capital gains.

The focus of this book is on the rate of CGT rather than the definitional issue of the CGT base. The definitional issue is outside the scope of this book, notwithstanding that tax reform aimed at redefining the CGT base in Australia may be worthwhile. The quantitative research in this book is concerned with how CGT rate changes affect the realisation decisions of personal taxpayers and, in turn, how these rate changes affect CGT revenue collected from personal taxpayers.

A comprehensive regime for taxing capital gains has been a feature of Australia's taxation system for more than 30 years. The 1975 report of the Taxation Review Committee (also referred to as the 'Asprey Report'[4]) referred to one of the primary arguments for a CGT: in a tax system such as Australia's, in which ability to pay is the primary test of liability, it would be inequitable to exempt capital gains from tax (Commonwealth Taxation Review Committee & Asprey, 1975). The *Draft White Paper*, which preceded the introduction of the Australian CGT in 1985, correctly identified that a tax system without a CGT violates the principles of horizontal and vertical equity and distorts investment decisions by encouraging investment in assets with returns in the form of capital gains over other types of investment (Commonwealth Treasury, 1985). Virtually all developed countries now have CGT regimes in place as a key part of their tax systems, as do most developing countries. According to Cooper and Evans (2014), 167 out of 219 countries had a CGT regime in place in 2014.

The Australian CGT regime commenced on 20 September 1985 as a statutory means of bringing capital gains into the income tax base. Prior to the introduction of CGT, tax avoidance in Australia was encouraged by the tax-free status of capital gains, which, in turn, led to an erosion of the tax base. The earlier legislative provisions that attempted to capture certain types of asset disposals—the former s 26(a) and the former s 26AAA[5] of the *Income Tax Assessment Act 1936* (Cth) (*ITAA1936*)—were, arguably, relatively unsuccessful in achieving this (Cooper & Evans, 2014).

2 For a useful overview of the comprehensive income versus optimal tax theory arguments, and their impact upon capital gains taxation reform proposals in six countries (Australia, Italy, the Netherlands, New Zealand, South Africa and the United Kingdom), see White (2015).

3 Another potential benefit of receiving income in the form of capital gains relates to the discretion that taxpayers have in the timing of realising their capital gains.

4 The Asprey Report first recommended a CGT for Australia.

5 The then Whitlam Government enacted section 26AAA in 1973. The provision was intended to bring into assessment casual profits that had been realised on assets held for less than 12 months.

The CGT provisions of the *Income Tax Assessment Act 1997* (Cth) (*ITAA1997*) have adopted a prescriptive approach to defining what is a capital gain. A capital gain is determined by reference to Division 104 of the *ITAA1997*, which contains a legislative list of 'CGT events' that can give rise to either a capital gain or capital loss.[6] The alternative approach, which the Australian legislators did not adopt in the 1997 Act, would have been to define a capital gain using broad principles. In Australia, taxpayers are liable for tax on their net capital gains under s 102-5(1) of the *ITAA1997*, which operates to include the net capital gains of taxpayers in their assessable income.

From 20 September 1985 until the introduction of the 50% CGT discount regime on 21 September 1999, the capital gains of Australian personal taxpayers were taxed at a taxpayer's highest marginal income tax rate. The indexation system allowed for an inflation adjustment to the cost base[7] of the CGT asset. Since 21 September 1999, the 50% CGT discount has applied to capital gains where the personal taxpayer has held the asset subject to the CGT event for at least 12 months (Div. 115 of the *ITAA1997*).[8] The former Howard Government introduced the 50% CGT discount on the recommendation of the 1999 Ralph Review of Business Taxation (also referred to as the 'Ralph Review').

Given that a separate tax for capital gains is not a feature of the Australian tax system, there is a relationship between the tax rate on ordinary income and the tax rate on capital gains. Since the enactment of the CGT discount in September 1999, capital gains have been subject to tax at half the taxpayer's top marginal tax rate on other taxable income. However, the term 'CGT discount' can be considered a somewhat inaccurate description, given Australia's approach to taxing capital gains. Rather than capital gains being taxed at a 'discount' rate, the taxpayer includes 50% of eligible net capital gains in their assessable income.

The research in this book is concerned with the effects of the 50% CGT discount for personal taxpayers in Australia. Chapter 5 notes that the marginal rates of tax, and rate brackets, have changed during the years of the study.

The introduction of the CGT discount for personal taxpayers did not eliminate the choice of using the indexation method.[9] However, since indexation was 'frozen' at the September 1999 quarter when the CGT discount was introduced, the benefit of using the indexation method has diminished over time. Most net capital gains of personal taxpayers are discount capital gains. At the individual taxpayer level, there are two possible reasons for this: (1) that the discount method gives a better result than the indexation method where a choice of methods is available; or (2) the choice between the two methods is not available because of the timing of the acquisition of the asset subject to the CGT event.[10]

---

6 It is also possible for a CGT event to give rise to neither a capital gain nor loss.

7 Cost base is an Australian term for what is referred to as basis in the United States and Canada.

8 Where a capital gain is calculated using the discount method, indexation does not apply. Certain CGT events are ineligible for the CGT discount.

9 Depending on the timing of the CGT acquisition event, taxpayers can choose either the discount or the indexation method. Where the discount method is chosen, the cost base cannot be indexed as per s 115-20(1) of the *Income Tax Assessment Act 1997* (Cth).

10 Furthermore, some capital gains do not qualify for the discount method or the indexation method.

The literature identifies two broadly competing ideological views on CGT rates. First, proponents of preferential CGT rates have argued for CGT rates that are lower than tax rates on ordinary income. As noted by the U.S. Congressional Budget Office (CBO) (1990), the case for preferential CGT rates is usually linked to providing an incentive for entrepreneurship and risk-taking, increasing the level of saving, investment and productivity and counteracting the 'lock-in effect'. The lock-in effect is the incentive for individuals to defer realisations when the marginal tax cost of selling the asset is more than the marginal gain arising from selling the asset (Zodrow, 1992). Gravelle (1994) identified the lock-in effect as the primary argument for reducing CGT. Nevertheless, it is only where the lock-in effect is found to be powerful that measures should be taken to reduce it (Gravelle, 1994). If the lock-in effect is modest, the case for reducing CGT rates is weaker on both welfare grounds and revenue yield grounds (Gravelle, 1994).

Second, there is the view that, in the interests of overall tax system integrity and horizontal and vertical equity, capital gains should be subject to the same rate of tax as ordinary income. If a tax jurisdiction adopted a pure comprehensive income system, the taxation of capital gains as these accrue would be required. However, the impracticalities of taxation on an accrual basis—because of liquidity and valuation issues—have prevented the adoption of an accrual-based CGT in Australia and most other comparable jurisdictions.[11]

The problems with horizontal equity arise partly because of differences in the taxation of capital gains compared to other forms of passive income, such as bank interest. In Australia, for example, bank interest is taxable at full marginal tax rates, whereas accrued capital gains are not subject to tax and realised capital gains are subject to tax at preferential rates. Given that from an economic perspective there is no difference between these accretions to wealth, an equitable tax system would require the same rate of taxation for each.

CGT preferences lead to vertical inequity because higher-income taxpayers accrue and realise higher proportions of capital gains. It follows that a tax system will not be vertically equitable if lower-income taxpayers are liable to tax on their income at a higher overall rate, simply because capital gains comprise a smaller proportion of their total income compared to higher-income taxpayers.

The remainder of this book examines the issues raised in this introduction in more detail.

## 1.2 AIMS OF THE RESEARCH

The research in this book aims to fill an empirical gap in the existing knowledge on the taxation of capital gains. The focus of the book is on the responsiveness of capital gains realisations to tax rate changes for personal taxpayers in Australia. This book examines

11 In Australia, the Asprey Report noted that 'the impracticability of taxing capital gains as they accrue is universally recognised: the tax can only attempt to deal with realised gains' (Commonwealth Taxation Review Committee & Asprey, 1975, p. 570). Despite the reluctance of tax jurisdictions to tax capital gains as they accrue, there are examples of accruals taxation of capital gains. For example, New Zealand taxes financial arrangements on an accruals basis, and it uses the comparative value method (an accruals basis) for the taxation of foreign investment funds.

an original research question in the Australian context: what are the effects of CGT rate preferences on the capital gains realisations of personal taxpayers? This book consists of a mixed methods research design in two phases. The first is a qualitative interview study that examines and analyses the views of experts on CGT. The second is an econometric capital gains realisations response study. The findings of each component are presented in separate chapters and the research findings from these two separate methodologies can be considered complementary.

The research in this book advances existing knowledge on the effect of CGT rate changes on capital gains realisations in Australia. Generally, tax reform in Australia has been undertaken with regard to the accepted traditional criteria of a 'good' tax system, namely efficiency, horizontal and vertical equity, simplicity and fiscal adequacy. Although it is usually not possible for each specific aspect of tax reform to meet all of these criteria, the tax system should ideally possess all these characteristics to some degree. There is a trade-off between some of the individual traditional tax system criteria and the choice of which criteria a specific tax reform should focus on. The priorities of the government of the day may be reflected in such a trade-off process. Cooper and Evans (2014) noted that, in relation to CGT, the criteria of equity, efficiency and simplicity could be better achieved in Australia than they are in the current regime.

Part of the motivation for this book is the view that the 50% CGT discount is a feature of tax policy that performs poorly against all of these traditional tax system criteria. In Australia, there has been a lack of empirical research on the revenue effects of the CGT discount. The results of this book are relevant to the revenue effects of the CGT discount and to whether the CGT discount achieves the tax policy goal of fiscal adequacy. The responsiveness of realisations to CGT rate changes is critical to efficiency analyses of CGT. Generally, the link between efficiency and CGT is that, where the realisations response is large, there are large efficiency costs caused by the lock-in effect of CGT (Zodrow, 1992). However, this is a simplification of overall efficiency costs given that the efficiency implications are broader, since CGT affects several economic decisions other than those related to the lock-in effect (Zodrow, 1992). An example of a more general efficiency issue is the extent to which changes in the CGT rate would change the allocation of capital in the economy (Zodrow, 1992).

The term elasticity, in the context of this book, refers to the responsiveness of the realisations of capital gains by taxpayers to a change in the effective CGT rate.[12] Cunningham and Schenk (1993) described the realisations response of capital gains as important on political, economic and fiscal grounds. According to Gravelle (2010), if capital gains realisations are found to be highly elastic in the long run (typically in excess of one or two years), there may be some justification for taxing capital gains at rates lower than those on ordinary income.[13] In theory, a capital gains realisations response that is high in magnitude may allow a reduction of the CGT rate at no cost to the

12 Specifically, it measures the percentage change in the rate of capital gains asset realisations relative to the percentage change in the CGT rate.

13 Such a justification would relate to the fiscal adequacy considerations of the CGT rate: it would not necessarily consider the other tax policy criteria.

Australian Government. The capital gains realisations response is an important area of CGT policy because taxpayers have discretion on whether and when to realise a capital gain.[14] Furthermore, the revenue effects of CGT rate reductions are an aspect of tax policy that has been subject to extensive debate, arguably more so in the United States than in Australia. The greater interest in this topic in the United States may be partly explained by the *Revenue Act 1978*; this legislation required the U.S. Treasury Department to complete a study of the economic revenue effects of the CGT rate reductions that were part of that Act.[15] Notwithstanding the absence of an equivalent statute to the *Revenue Act 1978* in Australia, empirical evidence on the capital gains realisations response should inform Australian policy makers' decisions on CGT rate changes. For example, in the event that a large rate reduction is likely to lead to revenue losses, there may be a case for not enacting the rate reduction or enacting a rate reduction of a lesser magnitude.

Despite the debate that has taken place in the United States, there is arguably a lack of conclusive empirical evidence for large capital gains realisations responses in the long run. Although some of the earlier U.S. capital gains realisations response studies estimated large responses, analysis of these results indicated that, in some cases, they were inconsistent with the actual response.[16]

The research in this book may be informative to forecasting the revenue effects of a future change in the 50% CGT discount rate or a change in the effective CGT rate achieved by other means; for example, the introduction of a separate CGT schedule and rates. Revenue effects have been, and continue to be, an important consideration for tax policy makers in deciding the level at which to set CGT rates, as they relate to the tax policy consideration of fiscal adequacy. However, there are several other tax policy considerations inextricably linked with CGT policy, including the traditional criteria for a good tax system of economic efficiency, vertical and horizontal equity and simplicity. It is arguable that these other tax policy considerations are of greater importance than revenue in the case of CGT. For example, according to Cooper and Evans (2014, p.18), 'from a policy perspective the essential role of a CGT is not to raise revenue.' Zodrow (1992) described the literature's focus on the revenue issues associated with capital gains as unusual, although not unsurprising given the interaction of the question of revenue with other areas of policy concern.

The mixed methods research in this book aims to be informative to CGT policy in Australia. Specifically, the interview study in Chapter 4 provides insights into taxing capital gains from CGT experts in three tax jurisdictions, including Australia. Although political considerations are often an influence on the formulation of tax policy, the Chapter 4 study explores the issue of taxing capital gains through a more objective perspective.

14 Because most CGT systems operate on a realisation basis, the tax can be avoided for as long as the taxpayer does not realise their capital gain. Despite this, in practice taxpayers choose to realise capital gains. This may be because of a need to realise capital gains for consumption purposes or because there are other assets that provide a better rate of after-tax return.

15 The report was not released until 1985; see U.S. Department of Treasury, Office of the Secretary of the Treasury, Office of Tax Analysis. (September 1985).

16 More detail on this point is contained in Chapter 2.

The quantitative research in Chapter 5 is concerned with estimating the capital gains realisations response, and the findings will allow policy makers to make informed decisions on future CGT policy. In particular, the findings will be useful for decisions about the rate at which to tax capital gains for personal taxpayers.[17]

## 1.3 SIGNIFICANCE OF THE RESEARCH

The research is significant because it can inform future CGT policy in Australia by providing empirical evidence on the capital gains realisations response and, in turn, the revenue effects of CGT rate changes. The potential audiences for the research include politicians, tax policy makers,[18] revenue authorities[19] and tax academics. The research may be of particular relevance to politicians and tax policy makers, as the revenue effects of the CGT are of increased importance in a deficit budget environment. Although, as explained by Dowd, McClelland and Muthitacharoen (2012), it is difficult to estimate the elasticity of capital gains realisations, the results of the quantitative study in this book provide an empirical basis for determining the accuracy of the Ralph Review's prediction of no loss of revenue resulting from the 50% CGT discount. The results of the Chapter 5 study may be broadly informative to the question of what impact CGT rate changes may have in the future. Moreover, research relating to the revenue collected from CGT for personal taxpayers will be of interest to tax policy makers and administrators.

The research is also significant because of its potential impact on the debate in the tax literature and in public policy on the most appropriate rate at which to tax capital gains. As noted earlier, there are two opposing views of the optimal rate for CGT. One view is that, in accordance with Schanz-Haig-Simons comprehensive income concepts and in the interests of overall tax system integrity, capital gains should be subject to the same tax rate as ordinary income.[20] Feldstein (1976) noted that the Haig-Simons[21] standards of comprehensive income are concerned with the tax base rather than the tax rate, with all departures from the standard considered tax preferences, tax expenditures or an erosion of the tax base. An example of a departure leading to a narrowing of the tax base is the 'realisation principle' whereby income is recognised only when it is realised rather than when it accrues (Auerbach, 2010).

There is no known example of a tax system that strictly applies the Schanz-Haig-Simons definition of income, given that this income concept necessitates the taxation of capital gains on an accruals basis. However, taxation of capital gains at full rates is as close to the Schanz-Haig-Simons standard as possible in a realisation-based CGT system.

17 The CGT discount determines the CGT rate in the current CGT regime for personal taxpayers in Australia.

18 In particular, the Australian Treasury.

19 In particular, the Australian Taxation Office.

20 Australia's CGT regime that taxed capital gains at the same rate as ordinary income from September 1985–September 1999 is not a 'pure' comprehensive income system. This is because such a system would require the taxation of capital gains as they accrue.

21 Although the book refers to Schanz-Haig-Simons where possible, in this case the cited article refers to Haig-Simons.

The opposing view is that capital gains should be taxed at lower rates than those applying to ordinary income, usually on the grounds of providing an incentive for saving and entrepreneurship and to prevent the flight of highly mobile capital. The arguments about capital mobility can be considered a low-order concern as Australian resident personal taxpayers are assessed on their worldwide income. Therefore, if an Australian resident taxpayer decided that their capital investments should be located in lower taxing jurisdictions than Australia, they would still be subject to tax in Australia on the capital gains from these investments.[22]

The research is significant in light of the fact that the introduction of the 50% CGT discount in 1999 was a tax policy change made in the absence of empirical evidence about the capital gains realisations response for personal taxpayers in Australia. Notwithstanding that there were no Australian data on the effect of CGT rate changes available at the time, the predicted revenue effects that the Ralph Review relied on were optimistic as they were predicated on short- and long-run elasticities that were high in magnitude.[23] Since there are now suitable data available for an empirical capital gains realisations response study, this would be an effective way of informing future CGT rate policy. It is preferable for any future CGT effective rate changes to be based on empirical evidence about the revenue effects of the rate change. The capital gains realisations response study in this book provides information to policy makers and others about the revenue effects of CGT rate changes. This is important if a loss of CGT revenue is an outcome that policy makers wish to avoid.

A CGT rate cut causes a loss of revenue where there is no accompanying behavioural response; such a revenue loss is referred to as the static loss. If a CGT rate cut is to be revenue neutral, this requires a level of behavioural response that is sufficient in magnitude to offset the static revenue loss. The behavioural response in this case is additional realisations induced by the rate cut.

The extent to which CGT rate cuts increase realisations is potentially confounded by the incentive for taxpayers to convert income receipts into capital gains, which can be considered a secondary behavioural response. If a proportion of taxpayers successfully undertake this conversion practice, the realisations response can be overstated, since these types of realised capital gains are not those induced by a CGT rate cut. It can be argued that the potential for overall tax revenue losses eventuating from the introduction of the 50% CGT discount, and the resultant tax avoidance and minimisation that it encourages, has not been given due consideration by the policy makers who introduced the reform. Ideally, policy makers would have taken a cautious view of any predictions of a potentially large realisations response since Australia had no previous experience with a change in the CGT rate in 1999,[24] and there was a lack of empirical research informing the introduction

22 In each case, this would depend on the applicable tax treaty, but in most cases tax on capital is on a residence rather than source basis. It is also notable that Australia limits the scope of the capital gains of non-resident personal taxpayers that are subject to taxation.

23 Furthermore, it is unclear whether the long-run elasticity forecast by the Ralph Review is, in fact, revenue positive. The later chapters discuss this point in more detail.

24 Arguably, an earlier CGT rate change occurred in 1985 when the CGT was introduced in Australia. That is, taxpayers who had previously had a CGT rate of zero were taxed at their top marginal tax rate following the

of the 50% CGT discount. Gravelle (1990) noted that where revenue forecasts are based on elasticities that are too high, the result is an increase in the budget deficit.[25]

The significance of the research in this book is that it empirically examines the question of the capital gains realisations response. The study in Chapter 5 uses the available data on CGT realisations in Australia to test the hypotheses as outlined in this chapter. This book is the first comprehensive study of its type in the Australian context.

The environment at the time of conducting the research is one where several broadly comparable OECD countries, such as Australia, Canada, the United Kingdom and the United States, are taxing capital gains at preferential rates. This may be due to tax policy reasons or to political imperatives for low tax rates generally or perhaps to a combination of the two factors. One of the aims of the research is to investigate the problem of how to tax capital gains. Although the literature has examined this question, this book is the first to examine the specific issue of the capital gains realisations response for personal taxpayers in Australia.

The rate at which to set CGT is part of a broader tax policy question on capital income taxation: how important it is to reduce tax rates on capital income (Gravelle, 1994). Bosworth (1984) identified that the average tax rate on capital income within the personal tax system is lower than the prevailing tax rate on capital gains. This is due to no CGT applying to gains that are deferred and because some items escape CGT altogether, such as a personal taxpayer's main residence.

The qualitative and quantitative research in this book is intended to be an influence on CGT policy in Australia. A motivation for the research is the fact that the 50% CGT discount has not been subject to empirical scrutiny. The research is highly topical given that, in the lead-up to the 2016 federal election in Australia, reform of the CGT discount was clearly a tax policy issue. Specifically, the Opposition Leader Bill Shorten announced a policy to reduce the 50% CGT discount to a 25% CGT discount, to take effect from July 2017, in the event that the Labor Party formed government.[26] This announcement was the first known instance where an Australian prime minister or opposition leader proposed a change in the rate of the CGT discount since its enactment in September 1999.

## 1.4 SCOPE OF THE RESEARCH

This book is concerned with CGT, particularly CGT rate preferences, in the Australian context. The scope of the book is limited to personal taxpayers; other entities (such as companies, partnerships, trusts and funds) are excluded.

introduction of CGT. This is notwithstanding the fact that there was no comprehensive CGT in Australia before September 1985.

25 Although Gravelle was referring to the U.S. context, the principle is the same for Australia.

26 This policy was announced as part of a tax reform package that included restricting negative gearing where the asset is a 'newly constructed home' (Keany, 2016). The Labor Party was not successful in forming government after the 2016 election. The policy to reduce the CGT discount from 50% to 25% remained a policy of the Labor Party during the 2019 federal election campaign.

Australia is the principal focus of the book. The quantitative study in Chapter 5 and the principal policy recommendations made in Chapter 6 are limited to Australia. The scope of the qualitative study in Chapter 4 is Australia, Canada and the United States. The results of Chapter 4 may be of greater interest to readers outside of Australia.

The quantitative study in Chapter 5 is concerned with the capital gains realisations of Australian personal taxpayers.[27] The 50% CGT discount is not available to companies. Given that partnerships and trusts are not separate taxable entities, the scope of the study does not include these entities. In most years for which *Taxation Statistics* (an annual publication of the Australian Taxation Office) are available, the amount of taxable capital gains realised by personal taxpayers is more than the amount realised by companies.[28] Funds typically realise a lower amount of taxable net capital gains than personal taxpayers and companies.

Although the 50% CGT discount applies to trusts, the taxation of trust income will fall to either the beneficiaries or the trustee of the trust, not to the trust entity. According to the Australian Taxation Office (2016), only a small proportion of net trust income is taxable to trustees,[29] with the largest proportion taxable to beneficiaries. Irrespective of these proportions, some of the capital gains made by trusts will be taxable to personal taxpayers who may be either beneficiaries or trustees. Beneficiaries can also be companies and these entities do not qualify for the 50% discount. The tax treatment of trusts is such that the results of the study in this book are not compromised by their non-inclusion. A trust is not a separate taxable entity in Australia.

The data used in the research are the CGT data for Australian personal taxpayers taken from *Taxation Statistics*. The quantitative study in Chapter 5 uses aggregate data for the taxpayer population, rather than micro data from personal tax returns.[30] The data are used in an empirical elasticity study to estimate the capital gains realisations response of personal taxpayers to the change in the real CGT rate that commenced in September 1999. Estimating the capital gains realisations response by way of an elasticity study is consistent with the approach used in other jurisdictions. The United States is a prominent example of where this has been the main methodological approach.

The capital gains realisations response study in this book includes all capital gains assets and is not limited to certain types of assets such as shares. This is consistent with the methodology used in recent studies conducted elsewhere. Although there are examples of earlier elasticity studies that limited the type of CGT asset to shares, these have been criticised on the basis that they may overstate the realisations response because they exclude certain types of assets.

27 Although these taxpayers are also referred to as 'individuals,' the term personal taxpayers has been used throughout the book for consistency.

28 For example, *Taxation Statistics* for 2013–14 indicates that personal taxpayers realised approximately $33 billion in net capital gains in 2013–14, compared to approximately $16 billion for companies in the same year.

29 In 2010–11, the net income of trusts was $151,240,897,717 and the taxable income assessed to resident trustee taxpayers was approximately $1,617 million.

30 Micro data were not available for use in the study, due to the work program of the Australian Taxation Office.

The results of the research in this book will be of relevance for Australian policy makers in terms of potential application to tax policy design. Specifically, the results provide empirical evidence of the realisations response of CGT rate changes for Australian personal taxpayers. This evidence is useful for imputing possible revenue effects of a proposed CGT rate change. At the time of the introduction of the 50% CGT discount, there was an erroneous attempt to selectively apply the results of capital gains realisations response studies from the United States to the Australian context. Reynolds (1999) suggested that an average elasticity estimate from various U.S. realisations response studies had some application to CGT policy in Australia.

The book does not claim to be an exhaustive analysis of all issues in the taxation of capital gains. The theoretically correct treatment of capital gains and the correctness, or otherwise, of the definition of capital gains under Australian tax law are outside the scope of this book. Although the principal relevance of the research in this book is to Australia, it will nonetheless have conceptual, if not empirical, relevance to other jurisdictions.

## 1.5 RESEARCH DESIGN

This section outlines the research design for the book. A detailed description of the methodology is contained in Chapter 3.

This book uses a mixed methods approach, consisting of a qualitative component—a series of interviews with CGT experts in three comparable tax jurisdictions—and a quantitative component—an empirical study of the capital gains realisations response for personal taxpayers in Australia. Each of these components is now briefly considered.

### Qualitative study

The first phase of the research reports the results of a series of interviews with CGT experts in three comparable tax jurisdictions—Australia, Canada and the United States. The interviewees are academics, tax practitioners and tax economists.

The purpose of the qualitative phase of the research is to lead into, and complement, the quantitative phase. The qualitative phase considers broader issues in the taxation of capital gains in comparison with the quantitative phase. The focus of Chapter 5 is on a specific aspect of CGT and the quantitative study in that chapter is informed by the qualitative research in Chapter 4.

Previous studies on capital gains realisations have exclusively used a quantitative methodology. The fact that this book includes a qualitative component is considered to add to its originality and contribution.

### Quantitative study

The second phase of the research uses a quantitative methodology in the form of an empirical study on the capital gains realisations response. The methodology for the quantitative study has been determined following a review of the literature regarding similar elasticity studies that previously have been undertaken in the United States. The methodologies used in the U.S. studies may require modification so they are relevant to the

Australian tax system.[31] The study uses aggregate time series data to estimate the capital gains realisations response for Australian personal taxpayers.

In providing an empirical estimate of realisations response, the research seeks to establish whether the 50% CGT discount has been successful in achieving its original objective of revenue neutrality. If the discount has caused lost revenue, a related question is whether a reduction in the rate of the 50% CGT discount would increase revenue.[32] Prior to the enactment of the 50% CGT discount in 1999, the level of CGT realisations for personal taxpayers fluctuated significantly without any corresponding change in the statutory rate of CGT. This implies that there are factors other than the CGT rate that are determinants of the realisation of capital gains by taxpayers. In recognition of this fact—and consistent with the approach used in previous realisations response studies—the quantitative study in this book is controlled for non-tax factors that influence capital gains realisations.

The approach of previously conducted realisations response studies has been a regression analysis of capital gains realisations against CGT rates as well as other variables that influence capital gains realisations. These may include wealth, a stock market index, income or gross domestic product (GDP) and, in the case of panel data studies, demographic information about personal taxpayers (Auten & Cordes, 1991). Regression analysis is a statistical technique that estimates the relationship between variables.

There are a number of methodological choices in relation to the data type used in capital gains realisations response studies. These include the use of cross-sectional, time series or panel data,[33] or pooled time series cross-sectional data. A study using cross-sectional data is concerned with the realisation behaviour of a large number of taxpayers in one year. Studies that use time series data analyse realisations over a number of years using aggregate tax return data. In a panel data study, the capital gains realisations of each taxpayer in the panel are observed for a number of years. A fourth alternative is using pooled cross-sectional time series data; these are separate samples of a taxpayer population for a sequence of years. As a new sample is drawn for each year of the study, individual personal taxpayers cannot be tracked between years.

Time series is the preferred type of analysis for the study in this book for reasons explained in Chapter 2.

## 1.6 STRUCTURE

This chapter provided an introduction to and overview of the book. A description of the structure of the remainder of the book is as follows. Chapter 2 is a review of the literature on taxing capital gains and CGT rate preferences, followed by a review of the literature on capital gains realisations response studies. Most of the existing literature on the capital gains realisations response has originated from the United States. Chapter 2 also considers

31 For example, state income taxes, which have been included in some of the U.S. studies, have no application to Australia.

32 A reduction in the rate of the CGT discount would result in an increase in the tax rate on capital gains.

33 Panel data are also referred to as longitudinal data.

the benefits of the main data choices for the capital gains realisations response study in this book.

Chapter 3 describes the mixed methods research design used in this book. The chapter includes explanations of the two phases of research—the qualitative component of the research and the quantitative capital gains realisations response study—and provides justifications for using a mixed methods research design. Following this, the application of research paradigms to the research questions and the hypotheses are set out in the chapter.

Chapter 4 reports on the results of the qualitative phase of the research: the interview study. In this chapter, the links between the interview responses and the existing literature are explored. The implications of the experts' views on CGT for tax policy makers are considered, and the themes that lead into the quantitative study that follows are identified.

Chapter 5 reports and explains the empirical results of the capital gains realisations response study. This chapter quantifies the long-run elasticity of capital gains realisations in the form of elasticity point estimates.

Chapter 6 presents policy options and recommendations based on the conclusions of the quantitative and qualitative studies in Chapters 4 and 5.

Chapter 7 is the final chapter of the book. This chapter discusses the contribution to knowledge, the limitations of the studies conducted and possible opportunities for future research.

# CHAPTER 2

# A Review of the Literature on Taxing Capital Gains

## 2.1 INTRODUCTION

The purpose of this chapter is twofold. First, it reviews the literature on the taxation of capital gains, with particular attention to CGT rate preferences. Second, it reviews the literature on capital gains realisations response studies in order to identify the main gaps in the knowledge that the book subsequently explores.[1]

The structure of this chapter is as follows:

- Section 2.2 contains a brief description of the issues in taxing capital gains relevant to this book.
- Section 2.3 is a critique of preferential rate capital gains and a discussion of the background to elasticity and capital gains.
- Section 2.4 sets out a review of capital gains realisations response studies.
- Section 2.5 considers the revenue effects of the 50% CGT discount.
- Section 2.6 draws on the preceding analysis to develop and specify the research questions and hypotheses for the book.

## 2.2 TAXING CAPITAL GAINS: THE DEFINITION AND BASE

The focus of the quantitative study in this book is the capital gains realisations response for personal taxpayers. One of the key elements of the research—the effects of CGT rate preferences on the capital gains realisations of personal taxpayers—is part of the broader issue of what capital gains are and the possible approaches to taxing capital gains. This is especially the case as the propensity of taxpayers to realise capital gains may be unrelated

1 Part of this chapter draws on and considerably extends a previously published journal article. See Minas (2014).

to other desirable characteristics of tax systems such as efficiency, vertical and horizontal equity and simplicity.

Although tax systems such as Australia's distinguish between capital gains and other forms of income, Krever and Brooks (1990, p. 1) noted that 'it is difficult to delineate the boundaries of the concept and invariably a highly diverse set of gains have to be included in the concept.' According to Avi-Yonah and Zelik (2015, p. 40) 'the main problems with (CGT) have been the difficulty of distinguishing between capital gains and ordinary income and taxpayers' attempts to convert ordinary income into capital gain.' On this point, they noted that taxpayers continue to use tax shelters to achieve such results notwithstanding the existence of tax provisions and judicial doctrines designed to prevent them (Avi-Yonah & Zelik, 2015).

Another issue that confounds the efficient, equitable and simple taxation of capital gains is that not all capital gains are realised annually (Krever & Brooks, 1990). The definition of a capital gain or loss is partly dependent on whether the accrual model or realisation model is used. Under the accrual model, a capital gain is the increased value of an asset, regardless of whether that asset is converted into cash or an equivalent (Avi-Yonah et al., 2011). Under the realisation model, a capital gain or loss is the income or loss resulting from the disposal of an asset or from any other realisation event (Avi-Yonah et al., 2011). Policy makers worldwide have been reluctant to adopt the accrual model in the taxation of capital gains, notwithstanding the fact that its merits are well documented in the literature (Burman, 2009; Krever & Brooks, 1990). According to Krever and Brooks (1990), there is no tax equity concept that requires a distinction between an accrued and realised gain. Most revenue authorities tax capital gains on realisation, and the definition of what constitutes a capital gain realisation can be complex.

Ault and Arnold (2010) identified three main approaches to the taxation of capital gains: the Continental approach, the Anglo-Saxon approach and the global approach. Under the Continental approach, business taxpayers are subject to the same rate of taxation on their capital gains and income. However, in the instance of capital gain unrelated to business, there is often no taxation, with possible exceptions for short-term gains or special circumstances (Ault & Arnold, 2010).

Under the Anglo-Saxon approach, there was a historical distinction, developed through case law, between taxable ordinary income and capital gains, which were not subject to tax. This applied to business and personal taxpayers. Legislation was required, sometimes in the form of a separate CGT regime, to bring capital gains into the tax base for countries using the Anglo-Saxon approach, and often these were taxed at preferential rates (Ault & Arnold, 2010). The Anglo-Saxon approach also applies to countries whose legal systems have been influenced by the U.K., such as Australia and Canada. Historically, English precedents have influenced Australia, although the primacy of the English courts is no longer recognised (Bentley, 1996).

Under the global approach, the concept of income developed through case law was broad enough to include capital gains, which meant that capital gains were always part of the jurisdiction's tax base (Ault & Arnold, 2010). Preferential taxation was common in these jurisdictions. The United States is an example of a country that has used a global approach, with capital gains included in the tax base whether they are from business or not.

A review of the literature indicates there is a lack of consensus on how capital gains should be taxed (Sandford & Evans, 1999) and that the difference of opinion reflects a debate over the appropriate tax base. This can either be the Schanz-Haig-Simons comprehensive income tax base, under which consumption and net accretions to wealth from all sources are taxed, or a consumption or cash flow tax base, under which savings are excluded from taxation and the measurement of capital gains is not required.

The tax literature has identified two broadly opposing views on the appropriate tax base. These are either an income tax base or a consumption tax base. Cunningham (1996) identified that the principal difference between these two tax bases is that while both tax consumption, an income tax base also includes changes in wealth or savings. More specifically, the Schanz-Haig-Simons comprehensive tax base requires the taxation of capital gains as they accrue. Nevertheless, proponents of a comprehensive income tax base consider the full inclusion of net capital gains in income to approximate a Schanz-Haig-Simons base, where it is not possible or practical to operate an accruals-based CGT. According to Cunningham (1996, p. 22), 'no one believes that a normative income tax based upon the Haig-Simons definition could ever be fully implemented; its importance is as an ideal.' The fact that most tax jurisdictions do not tax all capital gains as they accrue is consistent with this view. Fane and Richardson (2005) noted that an accruals-based CGT would be very costly to administer.



## 2.3 A CRITIQUE OF PREFERENTIAL RATES FOR THE TAXATION OF CAPITAL GAINS

### Background

Once policy makers have decided to tax capital gains and on what basis (either accruals or realisation) and base (all assets or assets subject to specified exceptions), a key consideration is the appropriate tax rate. This is a controversial issue and one that has never been resolved. Although the debate about CGT preferences is a politically charged issue, it is important to differentiate between the findings of relevant empirical research and arguments advanced in the popular debate.

The arguments for and against preferential CGT rates have been part of the tax literature for the last few decades. Blum (1957) set out these arguments several years before the topic attracted increased interest in the United States, following the enactment of the *Revenue Act of 1978*. Some of the arguments advanced as early as the 1950s are still part of today's debate. According to Minarik (1992), the debate is one that 'will go on forever'. The case for not taxing capital gains at all (Bartlett, 1985; Bracewell-Milnes, 1992; Grubel, 2000) is outside the scope of this book. This is because the research here is concerned with the revenue effects of CGT; clearly, in the absence of a CGT, there are no revenue effects to consider.

### The literature on CGT preferences

According to Kesselman (2005), the rate at which to set CGT is based on arguments about economic efficiency and revenue effects. Commentators in favour of lower CGT rates have argued that where CGT rates are too high, the formation and mobility of capital are discouraged (Bartlett, 1985). However, equity is an important consideration in deciding on a CGT rate and a justification for a CGT, as noted by the Commonwealth Taxation Review Committee and Asprey (1975). Arguments have been raised about the negative effects of capital gains preferences on simplicity. The arguments based upon each of these factors—economic efficiency, equity, simplicity and revenue effects—are now considered in more detail.

## Economic efficiency arguments

Proponents of CGT rate preferences have advanced several economic efficiency arguments associated with these preferences. First, some proponents have held that CGT rate preferences can increase the level of national saving and may have a positive effect on economic growth. Second, CGT preferences may increase tax system efficiency. This argument originates from the view that inefficiency may arise to the extent that taxpayers are 'locked in' to their investments because of CGT. Third, CGT preferences can be a proxy for inflation without the complexity of a CGT regime that applies indexation to the cost base of assets. Fourth, CGT preferences can encourage risk and entrepreneurship. These arguments are now critiqued in turn.

### National savings and economic growth

Minarik (1992) noted that in order to have any success in increasing economic growth, a CGT rate reduction must be able to increase national saving. However, a review of the literature shows that some of the claimed economic efficiency benefits of preferential CGT rates—such as those related to increasing the level of national saving and economic growth—may be contentious. According to Gravelle (1994), the evidence does not support claims that a CGT rate reduction is important to economic growth. A 1985 U.S. Treasury study estimated a 0.005% increase in economic performance over 50 years resulting from the 1978 capital gains tax rate reduction (U.S. Department of Treasury, September 1985). Furthermore, according to Gravelle (1995), estimates relating to the then proposed *Contract With America* CGT rate cut[2]—that were favourable to larger and positive effects on capital stock, labour supply and output—indicated only very small increases in economic growth. Gravelle was of the view that under less favourable assumptions the effect on economic growth could be negative. Gravelle also noted that in comparing the CGT rates and economic performance of other countries, the former did not appear to have much explanatory power in the latter.

Burman (1999) found there was no perceptible effect on economic growth of at least twelve CGT rate changes between 1954 and 1995. Specifically, the correlation between the percentage change in real GDP and the maximum CGT rate was –0.01 (Burman, 1999).

A large preference for capital gains may have a slightly depressing effect on the economy and is likely to have no positive effect on saving or investment (Burman, 1999). Cunningham and Schenk (1993) rejected the claim that a CGT preference stimulates

2 Under discussion at the time was a proposal to halve the CGT rate. The alternative proposals were to introduce an indexation system for capital gains or to allow taxpayers to deduct losses arising from the sale of personal residences.

economic growth. The claim is disputed given that in order to be correct, the preference must increase domestic investment, and its ability to achieve this is dependent on whether the preference is self-financing through increased realisations. According to Gravelle (1990), if the magnitude of the realisations response is overestimated, this leads to a reduction in national saving through an increase in the budget deficit and, consequently, a slowing of economic growth. Burman (1999) noted that concerns about the negative effects on saving and investment from taxing capital gains at ordinary income rates may be overstated. Furthermore, it was the view of Burman (2009) that a better solution for such concerns than CGT preferences is an overall lowering of tax rates.



The level of national saving comprises two components: private saving by households and firms and public saving by government (Hungerford, 2010). The ability of a CGT rate reduction to increase savings depends on whether the higher after-tax return leads to an increase in private saving and whether such an increase in private saving is greater than the increase in public debt[3] (Burman, 1999).

Since public savings take the form of budget surpluses, it follows that in order to have a positive effect on public saving a CGT rate change must raise more revenue than the previous rate. An increase in realisations that follows a CGT rate reduction does not necessarily mean that there has been an increase in revenue collected. There will only have been an increase in revenue where the behavioural response was large enough to offset the static loss in revenue caused by the rate cut.[4] According to Gravelle (1994), reducing a budget deficit or increasing a budget surplus is a more certain way of increasing savings compared to reducing the CGT rate. According to Avi-Yonah and Zelik (2015, p. 2) the argument that a lower CGT rate encourages savings is 'empirically dubious'. Gravelle noted that an increase in savings is not the same as an increase in well-being; where savings are increased present consumption is traded for future consumption, and economic efficiency will be determined by the value of that trade-off.

Although CGT rates have an effect on the rate of return after tax, the overall effect on savings is low (Auten, 2005). Minarik (1992) noted it may be impossible to isolate the effect of a CGT cut on household saving in the empirical data because of the large range of estimates.

According to Krever and Brooks (1990), the case for justifying CGT preferences on the basis that they may increase private saving is weak since capital gains are only one form of private saving and there is little justification for distinguishing between capital gains and other forms of saving or return on investment. Although there may be an effect on private saving because of a CGT preference, the effect is likely to be small since capital gains are only a small proportion of total investment income and any gains from increases in saving achieved this way are at the cost of distortions of investment decisions (Krever & Brooks, 1990). Burman (1999) estimated that capital gains result from only 40% of saving and that most capital gains assets pay part of their return in dividends, rents and other

3 From the reduced CGT rate.

4 The static loss in revenue accompanying a CGT rate cut is present where taxpayers realise gains that they would have absent the rate cut. In effect, the static loss represents a windfall from the perspective of these taxpayers.

forms of income. There is some evidence that savings are not sensitive to rates of return (Krever & Brooks, 1990). In addition, Krever and Brooks noted that a CGT preference may be available to taxpayers who do not increase their net savings, for example those taxpayers who finance their entire investment by borrowing.

In reviewing the literature on the effect of a CGT rate cut on private saving, Gravelle (1994) concluded that higher rates of return on saving have small positive effects on savings behaviour and, in some cases, negative effects.

In summary, there is a lack of empirical evidence for a significantly positive effect of a CGT preference on savings and economic growth, and it would be difficult to justify a CGT rate preference principally on these grounds.

## Tax system efficiency

In determining whether a tax or tax system is economically efficient, the most relevant question appears to be: to what degree does a tax or tax system distort the decisions that taxpayers would make in the absence of that tax? The potential for distortionary effects are evident in a tax system without a CGT, as an incentive is created for investment in assets that provide returns in the form of capital gains in comparison to assets with other forms of returns, such as bonds.[5] The same distortion occurs in the case of a tax system with a preferential rate CGT as it creates a preference for investments where most of the return is in the form of capital gains. Halperin (1993) argued that a CGT preference is only justifiable if one is of the view that the tax system improperly discriminates against certain investment types or that encouragement in particular types of investments is desirable. Halperin was of the view that favourable tax treatment should not extend to all items that meet the definition of a capital gain, as this may include items for which there is no case for special treatment.

Another important negative effect of a CGT preference is the distortions that it can create in tax planning, and these are more serious than they may appear (Halperin, 1993). There could be a significant simplification of the tax system and a greater allowance of capital losses on the permanent implementation of equal taxation treatment of ordinary income and capital gains (Halperin, 1993). It is important to note a significant difference between Australia and the United States on the treatment of deductions in respect of capital gains assets. In Australia, there is no system of quarantining the amount of the deduction for items such as interest expense. This means that a taxpayer can be in a net loss position in a given tax year and deduct the net deductible expenses, related to capital gains assets, from their taxable income. An example of where such a practice occurs is for rental property assets, where the interest on loans and other deductible expenses exceed the rental income. Such investments can be tax effective because income losses reduce the taxpayer's assessable income from the first year that the taxpayer holds the asset, while the capital gain will be preferentially taxed in a future income year and only in the event that the taxpayer decides to realise the gain. This is a tax planning opportunity that would not be as problematic if capital gains were taxed at the same rates as those applying to

5 The distinction here is between 'growth assets,' or those that appreciate without producing an annual income, and 'yield assets,' which provide their return through income rather than capital gains.

other income or if the amount of losses that could be claimed as a deduction were subject to a loss limitation rule. The United States, by contrast, has a rule in its tax code to limit the deduction of investment interest expense; essentially, the deduction is limited to the amount of investment income.[6] Given this significant tax policy difference, there is less of a case for a CGT rate preference in Australia due to the absence of a limit on deductible expenses pertaining to capital gains assets.



Where the CGT rate is lowered, the type of investments that will be favoured are those for which a large share of the total return is in the form of capital gains (Auten & Cordes, 1991). There is debate on whether these types of investments should be given preferential tax treatment. An argument in favour of preferential treatment of capital gains assets is that assets such as company shares become a more attractive investment relative to assets such as housing, which are already subject to significant preferential tax treatment in many jurisdictions (Auten & Cordes, 1991). One of the opposing arguments is that where capital gains are subject to preferential tax treatment, there is an incentive for companies to retain earnings rather than pay dividends, which may not represent the most efficient allocation of investment. There are also arguments about efficiency losses associated with the increased allocation of capital to the assets most favoured by the preferential treatment. It is important to note that the incentive for companies to retain earnings rather than pay dividends is unlikely to exist to the same extent in Australia as it does in the United States. This is because of Australia's dividend imputation system, which provides an incentive for Australian companies to pay dividends. In summary, where the Australian resident company pays dividends out of profits on which company tax has been paid, an 'imputation credit' is distributed to shareholders. For the shareholder, the imputation credit reduces tax payable at the personal taxpayer level by the amount of company tax already paid on the profits distributed as dividends.

As explained in Chapter 1, the impact of lock-in is one of the main arguments advanced in support of a CGT rate preference. The lock-in effect arises due to the taxation of capital gains on a realisation rather than on an accruals basis. It results in taxpayers choosing to hold their capital assets that have appreciated and, in doing so, deferring or altogether avoiding CGT on the accrued capital gain. For many taxpayers, incurring a CGT liability is voluntary because of the realisation basis of taxing capital gains. Essentially, a taxpayer can defer their CGT liability indefinitely, provided they do not need to realise a capital gain for consumption purposes. Auerbach (2010) described the discretion that taxpayers have over the realisation of capital gains as a deferral advantage. Auerbach (2012) referred to a complexity of realisation-based CGT being that which occurs where taxpayers attempt transactions aimed at liquidating or hedging positions without triggering a capital gain realisation. The deferral advantage for the taxpayer holding capital gains is exacerbated by the practice of governments lowering CGT rates as a way of counteracting the lock-in effect. If there were a strong lock-in effect, there would be an expectation of taxpayers being very sensitive to CGT rates (Burman, 2009).

6 Internal Revenue Code §163 (d) (United States).

One of the earlier studies to consider the lock-in effect of CGT was the work of Holt and Shelton (1962). The authors concluded that although there was a lock-in effect arising from CGT, its magnitude for most investors is quite moderate. In contrast, Avi-Yonah and Zelik (2015) suggested that lock-in is a serious problem in a realisation-based system, especially where a step-up in basis at death exists. In a realisation-based CGT system, an investor may decline to change investments even where a higher return is available in doing so (Cunningham & Schenk, 1993). Thus, there are contrasting views on the impact of the lock-in effect.

Jacob (2011) identified an 'additional' lock-in effect that occurs when taxpayers are temporarily in a higher income bracket. This implies that taxpayers who are temporarily in a higher tax bracket will, if possible, avoid realising capital gains until they return to a lower tax bracket[7] and that a high proportion of capital gains realisations among higher-income brackets are predominantly for those taxpayers who will be in that income bracket in the longer term. The decision by taxpayers with temporarily high incomes to defer their capital gains realisations until their income returns to its more typical levels can be characterised as a timing response. Furthermore, in a CGT regime with progressive tax rates, there is no policy response to this additional lock-in effect.

Although CGT preferences are characterised as a form of tax expenditure in Australia, some of the U.S. literature suggests these preferences can increase overall tax revenue due to an unlocking effect. According to Eichner and Sinai (2000), the 'something for nothing' argument associated with the possibility of lower CGT rates leading to higher tax revenue is a compelling one for policy makers.[8] Early empirical evidence from Seltzer (1951), however, indicated that the fluctuation of realised capital gains and losses was more closely aligned with changes in share prices, rather than with changes in the tax treatment of capital gains. According to Gravelle (1990), in some instances a rapid increase in capital gains realisations has resulted from a natural response to an increase in asset values rather than from an unlocking effect of a CGT rate reduction. Nevertheless, where a lock-in effect exists, a CGT rate cut may induce the realisation of capital gains that would not have been realised in the absence of the rate cut.

According to Auerbach (1989), the lock-in effect is not a distortion of the overall composition of assets; rather, its effect is on the distribution of assets across investors. The magnitude of the lock-in effect increases the longer appreciating capital gains assets are held; this is consistent with larger gains accruing over time together with a higher potential capital gains liability.

Although some commentators have referred to lock-in as a justification for a CGT rate preference, some of the literature identifies weaknesses in this line of argument. Halperin (1993) argued that the costs of preferential CGT rates are more than any justification for it, and he found that lock-in is an overstated problem since, although it deters individual asset holders from diversifying, it has an insubstantial effect on the economy-wide mix of

7 Some taxpayers, however, may be temporarily in a higher income bracket as a consequence of realising a large capital gain.

8 Eichner and Sinai, however, are not proponents of the 'something for nothing' argument.

investments. More specifically, any welfare loss to individuals resulting from lock-in is less than their welfare gain caused by a CGT system that uses a realisation basis of taxation (Halperin, 1993).

Some of the arguments on the importance of the lock-in effect appear to be predicated on what is effectively the worst-case scenario, under which the investor owns a single asset. Lock-in is less of a problem for investors who own more than one capital gains asset (Burman, 1999). Arguments portraying lock-in as a phenomenon that, of itself, necessitates a preferential rate of CGT appear tenuous. Moreover, the supposed importance of the lock-in effect appears diminished given that taxpayers, who would have the opportunity to avoid realisation of capital gains and the consequent CGT liability, have realised significant amounts of capital gains every year since the introduction of CGT in Australia in 1985. Notably, this phenomenon has occurred in the years before, as well as after, the enactment of the CGT discount.



According to Krever and Brooks (1990), lock-in is a problem that appears to apply primarily to the sale of company shares compared to other types of CGT assets. Furthermore, the economic concerns relating to the lock-in effect have no relevance to situations where a taxpayer sells for the purpose of personal consumption rather than for reinvestment, as realisations for consumption do not contribute to the mobility of capital (Krever & Brooks, 1990).

In conclusion, some of the economic efficiency arguments for a CGT rate preference are not entirely convincing. It is apparent that rate preferences for capital gains introduce a new type of distortion into the tax system as taxpayers may seek to invest more in assets where most of the return is in the form of capital gains than they would absent a preference.

## Proxy for inflation

An argument made in favour of a CGT rate preference is that it can operate as a proxy for an inflation adjustment to the cost base of an asset. However, a rate preference does not approximate the required inflation adjustment in most cases and, due to its imprecision, it is not the best method for dealing with inflation. Furthermore, deductible interest expense invariably includes an inflation component, and the deductible amount of interest expense should be reduced in the event that an inflation adjustment is made for the amount of capital gains subject to tax.[9] The justification for inflation adjustments for capital gains is weak given that other forms of capital income, such as rental income, receive no such inflation adjustment. The argument that one type of assessable income within the tax system should be taxed on real rather than nominal terms, while others do not receive this treatment, is less than compelling. This is especially the case since capital gains are taxed on a realisation basis and not as they accrue.

In the case of assets held for a long time, inflation is often not considered a problem since it becomes a smaller percentage of the nominal gain over time and can be offset by the benefits of deferral accruing to the taxpayer (Halperin, 1993). Furthermore, a preferential CGT rate cannot be justified on the grounds of high inflation, given that in this scenario,

9 Notwithstanding that not all capital gains asset purchases are subject to interest payments.

where an asset is financed by debt there is a countervailing inflation gain accruing to the taxpayer (Brannon, 1986). According to Auerbach (1989), a system of indexation of cost base, similar to that used in Australia before the introduction of the 50% CGT discount, is a superior alternative to a CGT preference. Specifically, keeping the CGT rate the same as the tax rate on ordinary income reduces the incentive for arbitrary conversion of income to capital gains, while the indexation ensures that inflationary gains are not taxed.

In a recent call for the CGT discount to be abolished, Chris Cuffe (in Mather, 2017) rejected arguments that the CGT discount was needed as a proxy for inflation, noting that:

> For much of the late 1980s, inflation was around 8%, and then in "the recession we had to have" in 1991, it fell significantly and then rose again. By 1999, it was approaching 6%. It is now closer to 2%. With inflation closer to 2%, and likely to stay low for many years, the 50% discount is extremely generous for assets realised after a relatively short period.

In summary, CGT rate preferences are not suitable as a proxy for inflation as they are an imprecise way of excluding the inflationary gain from the tax base.

## Risk and entrepreneurship

According to Gravelle (1994), the view that preferential CGT can encourage risk is a more prevalent argument in the popular debate than in the economics literature. Cunningham and Schenk (1993) were critical of capital gains preferences as incentives for risk-taking because they are untargeted and provide incentives for non-risky CGT assets as well. According to Slemrod and Bakija (2008), only a small fraction of the lost revenue that occurs as a result of a capital gains preference is going towards improving incentives for entrepreneurship. A reduction in the CGT rate provides a windfall for the existing assets of taxpayers at the time of the rate change. Apart from providing a higher after-tax return to this group of taxpayers, in the event they decide to sell these assets, it is unclear how such a reform increases the level of overall investment.

Although some proponents of preferential CGT rates have argued that these can encourage and increase investment, this view overstates the importance of CGT rates to decisions to invest. Although CGT may be a consideration in decisions to retain or dispose of an asset, the realisation of a capital gain may not occur until several years after the purchase of the same, if at all. The question of how successful capital gains preferences have been in achieving their objectives is explored in more detail in the qualitative interview study in Chapter 4.

There is little evidence in the literature about a CGT preference constituting an appropriate method for encouraging entrepreneurship and venture capital investments; a preference is a broad way of encouraging such investments. Zodrow (1992) called for more directly targeted measures as a better alternative to general CGT preferences. According to Poterba (1989, p. 384), 'there is very limited evidence of the extent to which the supply of entrepreneurial activity responds to the relative tax burdens on capital gains and labour income.' Another possibility is a CGT preference that is targeted at a particular type of investment. For example, in 1993, the United States enacted a 50% exclusion with a maximum tax rate of 14% for new investments in certain types of small business shares that the taxpayer had purchased at the time of their original issue and held for a minimum of five years (Clark & OECD, 2006). It was the view of Gravelle (1994) that a reduction in the rate of tax on corporate stock would be more likely to increase tax system efficiency than a tax rate reduction per se.

Auerbach (1988) identified that although in efficient capital markets there is no a priori argument for the encouragement of risk-taking, there is a specific problem concerning risk that investors face. Those who invest in risky assets may have no income or capital gains against which they may deduct capital losses (Auerbach, 1988). That is because most tax jurisdictions limit the deductibility of capital losses given the arbitrage opportunities that full deductibility of these losses would present. Taxing capital gains on an accruals basis would overcome this problem, although other problems with accruals basis CGT are such that this system has not been adopted by any jurisdiction. The reluctance of revenue authorities to adopt CGT on an accruals basis may be because of difficulties with valuing assets, which would be subject annually to CGT. Nonetheless, there are certain types of assets such as shares in public companies for which there would not be valuation problems.[10]

Another possible alternative to a preferential CGT rate for all capital gains is a better-targeted preferential CGT that only applies to certain types of investments, that is, those that policy makers consider necessary to encourage through the tax system. Examples may include investments in new assets and investments where there is a higher degree of risk. However, the use of the tax system to influence taxpayer choice and behaviour is a controversial issue in tax policy. The efficiency of a tax system can be evaluated according to the degree to which it remains neutral.

Gravelle (1994) disputed the view that a CGT discourages risk-taking and argued that a CGT, in fact, has the effect of increasing investment in risky assets. Furthermore, the claim that there is not enough risk-taking in society may be incorrect given the opportunities that exist for pooling capital in corporations and diversifying risk (Gravelle, 1994). Stiglitz (1969) noted it is unclear whether the preferential treatment of capital gains is the most desirable way of encouraging risk-taking.

In summary, the economic efficiency arguments in favour of CGT rate preferences may not be as strong as is sometimes contended. Although some policy makers may expect that CGT rate preferences can encourage investment in new ventures or riskier assets, they appear to be an ineffective means of doing so. A CGT rate preference is untargeted towards new or riskier investment. Indeed, the preferential tax treatment of capital gains is extended to the stock of existing accrued capital gains. Other economic efficiency arguments that have been posited in favour of preferential rates suffer similar shortcomings and drawbacks.

## Equity arguments

Gravelle (1994) identified the concentration of the CGT burden towards higher-income taxpayers and the skewing of any CGT rate reduction towards this group as major

10 Since there is no difficulty in ascertaining the value of shares in public companies at any given point in time.

arguments against reducing CGT rates. Consistent with this view are arguments against preferential CGT rates on the basis they are counter to the traditional tax policy principles of vertical and horizontal equity and can create incentives for inefficient tax sheltering whereby taxpayers seek to categorise receipts, which would normally be considered ordinary income, as capital.

Vertical equity is concerned with ensuring a fair tax burden is imposed on taxpayers with different levels of income and different taxable capacities. Essentially, it posits the notion that those with a greater capacity to pay tax should shoulder a greater tax burden than those with a lesser tax capacity. The question of what constitutes a vertically equitable tax system is, however, an unsettled one, as it is influenced by individual notions of what constitutes a fair tax burden at different levels of income. Concerns about vertical equity, related to CGT rate preferences, arise from the fact that taxpayers with high taxable incomes derive most of the benefits of CGT rate preferences, since these taxpayers accrue and realise most capital gains. Therefore, a CGT rate preference generally results in a vertically inequitable tax system—notwithstanding individual beliefs about what constitutes fairness—since the benefits of the preference are concentrated at higher levels of income, given the skewed way in which capital gains are distributed. Hungerford (2010) noted that this skewed distribution of capital gains applies specifically to realised capital gains that are subject to CGT and that the distribution of realised capital gains would not be as skewed towards higher-income taxpayers if untaxed capital gains, such as owner-occupied housing, were included in such an analysis.

The introduction of the 50% CGT discount in Australia in 1999 constituted a significant reduction of the prevailing CGT rate.[11] Notwithstanding the merits or otherwise of a CGT rate reduction, any discussion of the benefits should be considered in the context of vertical equity. One of the reasons that CGT is an area of policy interest is because of the fact that a high proportion of gains accrue to the highest income taxpayers. A review of *Taxation Statistics* confirms that most capital gains are realised by higher-income individuals.[12] Because of the skewed distribution of capital gains, a CGT rate lower than that on ordinary income distorts the progressivity of the tax system. Specifically, a personal taxpayer at the highest marginal tax rate can face a significantly lower effective tax rate in years in which they realise capital gains. Taxpayers who are at lower marginal income rates and without CGT assets cannot lower their effective tax rate by realising capital gains. According to Burman (1999), a CGT preference reduces revenue and although it probably does reduce lock-in, it is unclear whether this effect is significant.

CGT rate preferences may lead to horizontal inequity since there is an unequal distribution of the tax burden among those taxpayers with the same taxable income, but who have differing proportions of capital gains to total taxable income. Although horizontal equity is a fundamental objective of tax policy, the way capital gains are taxed presents

11 The actual reduction of the CGT rate is less than half the rate under the indexation method. This is because of the fact that a taxpayer who chooses the discount method cannot index the cost base of the asset.

12 Capital gains also accrue at higher levels among high-income taxpayers in other comparable jurisdictions such as Canada and the United States.

vexing problems that compromise the ability of the tax system to achieve horizontal equity (U.S. CBO, 1997).

According to Pederick (1984), horizontal equity is important to a self-assessment tax system since perceptions of unfairness can have an adverse effect on enforceability. If the Schanz-Haig-Simons definition of income is accepted, a CGT rate preference instils horizontal inequity given the highly skewed concentration of capital gains at higher levels of taxable income. Minarik (1992) believed that a 'burden of proof' falls on those who argue in favour of preferential rates of tax to demonstrate how these are appropriate.



However, Shaviro (1993) argued that horizontal equity is not a criterion against which CGT should be evaluated given that the existing horizontal equity standard is too narrow. It was the view of Shaviro that a broader definition of horizontal equity may be more appropriate and, if adopted, would require a heavier tax burden for those who benefit more from government expenditure (Shaviro, 1993).

Another argument against preferential rates of CGT relates to the benefits of deferral. This may be characterised as an equity argument in the sense that the deferral benefit only applies to taxpayers who have capital gains. Specifically, there are some asset types that pay out most or all of their return in the form of income, such as rent or dividends, whereas for other types of assets the income returns are low or nil and the return is accrued in the form of a capital gain (Burman, 1999). For the latter type of assets, deferral is seen as reducing the effective tax rate, since the money that would have been used to pay tax continues to earn returns until tax is paid (Burman, 1999). The benefit of deferral compounds over the time that such an asset is held. This benefit is an argument for taxing capital gains at ordinary income rates. Burman (1999) noted that even in the absence of a preferential CGT rate, the treatment of capital gains is more favourable than the treatment of other returns to capital such as interest and dividends.

Benge (1997) used a scenario to quantify the benefits of deferral in a realisation-based CGT regime. He assumed that an asset's pre-tax rate of return is a constant rate of 10% per annum and the tax rate 44.4% for 50 consecutive years. A taxpayer can choose to sell an asset in one of the years in the sequence. Here the taxpayer's post-tax rate of return increases for every year that the taxpayer holds the asset. In the scenario, the effective tax rate is 44.4% if the asset is sold in year 1 compared with 12.7% if the asset is sold in year 50 (Benge, 1997). Auerbach (2012) noted that the two main arguments in favour of realisation-based CGT—capital gains are unknown until they are realised, and taxpayers may face liquidity problems in an accruals system—do not extend to an interest-free deferral of CGT. Auerbach suggested the addition of an appropriate charge for interest when capital gains are realised as a way of offsetting the advantage of deferral.

There are references in the literature to methods whereby taxpayers can maximise the after-tax value of their asset portfolios apart from the postponement of realised capital gains. For example, Miller and Scholes (1978) detailed a simple arbitrage strategy for converting dividends from shares into capital gains to take advantage of the preferential taxation of the latter. This strategy requires the taxpayer to borrow, in each tax year, an amount that will generate an interest deduction large enough to offset their taxable dividends; the loan proceeds are then used to purchase more shares. Since all the taxpayer's income is taken in the form of capital gains, they receive a higher after-tax rate of return (Miller & Scholes,

1978). An even simpler arbitrage strategy aimed at reducing tax payable is that of realising capital losses immediately, while holding assets with capital gains (Constantinides, 1983; Stiglitz, 1969).[13]

In summary, a CGT rate preference does not perform well against the tax system criteria of vertical and horizontal equity. In relation to vertical equity, the fact that a large proportion of the benefit of a preference accrues to the highest income taxpayers undermines the overall personal income tax system that is, by design, progressive. Horizontal inequity is another consequence of a CGT preference. Specifically, an increase in the amount of preferential capital gains that a taxpayer has in their assessable income results in a lower overall real tax rate. The negative effects of a CGT preference on vertical and horizontal equity and the deferral benefits of taxation of capital gains on a realisation basis diminish the case for a preference.

## Simplicity arguments

A tax system that taxes capital gains and other forms of assessable income at the same marginal rates has obvious simplicity benefits. Such benefits are not apparent in the current CGT regime for personal taxpayers in Australia where the taxation of most capital gains is at a lower rate than other income. In the current regime, a small proportion of capital gains are subject to the indexation method. The indexation method is less than ideal from the perspective of simplicity, especially where different parts of a taxpayer's cost base are subject to different rates of indexation.

Preferential rate CGT can increase tax system complexity. Part of the complexity associated with CGT rate preferences arises from legislators seeking to counteract avoidance techniques such as the re-characterisation of income into capital.[14] This may include the enactment of new legislative provisions as a means of bringing CGT events that were not originally contemplated into the tax base.

It is important to note that, in Australia, the CGT discount is a cause of tax complexity, notwithstanding its apparent simplicity in concept. The complexities that arise from the CGT discount include, for example, the legislative complexities encountered in the interaction of the CGT discount provisions of Division 115 of the *ITAA1997* with rules relating to specific forms of entity, such as the trust provisions. Furthermore, there is the complex interaction with the small business concessions in Division 152 of the *ITAA1997* and the existence of a series of detailed integrity measures (Evans, Minas & Lim, 2015).[15]

13 In the United States, such a strategy could be effective without the need for the taxpayer to concurrently realise capital gains to the same value as the capital losses provided the total capital gain in a tax year did not exceed US$3,000. In Australia, however, capital losses can only reduce taxable income to the extent that they are offset against capital gains.

14 Notably, complexity itself can lead to tax evasion. Richardson (2006) found that complexity was the most important determinant of tax evasion.

15 Including those designed to ensure that the discount is not available where a corporate entity is used to hold newly acquired assets, thereby potentially circumventing the 12-month holding period rules that are required before the discount can be used.

Evans et al. (2015) noted that the removal of the discount for foreign residents in 2013 (with effect from 8 May 2012) neatly illustrated some of the complexity of the application of the provisions in practice. Where a CGT event occurs after 8 May 2012, the discount percentage applying to a discount capital gain from that event will depend on four factors: first, whether the asset was held on, or was acquired after, 8 May 2012; second, if the asset was held on 8 May 2012, whether or not the individual was a resident on that date; third, whether a choice is made by an individual who was a non-resident on 8 May 2012 to use the market value approach to determine the part of the discount capital gain that accrued on and prior to that date; finally, the residency of the individual during so much of the period that the asset was held after 8 May 2012 (Cooper & Evans, 2014). The myriad possible interactions of these four factors cause significant complexity for taxpayers, advisers and administrators and can lead to unanticipated and unintended outcomes not only from a planning perspective, but also in terms of tax compliance consequences (Evans et al., 2015).



Evans et al. (2015) noted that there are several other ways the CGT discount adds complexity to the regime. CGT is already a complex tax that imposes disproportionate compliance costs on personal taxpayers. Evans (2003) established that CGT compliance costs are significant in Australia: they are high in relation to the amount of tax payable, the amount of revenue collected and the compliance costs of other taxes. Furthermore, the compliance costs of the CGT regime are a concern to practitioners, and there is a serious problem of underbilling for CGT work. In that regard, almost one in two practitioners revealed that they could not recover the full costs of their professional work on CGT from clients, with the estimated average amount of underbilling 30% (Evans, 2003).[16]

## Revenue effects

In 1999, policy makers were of the view that one of the benefits of the enactment of the 50% CGT discount would be an increase in revenue from CGT collections or, at worst, revenue neutrality compared with the previous regime that taxed capital gains at full marginal tax rates. Although there was no Australian empirical evidence available at that time, a review of the literature from the United States would have cautioned policy makers against predictions of a large capital gains realisations response that would be required for the reform to gain revenue. The lack of empirical evidence meant there was a potential risk to government tax revenue in overestimating the realisations response. In the event that the realisations response was moderate, setting the CGT discount at a level that was not as generous as 50% would have been more appropriate from a revenue perspective. Introducing the discount at a more moderate level would have allowed the revenue effects of the rate change to be estimated in the years following the policy change.

Although policy makers did not describe the 50% CGT discount as a permanent tax policy change, the status quo is often afforded a privileged status in tax policy. Tax rate preferences, once granted, are difficult for governments to repeal. That the 50% CGT discount has been in place for longer than the original CGT may be an example of the

16 By way of contrast, average underbilling by tax practitioners in the United Kingdom was less than 15%.

difficulties of reforming the status quo in tax policy. Such difficulties are especially apparent in the case of proposals to reduce or eliminate an existing tax expenditure.

From a policy perspective, there is a case for taxing capital gains on accrual at the same rate as ordinary income. For practical reasons, capital gains are taxed as they are realised rather than as they accrue. This may be a compromise in the sense that it results in a CGT regime that is less than the tax policy ideal. The rate preference for capital gains is another departure from the tax policy ideal that is a feature of CGT in Australia and in the tax systems of many other jurisdictions.

The next section in this chapter discusses elasticity and capital gains realisations.[17]

## 2.4 ELASTICITY AND CAPITAL GAINS

### Overview

The principal focus of the literature review in this chapter is the capital gains elasticity studies undertaken in the United States; these are referred to in the literature as capital gains realisations response studies. The reason that the chapter is weighted towards the U.S. studies is because this is where the vast majority of studies on capital gains realisations response have been conducted.

Capital gains realisations response studies are concerned with how responsive realisations of capital gains are to a change in the tax rate. To date, elasticity has been the most common means of quantifying realisations response. Typically, an elasticity point estimate is a measure of the magnitude of the capital gains realisations response. Elasticity is not necessarily constant at all tax levels, and the expectation is that there would be a higher elasticity at higher tax rates (Gravelle, 1994). Zodrow (1992) noted that elasticity may be influenced by the prevailing CGT rate; where CGT rates are relatively high, there is a greater probability of higher realisations elasticity than there would be at lower CGT rates.

The revenue effects of CGT rate changes have been a topic of debate in the United States for several decades; however, interest in the topic appears to have intensified from the late 1970s onwards. An early study by Seltzer (1951), using U.S. data from 1917 to 1946, concluded that for the highest income earners, the realisations response of capital gains was highly sensitive to tax rates. This degree of responsiveness was not as pronounced for middle and lower income earners. This early literature contained a less sophisticated analysis than in the econometric capital gains realisations response studies from 1980 onwards, which are the principal focus of the remainder of this chapter. According to Gravelle (1994), the debate about the revenue effects of a CGT rate reduction, over the last few decades, has involved the various econometric approaches used in elasticity studies.

Generally, a small increase in the CGT rate will provide additional CGT revenue for the government if elasticity is less than 1.00 in absolute terms, whereas CGT revenue will

17 Elasticity is the responsiveness of one thing to another; it is the percentage change in one variable resulting from a 1% change in another (Burman, 1999). Elasticity in the context of capital gains describes the percentage change in realisations divided by the percentage change in the tax rate (Gravelle, 1994).

be lost from a small CGT rate increase if elasticity is greater than 1.00 (Gravelle, 2010). This general rule about the revenue effects of a certain elasticity point estimate refers only to CGT revenue; it is not a measure of the overall revenue effects of a CGT rate change. Importantly, where taxpayers are able to convert other forms of assessable income into capital gains, it is possible for lost revenue from other taxes to occur because of a CGT rate reduction.[18] The elasticity point estimate from a capital gains realisations response study does not measure whether there are overall tax revenue losses resulting from a CGT rate that is lower than the ordinary income tax rate. The specific behavioural response of re-characterising income as preferentially taxed capital gains is described in the literature as 'tax arbitrage' (Auerbach, 1988), a 'portfolio effect' (U.S. Congress, Joint Committee on Taxation, 1990), and 'income shifting' (Slemrod, 1995a). According to Mayhall (1980–81), the conversion of income into capital gains increases the complexity of a tax system.

Auerbach (1988) noted that much of the capital gains realisation activity represents tax arbitrage, characterised by taxpayers realising capital gains and incurring a CGT liability as a way of avoiding other, higher rate taxes. The term arbitrage is appropriate for describing this type of activity as these taxpayers may be attempting to re-characterise the legal form of their receipt without changing its economic substance. Burman (1999) noted that capital gains preferences hinder the economy by acting as an incentive for the artificial conversion of income into capital gains. Grote and Fletcher (2000) noted that the inclusion of capital gains in the tax base reduces the distortive behavioural effects that can arise if they are excluded from the tax base.

Seltzer (1951) explained the negative effect on revenue collected from the arbitrary conversion of income to capital. The literature has since revisited this issue. It is now recognised that a CGT rate cut that increases realisations through an increased arbitrary conversion of income to capital may have the effect of reducing efficiency due to a lowering of tax revenue overall as well as increases in other taxes that are distortionary (Burman, 1999). Eilbott (1985) referred to specific examples of tax sheltering activity under which increases in reported capital gains are accompanied by increases in partnership losses, which may imply an overall revenue loss.

Efficiency losses because of increased tax arbitrage are also explained in terms of the social resources expended in reducing an individual's tax liability (Auerbach, 1988). Although there is a revenue effect of taxpayers re-characterising ordinary income as capital gains, this has been considered an indirect revenue effect.

Another example of an indirect revenue effect of a lower CGT rate is companies paying fewer dividends (Bogart & Gentry, 1995). However, this revenue effect, identified in the United States, is unlikely to be as pronounced in Australia given that the imputation credit system provides an incentive for companies to pay dividends.

18 The lost revenue here refers to the difference between the tax rate on ordinary income and capital gains. It specifically contemplates cases where revenue is lost because an item that would usually be taxed as ordinary income is instead taxed as a capital gain.

## Issues in estimating the capital gains realisations response

Typically, a regression equation is used in an empirical study that estimates the capital gains realisations response. In such an equation (also referred to as a specification), the dependent variable to be explained is capital gains realisations and the independent variable of interest is a measure of the marginal tax rate that applies to capital gains (Zodrow, 1992). The regression equation also includes a number of non-tax variables that are theorised to influence the decisions of taxpayers to realise capital gains.

According to Gravelle (1994), a model of capital gains realisations has never been fully developed and the econometric studies on realisations response are based on reduced form estimates that assume a negative relationship between tax rates and realisations without a formal model to explain or confirm this relationship. An alternative to the view that lower marginal tax rates are the cause of increased realisations is that taxpayers who engage in behaviour that lowers their marginal tax rate are also the taxpayers who have more accrued capital gains (Zodrow, 1992). Furthermore, elasticity—to the extent that it can change according to tax rates, taxpayer income and the mix of assets being realised—is more akin to a convenient summary rather than a guide to all situations (Zodrow, 1992).

Although an elasticity point estimate may be informative to estimates of the revenue effects of a CGT rate change, there are potential difficulties associated with such revenue estimates. For example, as noted by Auerbach (1988), the unitary elasticity rule will not hold in every situation.[19]

According to Zodrow (1992), in order for the unitary elasticity rule to hold, the tax system must be proportional, with average and marginal tax rates that are equal, and individual personal taxpayers must have the same degree of responsiveness to the tax rate change. However, in a progressive tax system, it is unlikely that these two characteristics will be present. It is implied that a CGT rate cut can increase revenue, even though the elasticity is less than 1.00, in situations where the relative decline in average tax rates is less than that in marginal tax rates (Zodrow, 1992). Auten and Cordes (1991) noted that in a progressive income tax system, where the elasticity of realisations increases with tax rates, the break-even point is a value slightly less than 1.00 in absolute value.

An example of a capital gains realisations response study for which the unitary elasticity rule did not hold was a study by the U.S. Treasury (1985), which found that a CGT cut increased revenue, even though elasticity was less than 1.00 in absolute value. However, this finding was criticised on the basis that the U.S. Treasury's methodology incorrectly held that the gap between average and marginal tax rates had declined because of the changes in CGT rates (Auerbach, 1988).

Burman (1999) identified a trend in the relative estimates of realisation responses given by two types of studies: the estimates of elasticity are relatively small in time series studies, while cross-sectional estimates are relatively large. A U.S. Congressional revenue estimate prepared by the Joint Committee on Taxation (JCT) in 1990 argued that

19 The unitary elasticity rule can be described as the basic assumption about the relationship between elasticity and revenue. An example of where the rule holds is where a small CGT rate cut loses (gains) revenue where the elasticity is less (more) than 1.00 in absolute value.

estimates of realisation elasticity from time series data better described how taxpayers responded to a permanent change in the tax rate. The U.S. Treasury has argued that time series studies may underestimate realisations elasticity (Auten & Cordes, 1991).

An important consideration in estimating the realisations response of CGT rate changes is that the empirical model should allow for the possibility that taxpayers respond differently to changes in permanent and temporary components (Burman & Randolph, 1994). Specifically, there are three distinct responses that, in theory, can be identified: a transitory response to a temporary tax rate change, a short-run response to a permanent tax rate change and a long-run or permanent response to a permanent rate change. Notably, a transitory response can include the timing response of taxpayers. For example, the pre-announced CGT rate increase, in the case of the *Tax Reform Act* (*TRA86*), led to a surge in the level of realisations prior to the change in the CGT rate. Timing responses can also occur as a result of fluctuations in a taxpayer's taxable income, in which case they may have an incentive to realise capital gains in a year when income is low. Of the distinct responses to CGT rate changes, it is the long-run effect that is certainly of most interest to tax policy makers.



The response to temporary CGT rate changes is not relevant to this book, as Australia has not had a CGT rate change that has been temporary at the time of its enactment. Furthermore, Australia has not experienced a pre-announced CGT rate increase. As a result, the ensuing transient surge in asset sales has not been experienced in Australia.

Transitory elasticity can relate to the circumstances of the individual personal taxpayer rather than the entire taxpayer population. For example, it may result from the 'permanent' income of wealthy personal taxpayers varying from year to year. In accordance with this definition, transitory elasticity is not considered as important as permanent elasticity, to the extent that the former represents taxpayers realising capital gains at an earlier time, and that these capital gains still would have been realised absent a CGT rate reduction.

According to Stiglitz (1983), a reduction in tax rates can cause a surge of higher realisations in the short run followed by smaller increases in the long run. Auten and Cordes (1991) referred to the fact that in the short run, additional realisations include those that would have occurred anyway, albeit in a later year; this is contrasted with the long run, where realisations will only be significantly higher if they are primarily from capital gains that would otherwise have been unrealised.

Lindsey (1987a) characterised short-run elasticity as the additional effect of short-term increases or declines in realisations in the year of a CGT rate change. There is a degree of consensus in the literature about the short-run capital gains elasticity being relatively high (Eichner & Sinai, 2000).

There is a lack of consensus as to the time it takes for investors to move from the short run to the long run. Although the Ralph Review referred to the short run in the context of a realisations response as one or two years, it may be considerably less than one year. Importantly, there appears to be little guidance in the literature on what time period constitutes the short-run response.

The importance of separating the transitory response from the long-run response of CGT rate reductions is well documented in the literature, and some of the earliest capital gains realisations response studies were subject to criticism on the basis that they did not separate these two distinct responses. Some of the studies reviewed in this chapter reported a transitory elasticity of a greater magnitude than the long-run elasticity. In the event that the transitory effects on capital gains realisations are high and relatively elastic and the long-run effects are low and relatively inelastic, the long-run revenue effects, resulting from a CGT rate cut, are unlikely to be positive. Under this scenario, it is more likely that the timing of capital gains realisations is being brought forward, which is distinct from an increase in capital gains realisations over the long run.

It appears that some of the high elasticity estimates in the earliest U.S. studies should be regarded with a degree of caution given the recognised problems with the methodology used; specifically, there are doubts about whether a cross-sectional study can disentangle and estimate the permanent capital gains realisations response.[20] A particularly important reason why some of the high elasticity point estimates from these early studies have been disputed is that the level of realised gains can never exceed the level of accrued gains that exist in a population of personal taxpayers (Gravelle, 1991). Studies that reported an elasticity estimate of a very high magnitude incorrectly implied that, over time, the level of realised gains could exceed the level of accrued gains. Gravelle (2010) noted that revenue estimating entities in the United States have not relied on any of the studies that reported a very high elasticity point estimate.

The long-run realisations response is of most interest in elasticity studies because, unlike the transitory response, it does not reflect investors' timing behaviour alone. Since the amount of accrued unrealised capital gains is the limit to the overall amount of capital gains that can be realised, elasticity studies should also attempt to estimate the amount of accrued gains in the sample that is used for the studies. According to Mariger (1995), where time series data are used, the short-run elasticity can be identified by holding constant the stock of unrealised capital gains—an independent variable—in a regression equation. Including the stock of unrealised capital gains, as an explanatory variable, in a regression equation will provide an estimate of the elasticity of capital gains realisations that better represents the long-run response. Although it is not possible to directly measure accrued capital gains, they are likely to follow overall economic growth and the value of company shares (U.S. CBO, 1988).

In the case of capital gains rate changes that are not pre-announced, there will only be a transitory response expected in the case of a CGT rate cut, but not in the case of CGT rate increase. That is, although there may be a significant increase in realisations from existing accrued capital gains when CGT is reduced, there is no reduction to realisations expected as a result of a rate increase. The overall effect on realisations is nil since the stock of accrued gains that has not been realised due to tax considerations will remain unrealised in the event of a CGT rate increase (Gravelle, 2010).

The introduction, in the United States, of the *TRA86* reduced the number of personal income tax brackets from 14 to 2 (15% and 28%) and taxed capital gains at the same rate as ordinary income. Some commentators saw this as a watershed event in the taxation of

20 The thinking is that the results in these studies measure temporary as well as permanent responses and are therefore overstated, to the extent that they purport to be a measure of permanent realisations response.

capital income for reasons including that it rejected some calls for a move further towards a consumption-based tax and it removed what was seen as an entrenched feature of the U.S. tax code: differential tax treatment of capital gains (Gravelle, 1994). According to Pechman (1987), the *TRA86* reduced the incentive to disguise ordinary income as capital gains and it made the U.S. tax code simpler. It is important to note that the *TRA86* resulted in an effective CGT rate increase for U.S. personal taxpayers on the top marginal tax rate. Specifically, before the *TRA86* took effect, taxpayers had a 60% exclusion of long-term capital gains from taxable income. Thus, although the top tax rate on ordinary income was 50%, the top CGT rate for long-term gains was only 20%.



The *TRA86* provided an example of a large transitory effect of a CGT rate change.[21] Specifically, there was an increase in CGT realisations from $170.6 billion in 1985 to $324.4 billion in 1986, followed by a decrease in realisations to $144.2 billion in 1987 (Gillingham & Greenlees, 1992). This significant transitory effect was the result of a pre-announced CGT rate increase. Research on this topic examining taxpayer data found that long-term capital gains realisations in December 1986 were almost seven times the December 1985 level (Burman, Clausing & O'Hare, 1994). It would appear that in the absence of the pre-announced rate change, realisations would have been lower in 1986 and higher in 1987. Eichner and Sinai (2000) examined the effect on the elasticity point estimate of excluding 1986 and found that this cut the elasticity estimate by almost half. The realisations response to the pre-announced CGT rate change in 1986 was also found to vary according to the type of asset.

The significant increase in realisations in 1986 in the United States cannot be characterised as a permanent effect. Specifically, because there was no change in the CGT rate between 1985 and 1986, the timing effect that occurred was based on taxpayers' expectations about future CGT rates. That is, taxpayers knew at the time of the pre-announced CGT rate change that the prevailing CGT rate had become relatively lower than the future CGT rate that would apply in the following tax year. The 1986 experience serves as an example of the potential difficulties associated with modelling expectations of future CGT rate changes.

There are two common approaches to dealing with this problem: first, to assume that CGT rate expectations coincide with actual CGT rates; or second, to construct an expected tax rate variable that is a function of previous CGT rates (Zodrow, 1992). Furthermore, Jones (1989) identified future wealth expectations as a variable affecting capital gains realisations; specifically, where a taxpayer expects the value of their wealth that can be realised as capital gains to increase in the future, this will have a negative effect on the amount of capital gains realised in the present. Another factor that may cause taxpayers to delay the timing of their realisations is that the benefits of deferral of realisations increase over time.

The methodology used in econometric studies to estimate realisations response appears to have developed over time. The limitations of elasticity studies per se include

21 Specifically the rate change was a pre-announced CGT rate increase. The transitory effect observed was a rush of realisations timed to precede the known CGT rate increase.

that some of the econometric analysis of capital gains realisations behaviour has weak theoretical economic foundations (Auten, Burman & Randolph, 1989); for example, there are few predictions provided in the theoretical literature about how and why capital gains are realised (Zodrow, 1992). Furthermore, the type of data that are adequate for answering policy makers' questions can be difficult to determine, and in some studies, various econometric problems have been a limitation (Auten et al., 1989).

The elasticity studies on capital gains realisations have tended to produce a wide range of elasticity point estimates, and this is the case even where studies using a particular type of data are considered: for example, time series. Capital gains realisations response studies imply that there is some economic value in realising capital gains and that this value must be, at least, equal to the tax cost of doing so (Auten et al., 1989).

Mariger (1995) concluded that, based on the available empirical evidence, capital gains realisations are quite responsive to the tax rate in the short run, but that little is known about the long-run response. According to Minarik (1984), the debate on CGT policy in the United States, although depending crucially on the capital gains realisations response, has been conducted in virtual ignorance of the same. Furthermore, due to changes in rates and realisations having offsetting effects on revenue, a relatively small degree of uncertainty about the realisations response to tax rate changes can cause significant uncertainty about revenue effects (U.S. CBO, 1988). The short-run realisations response is of less importance than the long-run response given that it represents, at least to some degree, a mere change in the timing of realisations. That is, if taxpayers are choosing to bring forward realisations that they were planning for a later year, the overall long-term effect on revenue collected of such timing behaviour is neutral.

One of the common econometric problems in capital gains realisations response studies is simultaneity between the dependent variable being explained—the CGT rate—and the independent (explanatory) variables—consisting of all variables seen as affecting realisations (Zodrow, 1992). The simultaneity problem occurs when a change in the dependent variable affects the independent variable simultaneously to the expected relationship where the independent variable affects the dependent variable; the effect of this problem on the estimation process can be severe. Where there is a simultaneity problem, there will be systematically biased and inconsistent estimated coefficients on the explanatory variable in the regression equation (Zodrow, 1992). The simultaneity problem in econometric studies on the capital gains realisations response is that the marginal CGT rate depends positively on the level of capital gains realisations. More specifically, a taxpayer can face a higher marginal tax rate as a result of realising a capital gain (Zodrow, 1992). It follows that simultaneity problems tend to be associated with the use of a 'last-dollar' marginal tax rate in elasticity studies. Although some researchers have attempted to deal with the simultaneity problem by using a measure of the CGT rate that does not depend on the level of capital gains realisations, such corrections are not always successful in ensuring that the CGT rate variable is not endogenous (Zodrow, 1992).

## 2.5 REVIEW OF CAPITAL GAINS REALISATIONS RESPONSE STUDIES

This section will consider the major capital gains realisations response studies that have taken place, primarily in the United States, over the last few decades. The studies are considered by reference to the three distinct groupings of type of study—cross-sectional, time series and panel data—that have been undertaken between 1978 and 2015. The studies are organised on this basis as the type of data used can affect the estimates—especially in the case of cross-sectional studies.



### Cross-sectional studies

A cross-sectional data set consists of a sample of units in a population taken at a given point in time (Wooldridge, 2016). A cross-sectional capital gains realisations response study is one that uses data for a sample of taxpayers for a single year. The earliest capital gains realisations response studies were based on cross-sectional analysis, with the first being Feldstein and Yitzhaki (1978), followed by Feldstein, Slemrod and Yitzhaki (1980). This chapter also reviews Minarik (1984), which is a cross-sectional study using the same data as Feldstein et al. (1980).

The first part of this section considers the main capital gains realisations response studies that have used a cross-sectional data approach, adopting a chronological approach for the analysis. Subsequently, specific advantages and disadvantages of this particular approach are explored. The limitations of the approach are significant. The fact that cross section data are no longer used reflects these limitations.

#### Studies using cross-sectional data

Feldstein and Yitzhaki (1978) is a U.S. capital gains realisations response study that used cross-sectional data. Its focus was on how sensitive investors are to tax rates in the decision to realise corporate shares. The analysis differentiated between two types of capital gains realisations: 'switch' sales, where the proceeds are reinvested, and 'net' sales, where the proceeds are not reinvested. The taxpayer data used in the study were from 1963, and high-income taxpayers were deliberately oversampled (Feldstein & Yitzhaki, 1978). The research found that switch sellers were highly responsive to the CGT rate. Feldstein and Yitzhaki (1978) also included simulations of alternative CGT policies; one of the findings here was that if capital gains were taxed at ordinary income rates, rather than at the prevailing preferential rates in the year of the sample, there would be a dramatic decrease in the volume of realisations. In their conclusion, Feldstein and Yitzhaki (1978) referred to the importance of considering incentive and efficiency effects as well as equity criteria in a redesign of the CGT law. The authors made the case for taxation of capital gains at preferential rates as a way of improving economic efficiency and incentives for investment. In their basic estimate, they reported a coefficient for the CGT rate variable of –3.2. The authors concluded that the estimate indicated a very powerful effect of CGT and that higher tax rates are a significant disincentive to the sale of common stock.

Feldstein et al. (1980) is a U.S. cross-sectional elasticity study for 1973, which extended on the work in Feldstein and Yitzhaki (1978). The study was limited to one type of capital asset—corporate stock—and most of the analysis was limited to high-income taxpayers. The study imputed taxpayer wealth, as the tax return information itself contained no information about the portfolio value of individual taxpayers. The main analysis of the study was limited to those taxpayers who had dividends of at least US$3,000 in 1973 (Feldstein et al., 1980). Taxpayers who were in receipt of dividends in the year of the study were identified as those who owned shares, and they could be included in the sample. Sampling taxpayers in receipt of dividends was intended to include taxpayers who owned corporate shares, not only those that sold this type of asset during the year (Feldstein et al., 1980). In 1973, the dividend yield on company shares was approximately 3%; consistent with this, the minimum portfolio size of investors in the sample was imputed to be US$100,000 (Feldstein et al., 1980). The amount of dividends received by taxpayers in the sample was a proxy for estimating taxpayer share holdings. Selecting the sample according to this criterion of a minimum amount of dividends may be problematic, and there have been comments in the literature to this effect. Cook and O'Hare (1987) noted, for example, that many types of investments pay little or no dividends.

One of the problems that those researching the capital gains realisations response face is deciding which CGT rate to use; this may be a 'first-dollar' or 'last-dollar' CGT rate or another type of CGT rate. In a CGT realisations response study, the first-dollar CGT rate is the rate that applies to the first dollar of capital gains that the taxpayer realises. The advantage of the first-dollar CGT rate is that it is exogenous, specifically that it is independent of the taxpayer's decision on the amount of capital gains to realise (Feldstein et al., 1980). The last-dollar CGT rate is the rate that would be incurred if the taxpayer had increased their actual capital gains realised by one dollar. According to Feldstein et al. (1980), it is more appropriate to use a last-dollar CGT rate rather than a first-dollar CGT rate. This is partly because, in the case of wealthy taxpayers, there is the potential for substantial differentiation between the first-dollar CGT rate and the tax rate at which marginal decisions concerning capital gains realisations are made. Feldstein et al. (1980) used an instrumental variable estimation procedure whereby the average capital gains for taxpayers at a particular income level were used to predict the last-dollar CGT rate. The dependent variables used were the ratio of shares to dividends, the ratio of long-term gains on shares to dividends, and a dummy variable for the sale of shares. The instrumental variables were the first-dollar CGT rate and the last-dollar CGT rate.

Feldstein et al. (1980) reported an elasticity point estimate of –3.75. Subsequently, Minarik (1984) reviewed the study and concluded that it overestimated the realisations response. According to Gravelle (1994), where elasticity is high, the welfare cost—in the form of the distorting effects of the tax—is also high. This welfare cost can be characterised as one of the efficiency effects of the tax. The results in Feldstein et al. are in the upper range of reported elasticity point estimates. Notably, several commentators have disagreed with the high elasticity found in the study and asserted it is inconsistent with observation. The elasticity point estimate reported in Feldstein et al. implies that if the CGT rate were cut by 10%, realisations would increase by 37.5%. If this estimate were correct, it follows that a small increase in the CGT rate would cause a large decrease in realisations. According to Gravelle (1994), the actual experience of a small increase in the CGT rate did not cause the virtual cessation of realisations that the –3.75 elasticity point estimate in Feldstein et al. (1980) implies.

One of the inherent limitations of Feldstein et al. (1980) is that, because it used cross-sectional data, the estimates of the capital gains realisations response may be overstated. This is because the elasticity point estimate is likely to include a measure of transitory or timing responses that are distinct from the permanent response to a lowering of the prevailing statutory CGT rate. A consequence of cross-sectional studies with only one year of data is that there is no way of ascertaining to what extent the elasticity point estimate is a measure of timing behaviour by individual taxpayers. The potential for overstatement of the sensitivity of realisations to a temporarily low tax rate was referred to in the discussion of the results in Feldstein et al. (1980). According to Burman (1999), cross-sectional studies may reveal more about timing strategies rather than the response to statutory changes in tax rates that are expected to be permanent or long lasting. Perhaps the main criticism of cross-sectional studies is that to the extent it is not possible to disentangle timing responses from the permanent response, the estimates will be overstated.

Feldstein et al. (1980) found that older taxpayers are more likely to engage in net selling rather than switch selling. Part of the rationale for this conclusion was that retirees are likely to have lower incomes and are more likely to want to use rather than reinvest the proceeds of their net sales of shares (Feldstein et al., 1980). The data used in the Feldstein et al. study did not allow switch selling and net selling to be distinguished.

Feldstein et al. (1980) identified two other variables that are likely to have an effect on the taxpayer's decision to sell shares: the value of shares in their portfolio and the level of income. Feldstein et al. found that the probability of a taxpayer selling some of their share portfolio increases with portfolio size. They noted that the effect of the taxpayer's age on the realising of capital gains,[22] although difficult to interpret, is not statistically significant when tax rate, income and portfolio size are taken into account (Feldstein et al., 1980).

Feldstein et al. (1980) identified a limitation of their study being the effect of the change in rules for assets transferred in the event of a taxpayer's death. Specifically, in 1973, the year of the study, U.S. tax law allowed for a full revaluation of these assets. In subsequent years, the law was amended to allow for only a step-up in basis on the transferred asset. Feldstein et al. acknowledged that this change in tax law meant that the advantage of holding rather than selling a CGT asset was reduced in the years subsequent to their study, which means that investor behaviour may be less sensitive to tax rates as a result. Caution should be taken in how the Feldstein et al. elasticity estimate may apply to tax years after 1973, as the elasticity estimate might be lower in those years.

Feldstein et al. (1980) noted that although their regression analysis should include an explanatory variable for accrued capital gains available for realisation, it does not, as the information was not available. The elasticity reported by Feldstein et al. is higher in magnitude in comparison with most other realisations response studies. According to McCarten (1988), the estimated parameters in the Feldstein et al. study are highly

22 As distinct from the selling of shares, which may be at a loss.

biased, and this might be due to the use of an inappropriate estimation procedure given the characteristics of their data.

Minarik (1984) presented an alternative functional form using the same data as Feldstein et al. (1980) and a weighted least squares regression technique, which resulted in a significantly smaller elasticity point estimate. According to Minarik, the sensitivity of capital gains realisations to marginal tax rates is vitally important. Minarik used a series of steps to present and apply what he considered a superior methodology to Feldstein et al., the result of which is a significantly lower elasticity estimate.

According to Minarik (1984), the high elasticity point estimate in Feldstein et al. (1980) was due to an econometric error related to the weighting of the observations. A significantly lower elasticity could be found using similar data and a different weighting method. Minarik argued it was not appropriate for Feldstein et al. to have used ordinary least squares to fit their equations given that their sample was not stratified according to the independent variable in the regression. According to Minarik, the combination of Feldstein et al. using unweighted ordinary least squares and their sampling technique resulted in an oversampling of individuals who realised large capital gains. Minarik noted that because their sample was stratified according to the dependent variable, the use of weighted least squares was appropriate.

Minarik (1984) did not agree with the use of unweighted summary statistics in calculating the elasticity, especially since Feldstein et al. (1980) used their coefficients to simulate the revenue effects of a change in the CGT rate using a weighted data file.

Minarik (1984) was critical of the use of a positive age dummy variable by Feldstein et al. (1980), and argued the negative age dummy variable used in his own study was more appropriate. According to Minarik, the fact that capital gains escape tax at death is a more powerful effect than the need for cash among taxpayers aged 65 and over who hold at least US$100,000 of corporate shares.

According to Minarik (1984), the elasticity point estimate in the Feldstein et al. (1980) study implies that an increase in the CGT rate of 0.6% from 20.6% to 21.2% would cause the average shareholder with at least US$1,500,000 of shares to completely stop realising capital gains on those shares. Minarik noted that the Feldstein et al. elasticity point estimate implies that in the event of a 0.6% CGT rate cut from 20.6% to 20%, the same taxpayer would double their realisations. Minarik argued that the use of a last-dollar tax rate by Feldstein et al. was not appropriate, given that this is relevant to the taxpayer's decision to realise additional gains rather than a CGT rate that reflects the amount of capital gains that they did realise. According to Minarik, the use of an average tax rate for predicted gains would have been more appropriate. According to Auerbach (1988), although Minarik's comment on the rate used in Feldstein et al. highlighted the difficulty of having to use a single tax rate in an elasticity study to represent an entire tax schedule, there is no theoretical justification for any one type of such a tax rate.

After applying all his suggested changes to the Feldstein et al. (1980) equation, Minarik estimated an elasticity of realisations of long-term capital gains of –0.6; this implies a level of realisations response that is too low to cause an increase in CGT revenue in the event of a small rate reduction.

Minarik (1984) appears to have improved on the methodology used in Feldstein et al. (1980) in two ways. First, Minarik's sample was weighted to reflect the taxpayer population; and second, Minarik's equation included more non-tax variables thought to influence realisations than Feldstein et al. Notwithstanding these improvements, Minarik was still unable to differentiate between permanent and timing effects given the use of cross-sectional data.

In a reply to Minarik (1984), Feldstein et al. (1984) sought to justify the appropriateness of their higher elasticity point estimate on the basis that higher-income taxpayers are more responsive to tax rate changes and their elasticity is appropriate for evaluating tax rate changes that largely affect high-income taxpayers. Feldstein et al. disputed the example provided by Minarik of the effect of a CGT rate increase from 20.6% to 21.2% being the complete cessation of capital gains realisations by higher-income taxpayers. According to Feldstein et al., this example is extremely misleading, and they explained that a more likely scenario is that, although a few wealthy taxpayers would be more likely to hold assets with very large accrued capital gains, most shareholders would not change their realisation behaviour.

Given these examples of cross-sectional data studies, the analysis now considers the strengths and weaknesses of this particular approach.

## Advantages of cross-sectional data

Although cross-sectional data may have some advantages, these can be described more accurately as advantages of micro data generally and of panel data in particular.

One of the advantages of a cross-sectional study is the number of observations it includes. Zodrow (1992) noted that this high number of observations means that the marginal tax rate variable can be calculated for specific individual taxpayers, resulting in an overall tax rate that is more accurate than for the time series approach. The use of cross-sectional data can more accurately gauge the revenue consequences at the individual taxpayer level, with these results aggregated to obtain the overall revenue response (Zodrow, 1992). These advantages are in contrast to the time series method, where the marginal tax rate used is effectively an estimate derived from aggregate taxpayer data. Cross-sectional studies typically have a large number of observations, as the taxpayer data are from individual tax returns (Zodrow, 1992). By contrast, time series studies have a small number of observations, as they are restricted to aggregate taxpayer data.

## Limitations of cross-sectional data

Cross-sectional studies have been criticised on a number of grounds. First, they fail to distinguish between transitory and permanent effects. Second, they include effects specific to individual taxpayers and the studies cannot disentangle these effects. Third, they fail to include a measure of accrued unrealised capital gains (Gravelle, 1994). A fourth problem is the correlation between the tax rate and income and wealth variables, which may cause difficulty in separating the price and income effects (Gravelle, 1994). A fifth problem is the lack of information about the components of the model specification, and a sixth problem is they are prone to 'heterogeneity bias'. Auerbach (1989) and Gravelle (1994) suggested that the problems are such that the results do not provide evidence on the capital gains realisations response. Each of these criticisms is now explored in turn.

The inability of cross-sectional studies to separate temporary and permanent effects is because they include only one tax rate per taxpayer: the tax rate that the taxpayer faces in the year of the study. Cross-sectional studies may attempt to estimate the relationship of the tax rate to the taxpayer's tax rate in other years by comparing it with the tax rates of similar taxpayers in the same sample and year (Auerbach, 1988). This is clearly not the same as comparing a taxpayer's tax rate in the one year with other years before and after that year. Due to the inability of cross-sectional studies to estimate temporary effects separately, these studies can show a negative relationship between CGT rates and realisations even in instances where there is no permanent effect. On this basis alone, the cross-sectional methodology is inferior compared to the alternative methodologies explored later in this chapter—all of which use more than one year of data.

Cross-sectional studies incorrectly include individual-specific effects as part of the elasticity point estimate. Consequently, where timing effects are present, the permanent realisations response in a cross-sectional study will be overstated. This inability to accurately measure the permanent elasticity is an inherent feature of cross-sectional studies, since the absence of data from several tax years means there is no information on taxpayers' timing behaviour. Timing behaviour refers to taxpayers choosing to realise capital gains in years when income is unusually low. The incentive to time capital gains realisations in this way applies especially to taxpayers with high permanent incomes, which fluctuate between tax years. Timing of capital gains realisations to coincide with years when the taxpayer's income is unusually low is not a permanent response to the CGT rate.

Cross-sectional elasticity estimates are likely to include a transitory response given that a personal taxpayer's income can fluctuate over time. Cross-sectional data contain no information about the difference between a taxpayer's income in the year of the study and their permanent income. By contrast, a panel of taxpayer data allows for a measure of permanent income by way of an average of taxpayer income over several years. By using such an average to determine permanent income, the researcher can then compare it to income in a single year to ascertain whether income is unusually low in the year concerned. Revenue estimating agencies in the United States (JCT and Treasury) have chosen not to rely on cross-sectional elasticity studies that produced very high elasticity estimates.

Gravelle (1991) explained the need for a measure of accrued capital gains in estimating the capital gains realisations response. Nevertheless, several capital gains realisations response studies have not included a measure of accrued gains in the estimating equations. The need for a measure of accrued gains originates from the fact that in the long run, the amount of capital gains realisations cannot exceed the stock of accrued gains (Gravelle, 1991). Some of the highest reported estimates of elasticity—such as the –3.75 estimated by Feldstein et al. (1980)—imply that a level of realisations in excess of the stock of accrued gains is possible. According to Gravelle, even in a hypothetical scenario where there are no transaction costs associated with trading CGT assets, it is unlikely that all of these assets could be realised in a single tax year. This is due to a number of factors such as the intrinsic worth of certain types of assets to taxpayers and the incentive to hold assets until death in the United States (Gravelle, 1991).

Zodrow (1992) highlighted another problem with cross-sectional studies: the difficulty in identifying the separate effects of income and CGT rates on capital gains realisations behaviour. This is because these are two closely related explanatory variables in a realisations response equation. Personal taxpayers with the same economic income may face different tax rates because of factors such as the amount of losses carried forward to the current tax year and differences in deductions claimed (Zodrow, 1992). Although such differences provide a source of independent variation in tax rate and income, it is unclear whether it is possible to accurately separate the effects of income and tax price (Zodrow, 1992).



Zodrow (1992) identified a further problem associated with cross-sectional studies being the lack of accurate data on the explanatory variables in the equation. Where data from a source other than individual tax returns are used, these data are often imputed from an aggregate source, which can lead to measurement errors, resulting in biased estimates of the coefficients in the regression equation.

Cross-sectional studies suffer from the problem of 'heterogeneity bias'. This term describes the lack of a variable in the estimating equation to control for the investment preferences of individual taxpayers. The problem is that observed changes in the tax rate variable are not independent or exogenous but are dependent on—and determined endogenously by—differences in individual behaviour reflecting differences in taxpayer investment preferences that are not captured by the explanatory variables in the equation (Zodrow, 1992). The endogeneity of the explanatory variable is a problem in cross-sectional studies, where much of the variation is due to circumstances of the individual taxpayer; this is in contrast with time series studies where the problem is not as apparent because the major source of variation is due to tax law changes (Gravelle, 2010). According to Bogart and Gentry (1995), the fact that in a cross-sectional study, the individual's tax rate is endogenous to their behaviour can result in a spurious correlation between tax rates and realisations. One way of explaining this problem is that differences in taxpayers' investment preferences can simultaneously affect taxpayers' tax rate and the amount of their capital gains realisations, thus the independent variable—the tax rate—is dependent on taxpayer behaviour (Gravelle, 1990). For example, where tax rates are progressive, a taxpayer who realises a large amount of capital gains may be in a higher-income tax bracket as a result (Bogart & Gentry, 1995).

## Summary

The review of the literature on cross-sectional capital gains realisations response studies has revealed that the results from these studies have a number of shortcomings. This is due to their unreliability in estimating the permanent elasticity of capital gains realisations, as confirmed in the wide range of results produced and the known problems with the methodology. This section highlighted the problems with and criticism of cross-sectional analysis as well as some of the challenges for regression analysis. Although cross-sectional studies have the advantage of many observations, these studies have the distinct disadvantage of being restricted to a single tax year. This inherent problem in cross-sectional studies is considered to outweigh any advantages that there are and makes cross-sectional studies the least preferred of the possible data types.

The review of the literature on cross-sectional studies demonstrates that timing behaviour is an important consideration in capital gains realisations response studies. Without data spanning several tax years it is not possible to ascertain whether taxpayers in the sample are responding to the statutory CGT rate or the fact that their income in the year of the study may be atypically low. According to Burman (1999), the main identifying assumption underlying cross-sectional studies is invalid. Specifically, while these studies assume that the tax rates of individual taxpayers are roughly constant over time, they are in fact highly volatile.

In conclusion, the criticisms of cross-sectional realisations response studies and the unreliability of the estimates they produce are such that cross-sectional data have not been considered for the quantitative study in this book. The review of cross-sectional studies in this chapter has been included for completeness, given that there are published studies that used this method. It is important to note that the literature reviewed in this section confirms that this data type is unsuitable for a capital gains realisations response study.

## Time series

A study using time series data relates total capital gains realisations, on a year-by-year basis, over several years to the CGT rate in each particular year. Time series studies typically do not use individual tax return data, relying instead on aggregate tax return data. According to Mariger (1995), aggregate time series data contain all the empirical evidence on capital gains realisations response. This is notwithstanding that some of the models used to estimate the capital gains realisations response can be quite simple due to data limitations (Mariger, 1995).

In the United States, time series capital gains realisations response studies have produced elasticity point estimates that are lower than for those reported in cross-sectional studies. The range of results from what the literature characterises as a 'core' of time series studies ranges between results that are not statistically significant to those of approximately 1.00 in absolute value. These studies, commencing with Auerbach in 1988 and concluding with Eichner and Sinai in 2000, are now considered in more detail.

### Studies using time series data

A study by Auerbach (1988) consists of a main paper authored by Auerbach and a separate comment and discussion section authored by Poterba. The paper contains a commentary on the time series evidence available at that time. Auerbach referred to the problem of how to model the effects of tax rates on realisations to permit a realistic characterisation of taxpayer behaviour. Auerbach noted the nonstationary nature of capital gains realisations and the variables used to explain realisations; specifically, in the estimating equation, it is necessary to take into account the fact that these vary systematically with time. One of the problems associated with nonstationary time series regressions identified by Auerbach is that *t*-ratios and other test statistics are incorrectly estimated, and significance levels may be greatly overstated. It follows that there is a need to test the variables in the equation for nonstationarity. Although using first-differenced variables in the equation would be expected to eliminate a unit root, instances where first differencing may create its own problems have been referred to in the literature. For example, Shumway and Stoffer (2011) noted that the use of first differencing can result in too severe a modification and may result in an 'overdifferencing' of the original process.

Auerbach (1988) found that when the time series equations were corrected for nonstationarity and expectations of changes in tax rate were correctly accounted for, there was no measurable response of capital gains realisations to changes in CGT rates.

Auerbach (1988) also highlighted the difficulty in ascertaining the theoretical importance of the lagged tax rate variable, which is a feature of the equation in several time series studies. In previous studies, the inclusion of a lagged tax rate variable had been justified according to its usefulness in determining to what extent the CGT rate responsiveness of capital gains is temporary rather than permanent (Auerbach, 1988). A second reason for the inclusion of a lagged tax rate variable is to use it as a proxy for the past realisation behaviour of taxpayers. According to Auerbach, the theoretical importance of such a variable is difficult to ascertain given that it does not play a clear role in the individual taxpayer's problem of the trade-off between the gains of portfolio adjustment and the tax costs of realisation.

According to Auerbach (1988), although tax considerations are a strong influence on taxpayers' decisions on when to realise capital gains, it is the timing effect that is the most noticeable, and there is a lack of convincing evidence of a strong permanent effect. In testimony to the Australian Senate Committee Inquiry, Auerbach (1999) noted that some of the previous CGT rate reductions in the United States might have been driven more by wishful thinking than by evidence and that the lack of support for a CGT preference on its own merits had led to proponents advancing 'free lunch' arguments.

Auerbach (1988) demonstrated that, in time series studies, the responsiveness of capital gains realisations to tax rate decreased when expected tax rate changes were incorporated into the specification. More specifically, when tax rate changes are controlled for, it is impossible to reject the hypothesis that in the long run, the tax rate has no effect on realisations (Auerbach, 1988). Furthermore, the data in time series studies prefer equations based on the change in tax rates only, rather than on the level of tax rates, suggesting that time series studies may not be robust to minor specification changes (Auerbach, 1988).

Auerbach (1988) referred to two factors that may be of relevance to potential increases in revenue from lower CGT rates: first, the perception that lower tax rates in general may reduce the level of tax evasion; second, bringing forward capital gains realisations may increase the present value of a government's tax receipts (Auerbach, 1988).

In a separate study, the U.S. CBO (1988) found that higher marginal tax rates on capital gains had the effect of reducing realisations. It was noted in the CBO study that the finding suggests that CGT rates cannot be raised to a level that is 'too high' without ultimately reducing revenue. Despite this, the CBO found that the increase in tax rates in the *TRA86* would most likely have the effect of increasing revenue, while a reduction in the top tax rate to 15% would be likely to reduce revenue.

The CBO (1988) emphasised that there are many factors other than revenue effects that should be considered in deciding how to tax capital gains. Because of these there may be a justification to tax capital gains at a rate above or below the revenue maximising rate.

A study by Gillingham and Greenlees (1992) was described by the authors as one that addresses the response of revenue to the CGT rate, rather than the response of capital gains realisations to the tax rate, as this study considered the former more relevant to the specific question of whether a tax cut can pay for itself. The study by Gillingham and Greenlees was based on a previous CBO time series study for the period from 1954 to 1985, extended to include subsequent years up to and including 1989. Gillingham and Greenlees used an instrumental variables technique concerned with taxes on predicted gains as an instrument; the authors regressed actual effective tax rates on predicted rates and used the fitted values in the realisations regression. According to Gillingham and Greenlees, the instrumental variables technique is preferable to the ordinary least squares technique used by the CBO and Auerbach. Instrumental variables use a two-stage least squares method, where a preliminary regression treats the CGT rate as the dependent variable and then estimates this variable using other predetermined instruments (Gravelle, 2010). The actual CGT rate could be regressed on a predicted rate, first-dollar rate or maximum rate, with the fitted values used in the final regression (Gravelle, 2010).

Gravelle (2010) identified that there may be problems in using the maximum tax rate as an instrument in the Gillingham and Greenlees (1992) time series regression, as there were several tax law changes over the time period that affected the relationship between the maximum and average tax rates. More specifically, there were years when a large fraction of taxpayers faced the maximum tax rate and other years where it affected only a small fraction of taxpayers (Gravelle, 2010). When the Gillingham and Greenlee equations included a variable for the stock of accrued gains, their elasticity point estimates ranged from –0.71 to –1.78 at a 20% tax rate; from –0.89 to –2.23 at a 25% tax rate; and from –1.06 to –2.68 at a 30% tax rate.

Bogart and Gentry (1995) completed a time series study spanning the years 1979 to 1990. The study used state-level aggregated data,[23] rather than data on individual taxpayers, to overcome the problem of the individual marginal tax rate being endogenous to the amount of capital gains realised while still allowing for the use of panel econometric techniques. Bogart and Gentry referred to the endogenous relationship between an individual's tax rate and their capital gains realisations behaviour as the biggest problem in estimating realisations behaviour using data on individuals. Although the Bogart and Gentry study was focused on results from a random sample of the taxpayer population, the authors reported the results for high-income taxpayers separately so that these can be compared with earlier studies focused on high-income taxpayers such as Feldstein et al. (1980). For the whole population of taxpayers in the panel, the average capital gains realised per tax return was US$1,203 per annum (Bogart and Gentry, 1995).

Bogart and Gentry (1995) outlined the advantages and disadvantages of studies focused on high-income taxpayers. One of the advantages is that lower-income groups may have less discretion in the timing of their capital gains realisations. Specifically, lower-income taxpayers may be more likely than higher-income taxpayers to realise capital gains

23 The result of this approach is that there were several observations for each tax year, with each observation being the aggregate data for each state.

for consumption purposes, as their need to do so arises, independent of any lowering of the CGT rate. According to Bogart and Gentry, to the extent that taxpayers in the higher-income group have a relatively lesser need to realise capital gains for consumption purposes, they may be considered a demographic for which the capital gains realisations response can be better observed. Furthermore, given that accrued capital gains and realisation of these gains are more concentrated at higher levels of income, there appears to be some merit in oversampling this particular group of taxpayers.



Bogart and Gentry (1995) referred to the non-tax factors that influence taxpayers' decisions of whether to realise capital gains. Typically, these non-tax factors are the control variables in capital gains realisations response studies. Examples of these variables include the variation in the stock of accrued capital gains and variation in the propensity of taxpayers to realise capital gains. Other examples of variables that are likely to affect an individual taxpayer's decision to realise capital gains include permanent and transitory income, wealth, marital status, age, family size and region of residence (Bogart & Gentry, 1995). The factors controlled for in studies using aggregate time series data are the macroeconomic variables that affect aggregate capital gains realisations (Bogart & Gentry, 1995).

The focus on state tax rates in Bogart and Gentry (1995) has several advantages. First, in the instance of a taxpayer relocating from a U.S. state with a relatively high state tax rate to a state without a state income tax, the effect on capital gains realisations can be examined (Bogart & Gentry, 1995). Bogart and Gentry considered that since U.S. state tax rates rarely change, a taxpayer who experiences a drop in their marginal CGT rate as a result of moving states is subject to a permanent rather than transitory tax rate change. Furthermore, they considered that state tax rates can be considered an exogenous source of rate variation, assuming that taxpayers do not base their decision to relocate between states on the variation in state tax rates (Bogart & Gentry, 1995). Bogart and Gentry qualified their use of state tax rates by noting there are still some transitory effects to consider related to state tax rates. Bogart and Gentry used the total of the highest federal and state tax rates as the marginal tax rate in their study. Although this calculation of a marginal tax rate was something of an assumption, it can be seen as reasonably accurate given that most capital gains are realised by taxpayers with high incomes. Bogart and Gentry noted that because the highest state marginal tax rate usually commences at a relatively low level of income compared to the federal top marginal tax rate, interstate variation—an integral component of the study—is not adversely affected.

Bogart and Gentry (1995) included controls for cyclical macroeconomic conditions, as was the practice in other studies. Bogart and Gentry used the unemployment rate as one such control; the authors considered that if a high unemployment rate is indicative of poor business conditions leading to a slower appreciation of capital assets, the propensity of taxpayers to realise capital gains will be reduced. Another example of a control factor that Bogart and Gentry used in their study was housing wealth for each state, determined by the decennial U.S. census median house values for owner-occupied, non-business-related housing. The housing ownership variable in the Bogart and Gentry study was used as a control for differences in portfolio consumption across states.

Bogart and Gentry (1995) also included controls for the age distribution of the taxpayer population in each state. This was achieved by determining the proportion of the population aged 65 years and over; the average proportion of taxpayers in this category for all states and all years is 11.6%. According to Bogart and Gentry, there are two competing effects associated with taxpayers aged over 65. The first is that they may be more likely to realise capital gains, and the second is that because of the step-up in basis at death—allowed under U.S. tax law—they may have an increased likelihood of not realising capital gains (Bogart & Gentry, 1995). In the Bogart and Gentry study there is a negative relationship between the fraction of a state's population that is over 65 years of age and the amount of capital gains realised. This is consistent with the approach taken by Minarik (1984) to the question of the overall propensity of older taxpayers to realise capital gains; whereas according to Feldstein et al. (1980) there is an overall increased likelihood of older taxpayers realising capital gains. Bogart and Gentry described the negative relationship between the proportion of the taxpayer population aged over 65 and capital gains realisations as somewhat counterintuitive.

Share ownership by state was also considered in the study; the information used here was from a random survey on the topic conducted by the New York Stock Exchange that estimated the incidence of share ownership by state (Bogart & Gentry, 1995). Bogart and Gentry (1995) explained that there is likely to be a positive correlation between share ownership and wealth and that sales of shares that are tax-motivated may be more prevalent in states that have a higher proportion of share ownership. Bogart and Gentry (1995) also noted that states with high levels of other capital income[24] tended to have more capital gains as well.

In their analysis of the results of their study, Bogart and Gentry (1995) noted that there are indirect revenue effects relevant to the elasticity of capital gains realisations, but these were not considered in their study. Bogart and Gentry referred specifically to the fact that their study did not take into account revenue effects of a progressive tax system; that is, while their study assumed realisations are at a flat tax rate,[25] in practice the realisation of a large capital gain could place a taxpayer in a higher tax bracket.[26] Bogart and Gentry also noted the potential for a response to changes in tax rate in the form of a change in the level of investment or a change in the rate at which tax shelters are used.

Bogart and Gentry (1995) explained they attempted to control for temporary timing effects by adding two variables to some of their specifications: a 'lag change' variable[27] and a 'lead change' variable.[28] The former described the change in the tax rate from the previous to current year and the latter the change in the tax rate between the subsequent and current year (Bogart & Gentry, 1995). This was also the approach used by Auerbach

24 Defined in the study as dividends plus interest received.

25 The marginal tax rate used in the study.

26 It would follow, in this case, that an elasticity of less than 1.00, in absolute value, could result in increased revenue where there is a reduction to the capital gains tax rate.

27 The change in the tax rate between the current year and the previous year.

28 The change in the tax rate between the subsequent year and the current year.

(1988). Using their basic specification, Bogart and Gentry estimated an elasticity of capital gains realisations of –0.65; they noted that their estimate casts doubt on the argument that reducing the CGT rate is self-financing.

Bogart and Gentry (1995) identified three qualifications to the results of their study. First, the results are sensitive to the econometric specification of year effects and this is not statistically significant for some specifications. Second, because the study used a reduced form specification, it does not account for some of the indirect revenue effects of a CGT rate change. Third, Bogart and Gentry noted that the importance of the CGT rate is not limited to revenue as there are implications for fairness and economic efficiency.



Bogart and Gentry (1995) also explored the use of alternative specifications to those in their main estimating equation. In one example of varying the main equation, they included a dummy variable for each state, but did not control for year-specific effects. Under this alternative equation, the elasticity estimate was –2.26. Bogart and Gentry concluded that this alternative estimate includes transitory effects of changes in tax rates and it illustrates the importance of controlling for year-specific effects that have a common influence on all states. The authors noted that their elasticity point estimate, from their main equation, of –0.65 is robust to the alternative specifications outlined in their paper.

In a review of elasticity studies since the 1980s, Gravelle (2010) noted that the techniques used in Bogart and Gentry (1995), including the use of differentials between states and dummy variables to control for fixed year effects, should identify a permanent elasticity.

Eichner and Sinai (2000) completed an aggregate time series study using aggregate tax return data from 1955 to 1997. Eichner and Sinai explained that time series studies are the best way to estimate the long-run realisation elasticity, one reason being that panel data typically span a lesser number of years than time series, so that the former are not as useful for separating out long-run and transitory elasticities. Eichner and Sinai referred to the sequence of previous tax changes as an influence on the level of accrued capital gains that taxpayers can realise. Specifically, where previous tax changes encouraged realisations of capital gains, the stock of capital gains remaining in later years is diminished and fewer asset portfolios are in need of rebalancing (Eichner & Sinai, 2000).

Eichner and Sinai (2000) reported several realisation elasticities; using their main equation the elasticity point estimate was –0.64 with a 1955–85 sample period and –0.81 with a 1955–97 sample period. In their specification, which attempted to model anticipated changes in the CGT rate, the point estimate is –0.74. However, Eichner and Sinai noted that their estimate was sensitive to the inclusion of 1986, a year in which there was an extraordinarily high level of capital gains realisations due to the pre-announced increase to the CGT rate. Eichner and Sinai found that by including a dummy variable for 1986—effectively excluding that year from the regression—the elasticity point estimate was –0.45. It may be that the latter model specification is preferred, especially considering that timing effects are known to have been an influence on the realisations that occurred in 1986 before *TRA86* took effect in 1987. *TRA86* resulted in what was effectively a pre-announced CGT rate increase, given that before it took effect the top rate on CGT was 20% and after it took effect the top rate of tax on capital gains was set at 28% (Burman, 1999).

Eichner and Sinai (2000) examined the specific question of the revenue effects of the *Taxpayer Relief Act of 1997* (*TRA97*), under which the top rate of CGT was reduced from 28% to 20% and the 15% rate was reduced to 10%. Eichner and Sinai used a range of elasticity estimates to examine revenue effects of the 1997 CGT rate reductions. Eichner and Sinai (2000) found that although there was an increase in realisations in 1997 compared to 1986, there was also a significant decrease in the average tax rate weighted by predicted 1996 realisations—from 23.4% to 16.5%. Eichner and Sinai considered the offsetting effects of *TRA97* leading to additional capital gains realisations and the decrease in revenue collected as a result of the CGT rate change. They concluded that the net revenue loss for 1997 was US$2.8 billion per year, approximately 5% of 1996 CGT revenue. Eichner and Sinai (2000) noted the unusual realisation dynamics of the years around *TRA86* resulting from the pre-announcement of the higher CGT rates to take effect in 1987. Specifically, even though $165.5 billion of capital gains realisations in 1985 was a record at that time, taxpayers realised $317 billon of capital gains in 1986 in order to take advantage of the lower rate relative to the increased CGT rate to take effect in the following year (Eichner & Sinai, 2000). According to the authors, there is evidence of some of these realisations in 1986 being a result of timing behaviour, which of itself interferes with the measurement of estimated long-run elasticity. The aggregate data give the appearance of low tax rate periods being associated with higher realisations and high tax rate periods being associated with lower realisations, whereas the true situation is representative of a reshuffling of the timing of capital gains realisations with no effect on the aggregate amount realised over the years concerned (Eichner & Sinai, 2000).

Eichner and Sinai (2000) referred specifically to the issue of 'path dependence,' which describes the dampening effect of previous CGT rate reductions on the future unlocking effects in subsequent years of additional rate reductions. The implication of this is that if path dependence is not considered in an elasticity equation for a period in which there are several CGT rate cuts, the elasticity point estimate will be overstated for the later years of the study. By way of example, Eichner and Sinai explained that a CGT rate reduction in the United States shortly after *TRA86* may not generate the same realisations response as a comparable rate reduction in 1997 given the high amounts of capital gains that taxpayers had already realised in 1986 before the *TRA86* took effect in 1987.

Eichner and Sinai (2000) identified another factor that caused a lowering of the sensitivity of capital gains realisations to the CGT rate over the period of their study: the increase in the share of household equity held in mutual funds. This is suggestive of mutual fund managers realising more gains than would individual taxpayers, which may lead to the conclusion that fund managers are not as tax efficient as individual investors (Eichner & Sinai, 2000). However, according to Gravelle (1990), mutual stock funds have higher turnover rates because of their professional management and lower brokerage fees. Eichner and Sinai noted that extending their sample caused the elasticity point estimate to fall and that this is consistent with mutual funds comprising only a small proportion (5.8%) of equities between 1954 and 1985 and a larger proportion (22.8%) of equities after 1985.

In one of their alternate specifications, Eichner and Sinai (2000) used the instrumental variable of the top marginal tax rate on capital gains, in an attempt to address the problem of endogeneity. The use of instrumental variables had the effect of increasing the magnitude of the elasticity point estimate to –1.21, compared to –0.81 in their ordinary least squares (OLS) regression. According to Eichner and Sinai, the instrumental variables regression does not necessarily solve the problem, and for this reason they reported the results of both OLS and instrumental variables regressions.

In their conclusion, Eichner and Sinai (2000) commented on the sensitivity of their results to how 1986 is modelled, and they identified a need for future research that uses micro data, rather than time series data, in a more structural framework.



## Advantages of time series studies

The principal advantage of time series studies, compared to cross-sectional studies, is that they are based on responses to actual tax rate changes (Auerbach, 1989). According to Eichner and Sinai (2000), time series data provide a better mechanism for identifying behavioural responses resulting from tax changes than micro data.

## Limitations of time series studies

Gravelle (1994) expressed concerns about the limited number of observations in time series studies and problems with the imperfect aggregation of tax rates where sub-national taxing jurisdictions—for example, individual states in the United States—are involved. However, the problem of constructing one national tax rate, while an issue for capital gains realisations response studies in the United States, is not of concern in a study that uses Australian data given that state taxes are not levied on capital gains in Australia.

One of the general issues associated with time series studies is that they require the researcher to compress a complex tax system into a single measure of tax rate. There is also the possibility that the estimates from time series studies are influenced by time-dependent unobservable factors. According to Shobe (1991), there is a lack of an empirically tractable behavioural model to guide the design, estimation and interpretation of realisations response studies and this is more problematic for time series studies.

Eichner and Sinai (2000) noted that in the United States, time series studies have guided the policy process. Part of the reason for this may be the lower elasticity point estimates that they have tended to produce. From a policy perspective, in a budget deficit environment, it may be more prudent to underestimate than overestimate revenue gains following a CGT rate cut.

According to Zodrow (1992), caution should be taken in basing tax policy prescriptions on any particular set of time series estimates. However, this does not imply that an average elasticity point estimate derived from a number of time series studies is of any use in informing tax policy. Given the diversity of approaches used in each study, an average does not necessarily provide any meaningful information. Furthermore, time series studies are highly sensitive to minor changes in specification and sample period (Zodrow, 1992). The U.S. CBO (1988) warned that because of this problem, revenue estimators must necessarily supplement any conflicting statistical information from such studies with their own judgment as to how markets are likely to work.

Auerbach (1988) identified time series studies as being sensitive to the sample period. Specifically, in some capital gains realisations response studies where there was the addition of data for one year to the time series, the effect was a significant change to the elasticity point estimate (Auerbach, 1988). There is something of an implied assumption in studies using time series data that the characteristics of the taxpayer population are static over the duration of the years in the time series (U.S. CBO, 1988). In long time series that span several decades, such an assumption is unlikely to hold given that characteristics of the taxpayer population are likely to change over time.

Another problem with time series studies relates to the choice of variables and the specific issue of omitted variables (Zodrow, 1992). An example is the fact that many time series studies do not include a variable for legislation that has reduced the range of tax avoidance techniques available to taxpayers (Zodrow, 1992). According to Zodrow (1992), the absence of a demographic variable capturing the age structure of the taxpayer population in some studies may constitute an omitted variable.

Furthermore, because time series studies include a smaller number of observations than the micro data studies, there is a high dependency on factors hypothesised to influence realisations of capital gains other than tax rates (U.S. CBO, 1988). The small number of observations in time series studies limits the number of variables that can be included and leads to an incomplete representation of the dynamics of adjustment (Gravelle, 1990). In many cases, where important variables are omitted from a time series study, the resulting tax rate variable will be too large and will overestimate the realisations response (Gravelle, 1990).

Another problem with time series studies identified by Auerbach (1988) is that of heterogeneity bias arising from the fact that aggregate data will not allow for the marginal CGT rate to vary according to the situation of individual taxpayers. For example, taxpayers with net capital losses face a marginal CGT rate of zero, therefore the extent to which taxpayers in aggregate face a net capital loss position should be an influence on the marginal CGT rate chosen in a time series study.

According to Jones (1989), time series cannot be relied on to produce a definitive elasticity estimate since the elasticity can be large or small according to how the estimating equation is specified. However, this criticism may be of some relevance to all capital gains realisations response studies. According to the U.S. Joint Committee on Taxation (1990), elasticity estimates derived from time series studies were the most appropriate for the purpose of revenue estimating. By contrast, Jones (1989) argued that because of the statistical uncertainty of time series estimates, it would be more prudent to use estimates from panel or cross-sectional studies in combination with those from time series studies.

## Summary

The review of the time series literature has revealed that several capital gains realisations response studies in the United States have used time series data and that there are a series of results centred upon a range of estimates between –0.5 and –0.9. In the context of this book, one of the benefits of a time series study is that the taxpayer data are readily available.[29] There are a few disadvantages associated with time series studies to consider.

29 This is of specific relevance to Australia, where a panel of taxed return data spanning the pre- and post-CGT discount years is not available to tax researchers.

Two of the main potential shortcomings of a time series study relate to the possibility for aggregation bias and the low number of observations. Acknowledgement of these shortcomings, as well as others, helped to inform the design of the research approach ultimately adopted for this study (see Chapter 3).



## Panel data studies

A panel data study is one that includes data on a sample of taxpayers for several consecutive years. One of the most apparent advantages of a panel data study, in comparison to the other types of study reviewed in this chapter, is the high number of observations it includes. Furthermore, a panel data set is information-rich, given that the data are on individual taxpayers for several successive years. Notwithstanding this point, panel data do not contain information on the individual capital gains transactions for the taxpayers in the panel. Such information, were it available, may improve the existing models on capital gains realisations response that are based on panel data.

Panel data studies constitute a significant improvement on cross-sectional studies given that the former can address the problem of transitory responses to rate changes being captured in the reported estimates;[30] it is the long-run or permanent response to CGT changes that is the effect of interest (Gravelle, 1990). Some of the earlier panel data studies that attempted to separate permanent and transitory effects were not completely successful in achieving this, as the panels used were too short (Gravelle, 1990).

### Studies using panel data

There have been several panel data studies completed between the early 1980s and the present. As with the other approaches considered thus far, predominantly these studies have taken place in the United States. In addition to the U.S. studies, there is a recent panel data study that used Swedish taxpayer data, although it did not include point estimates of the elasticity of capital gains realisations. These key panel data studies are now considered, again adopting a chronological approach to the analysis.

Auten and Clotfelter (1982) conducted a seven-year panel data study (1967 to 1973) in which they used a random sample of individual taxpayers. In the introduction to their paper, Auten and Clotfelter discussed the Feldstein et al. (1980) study and noted that the estimating equation used did not distinguish between permanent and transitory effects, in part because cross-sectional studies lack information on the variation in individual tax rates over time. Although Feldstein et al. recognised the problem of separating the two effects, the fact that they did not have information on the variation in individual tax rates over time prevented them from doing so. Auten and Clotfelter is a notable study in that it was one of the first studies to separately measure the permanent and temporary responses to changes in the tax rate. The elasticity estimates from the Auten and Clotfelter study are in the range of –0.37 to –0.55.

30 Specific to the individual taxpayer's income being relatively lower in a particular year.

Auten and Clotfelter (1982) described the purpose of their paper as distinguishing between transitory and permanent tax effects using their panel data set. The authors noted that it is important to include both permanent and transitory components of income as explanatory variables in their equation, as movements in transitory income can cause movements in marginal tax rates. The study used capital gains from all sources as its dependent variable; part of the rationale for using capital gains from all sources was that the data set did not contain information on the type of capital gains asset (Auten & Clotfelter, 1982). The explanatory variables in the study were permanent and transitory income, current capital income, age, retirement, marital status and the carryover of long-term capital losses (Auten & Clotfelter, 1982). The panel of tax returns used in the study included information on the exact age of taxpayers.

As part of their study, Auten and Clotfelter (1982) examined the extent to which marginal tax rates varied over time, given the importance of transitory effects and the timing of realisations by taxpayers when their tax rate is temporarily low. Auten and Clotfelter (1982) used a basic income measure as a value in their study, a predicted adjusted gross income (AGI), intended to be independent of the capital gains for an individual taxpayer. The predicted AGI is AGI minus capital gains plus the average capital gains of the taxpayer's income class. Auten and Clotfelter then used this predicted AGI to calculate a measure of permanent income: the logarithm of the average value of the predicted AGI for the current and previous two years. The Auten and Clotfelter study included dummy variables for individual years for exogenous factors affecting capital gains realisations such as the change in share prices. The Tobit[31] method of estimation was used, which the authors consider the most appropriate method given the discretionary nature of capital gains realisations.[32]

Auten and Clotfelter (1982) defined the permanent tax rate as the taxpayer's average marginal rate for the current and previous two years, and they defined the transitory tax rate as the difference between the current rate and the permanent rate. Burman and Randolph (1994) subsequently identified this three-year average approach as inadequate for estimating separately the effects of permanent and transitory tax rates since it, in itself, is a combination of the two. Lindsey (1987a) noted that Auten and Clotfelter and others used a retrospective calculation of the transitory component of rate change effects and that these were consistent with theory on the lock-in effect.

One of the findings of the Auten and Clotfelter (1982) study was that the elasticity of capital gains realisations for all asset types is not as large as the elasticity of capital gains realisations from company shares, estimated in previous studies such as Feldstein et al. (1980). This finding is consistent with Gravelle (1991), who noted that where transaction costs are lower the realisations response is likely to be higher. Auten and Clotfelter included a number of additional equations in order to estimate the variation in responsiveness to marginal tax rates for different taxpayer groups. They found that the transitory and

31 Tobit describes a maximum likelihood method of estimation. Earlier studies such as Feldstein et al. (1980), which used ordinary least squares (OLS) as an alternative method of estimation, have been criticised as containing an econometric error, which is, in part, a comment on the use of OLS.

32 Auten and Clotfelter (1982) noted that approximately one-third of the sample realised net gains in any given year.

permanent tax rate effects were larger for taxpayers aged under 65 than for the total sample. The sample was also divided into two classes of taxpayer income: taxpayers with income[33] less than US$25,000 and those with income more than US$25,000. One of the findings here was that the transitory tax rate effect was slightly higher for the high-income group, whereas the permanent tax rate effect was only significant for the low-income group. This result is somewhat unexpected, and Auten and Clotfelter explained it may reflect that there were few high-income taxpayers included in their panel, which may make the results for these taxpayers less reliable and more sensitive to extreme values.



In their conclusions, Auten and Clotfelter (1982) identified the difficulties involved in undertaking empirical research on tax-induced behaviour. First, there is the problem of attempting to calculate a correct marginal tax rate. In the U.S. context, such a calculation requires assumptions about the order in which a taxpayer realises their short-term and long-term gains as well as the use of loss carryovers. Auten and Clotfelter noted that taxpayers may not be able to estimate the tax consequences of a particular transaction given the complexity of the CGT law. This point may have implications for this type of research generally to the extent that it is correct. The study in this book is also subject to the problem of attempting to calculate a marginal tax rate for capital gains.

Auten and Clotfelter (1982) found that capital gains taxes cause a significant effect on the timing of realisations, as reflected by the transitory effect that they estimated; they also concluded that it is likely there is a permanent lock-in effect of capital gains taxes, but that the coefficient is not always significant. Auten and Clotfelter concluded that the absolute level of realisations increases with permanent income, but that the increase is not proportionate. Auten and Clotfelter estimated short-run elasticities for a range of specifications as well as a long-run elasticity of –0.5.

According to Auten and Clotfelter (1982), it is important to determine how much marginal tax rates vary over time given the importance of transitory effects. The authors found that although CGT rate reductions may produce increases in realisations of long-term capital gains, their study does not provide strong support for the hypothesis that such rate reductions lead to increased revenue for the U.S. Treasury. According to Shobe (1991), the Auten and Clotfelter regression suffered from similar heterogeneity and misspecification bias as that in Feldstein et al. (1980).

Lindsey (1987b) stratified the taxpayer population into six income classes of adjusted gross income. Lindsey found that capital gains realisations were highly sensitive to tax rates, and he estimated that a revenue-maximising tax rate was within the range of 14% to 20%. Lindsey also conducted a revenue simulation to estimate the revenue effects of the *TRA86*, and reported that the increase in the maximum CGT rate from 20% to 28% would result in an overall loss of tax revenue collected.

Subsequently, Auten et al. (1989) conducted a five-year panel data study. Auten et al. referred to a number of advantages of panel data over cross-sectional data; one such example is that panel data allow the dynamics of the individual response to CGT rate changes to be estimated due to the availability of lagged data. Another advantage of using

33 Adjusted gross income less capital gains.

panel data is that it provides information about permanent income of taxpayers and it allows for corrections for individual-specific fixed effects (Auten et al., 1989).

Auten et al. (1989) considered taxpayer wealth to be an important component of a model that measures elasticity and noted that such information is not available from tax returns. Auten et al. used the results of the '1981–82 U.S. Treasury Estate-Income Tax Match Study' to impute the total wealth of the taxpayers in their sample since there was no direct information on taxpayer wealth available in the tax return data they used. Auten et al. included a number of demographic variables in their equation in an attempt to control for variances in trading strategies as a result of taxpayer preferences. They noted that for wealthier taxpayers there is a decision of whether or not to realise capital gains, which is distinct from the decision on the amount of capital gains to realise, and that failure to model this distinction may have led to biased estimation results in some previous micro data studies (Auten et al., 1989).

Auten et al. (1989) noted that previous realisations response studies that used a fixed marginal tax rate might have overstated the response of taxpayers to changes in CGT rates. Furthermore, the authors asserted that focusing on individual capital gains realisations behaviour might ignore some important determinants of the aggregate revenue effects of CGT rate changes.

Part of the purpose of the Auten et al. (1989) study was to gain an understanding of why capital gains realisations equations from previous studies have yielded a wide range of varying results as well as the relevance of panel data to answering this question. The results of Auten et al. suggest that one of the main reasons for the past variance in elasticity point estimates could be the simultaneity between marginal tax rates and capital gains realisations and the failure of previous studies to correctly deal with bias in sample selection. Auten et al. used a simulation method to examine the effect of changes in the individual income tax on aggregate capital gains and tax revenue. Jones (1989) confirmed the problem of simultaneity between realisations and tax rates.

Auten et al. (1989) identified that using a lagged tax rate detected a short-run capital gains realisations response that was significantly greater than the long-run response. Auten et al. argued that data from a long panel are essential to unravelling the components of capital gains realisations response that are due to tax policy from the component that is due to individual-specific factors. They noted that the five-year panel used in their study is not long enough and that one of the problems this poses is that it cannot identify the differential between CGT rates and tax rates on other income (Auten et al., 1989).

Auten et al. (1989) identified deficiencies associated with panel data that a longer panel would not remedy. One example is that focusing on individual capital gains realisations behaviour may ignore important determinants of the aggregate revenue effects of CGT changes. This is notwithstanding another point made by Auten et al. that panel data have the advantage of a lack of aggregation bias. The view of Auten et al. on a long panel is not universal. Eichner and Sinai (2000) claimed that there is no doubt that a long panel data set would be preferable to a long time series.

In their discussion of the estimation results, Auten et al. (1989) noted that older taxpayers are more likely to realise capital gains than younger taxpayers, but that older taxpayers realise lower levels of capital gains. They noted that taxpayers with higher permanent income are more likely to realise higher amounts of capital gains. As part of their study, Auten et al. used a simulation model to examine the effects of changing the inclusion rate on long-term capital gains. Auten et al. found that where there was a small change in the inclusion rate, the long-run elasticity was –1.63 and the short-run elasticity was –1.98; in the case of increasing the inclusion rate to 60%, the long-run elasticity was –1.67.

In their conclusion, Auten et al. (1989) argued that there should be more research undertaken on the effects of CGT policies on growth and rates of return in financial markets. They noted that predictions about revenue consequences of CGT are tenuous in the absence of an understanding of the effects of CGT on gross national product, interest rates, dividend payouts and asset values (Auten et al., 1989).

At about the same time as Auten et al. (1989) were conducting their panel data study, Slemrod and Shobe (1990) undertook another six-year panel data study. In their discussion of heterogeneity bias, Slemrod and Shobe noted that capital gains realisations behaviour is influenced by factors not observable by the econometrician and that unobservable explanatory variables can lead to inconsistent estimates of parameters. Notwithstanding this, Slemrod and Shobe asserted that where the unobserved influences are specific to the individual taxpayer, it might be possible to minimise or avoid heterogeneity bias in panel data studies. Slemrod and Shobe attempted to achieve this by using a fixed effects model to control for differences in permanent tax rates and other unobservable fixed effects that may have an effect on parameter estimates.

The panel used by Slemrod and Shobe (1990) was non-stratified and randomly selected. The number of individual taxpayers who were present in all six years of the initial sample was 6,152. The authors limited their study to a 5% subsample of tax returns consisting of 307 taxpayers. The 5% sample selected those taxpayers having the highest values of real positive income, excluding capital gains, when averaged over the six-year period of the study. The subsample of 307 taxpayers in Slemrod and Shobe realised 52% of total net capital gains.

The panel data were analysed by Slemrod and Shobe (1990) using a slightly modified version of the model estimated in Feldstein et al. (1980). The dependent variable in the Slemrod and Shobe study was the long-term gains or losses divided by the sum of dividends and interest receipts. Although it was a panel data study, Slemrod and Shobe did not attempt to separate the transitory and permanent responses. The study used ordinary least squares as the method of estimation for all four specifications.

Slemrod and Shobe (1990) concluded that there is consistent support for an inverse response of capital gains realisations to changes in the rate of taxation. Although their elasticity point estimates are high in magnitude—greater than –1.00 and greater than –5.00 in some cases—Slemrod and Shobe qualified their findings by reference to a standard error quantum whereby, even in the case of an elasticity that is in excess of –1.00, the coefficient may not be statistically different from zero. In secondary commentary on the Slemrod and Shobe study, Gravelle (2010) referred to the fact that the results appear to have captured transitory effects and that this is a limitation of the study. Slemrod and Shobe referred to further limitations, such as the fact that their study is restricted to higher-income taxpayers and that elasticity studies generally are very sensitive to many dimensions of specifications. Slemrod and Shobe acknowledged that their estimates may capture some transitory effects.

Burman and Randolph (1994) reported the results of a panel data study that used a semi-log functional form to model the long-run relationship between capital gains realisations and rates as well as two transitory or timing effects. One of these transitory effects considers the tax cost of realising a capital gain in the current year, compared to waiting to do so in a later year. The second transitory effect relates to the influence of prior year CGT rates on realisations. The rationale for the inclusion of this effect appears to be that past CGT rates can influence the stock of unrealised capital gains.

Burman and Randolph (1994) separated the transitory and permanent responses by using the variation in state tax rates to estimate the permanent elasticity; the authors considered state tax rates to be an easily measurable exogenous source of variation. They reported a very large transitory elasticity of –6.42 and a small permanent elasticity of –0.18 (Burman & Randolph, 1994). The authors noted that although the transitory elasticity is a large in comparison with most other estimates that had been completed at the time of the study, it is consistent with the volume of the increase in realisations that occurred as a result of the *TRA86* (Burman & Randolph, 1994). According to Burman and Randolph, given the relatively large standard error, the hypothesis that permanent changes in CGT rates have no long-term effect on capital gains realisations cannot be rejected.

The Burman and Randolph (1994) study used a panel of approximately 11,000 individual income tax returns for the years 1979–83. Generally, a panel study of five years is considered a short panel. Burman and Randolph (1994) stratified the sample of taxpayers according to income, and although their study used unweighted data, testing was conducted to ascertain whether endogenous stratification biased the estimates.

The elasticity point estimates in the Burman and Randolph (1994) study imply that the permanent elasticity is significantly lower than the transitory response. Burman and Randolph used a lagged tax rate as a proxy for the unobservable size of accrued gains; they noted, by way of example, that if the previous year's CGT rate was unusually high, then accrued gains in the current year should be higher than usual, as a proportion of realisations would have been postponed. The Burman and Randolph sample included the year 1981, in which the *Economic Recovery Tax Act* reduced the tax rates on ordinary income and capital gains. Burman and Randolph identified an advantage and disadvantage of including this year. The advantage is that significant variation in tax rates is introduced into the study, while the disadvantage is that some of the response to the CGT rate reduction may have been transitory (Burman & Randolph, 1994).

Observations on individual taxpayers were included in Burman and Randolph (1994) whenever the current and lagged data were considered valid, and this process yielded 42,406 included observations. The dependent variable in Burman and Randolph was net long-term capital gains before the carryover of prior year losses. The tax rate measure used in the Burman and Randolph study was determined with reference to the taxpayer's income and deductions and the applicable tax law for the year concerned. Burman and Randolph calculated the marginal tax rate on capital gains transactions using defined realisation transactions rather than a single dollar of capital gains. The capital gain on each defined transaction was the maximum of US$1,000 or the square root of imputed wealth (Burman & Randolph, 1994). Burman and Randolph imputed permanent income by using the panel sample to regress the logarithm of a five-year average of real positive income on taxpayer characteristics.

Burman and Randolph (1994) noted that previous micro data studies lacked appropriate instruments for the permanent tax rate and that the estimates of tax effects in those studies could only be considered consistent if transitory and permanent responses were the same. Burman and Randolph found that capital gains realisations are significantly positively related to permanent income, but negatively related to transitory income, which suggests a consumption motive for realisations. Their study concluded that wealthier taxpayers are more likely to realise capital gains and that this demographic realises larger capital gains than the average. According to Burman and Randolph, the composition of capital gains assets was an influence on whether taxpayers were more likely to realise gains; where shares comprised a larger proportion of the overall asset portfolio, the taxpayer was more likely to realise capital gains. Burman and Randolph reported an elasticity point estimate of –0.18 at an 18% CGT rate.

Burman and Randolph (1994) concluded that there is a large and statistically significant difference between the transitory and permanent responses to CGT rate changes. Burman and Randolph used a first-dollar tax rate to estimate the transitory effect. They also concluded that the lagged tax rate coefficient in their study was insignificantly small and that this implies that lagged taxed rates do not affect capital gains realisations decisions, provided current and permanent tax rates are held constant (Burman & Randolph, 1994).

Burman and Randolph (1994) identified a number of limitations of their study. First, the effects of CGT on the cost and allocation of capital are ignored. Second, a reduced form model is used, as per other capital gains realisations response studies, and this has the limitation of the estimated parameters being subject to change over time since they are a function of the macroeconomic environment and the tax law. Secondary commentary on the Burman and Randolph study by Dowd et al. (2012) referred to the imprecision of their estimates to the extent that their permanent elasticity of –0.18 may not be significantly different from zero and –1.00. According to Dowd et al., the imprecision in the study may have been caused by using the same set of explanatory variables in modelling the decision to realise capital gains as well as the amount of capital gains to be realised. Gravelle (2010, p. 15) described the Burman and Randolph study as 'perhaps the most innovative study done since the 1980s'.

Auerbach and Siegel (2000) completed a panel data study that used the same empirical model as Burman and Randolph (1994), applying it to a panel of taxpayers over the years 1985 to 1994. Auerbach and Siegel estimated a long-run elasticity of –0.34 and a transitory elasticity of –4.91; their study does not report the marginal tax rate used in determining the elasticities. Auerbach and Siegel referred to an improved precision of their elasticity estimate compared to earlier studies due to the large sample size and the improved spread of state tax rates over the sample period. Auerbach and Siegel noted that they were able to reject an elasticity of zero with a high confidence level but could also exclude much above 0.5 in absolute terms.

The Auerbach and Siegel (2000) study included an alternative specification under which the elasticity estimate increased, in absolute terms, from –0.34 to –1.75. This estimate for the alternative specification is similarly high in magnitude to some of the panel and cross-sectional studies of the 1980s. The higher elasticity estimate may be partly due to the inclusion of a current first-dollar tax rate,[34] which is likely to add a transitory element to the measurement of the permanent tax rate (Auerbach & Siegel, 2000).

An important finding of the Auerbach and Siegel (2000) study was that a small group of taxpayers identified as wealthy and sophisticated exhibited significantly smaller realisation responses than other taxpayers. Auerbach and Siegel considered that this was because a large proportion of their response related to timing and tax-avoidance strategies. Furthermore, the authors considered that these taxpayers were likely—relative to the whole taxpayer population—to be less subject to liquidity restraints, to face lower transaction costs for buying and selling assets and to have a different consumption pattern of their assets over their lifetime (Auerbach & Siegel, 2000). Auerbach and Siegel compared taxpayers with imputed wealth of over US$10,000,000 with their general taxpayer sample and they rejected at the 1% level the hypothesis that these wealthy taxpayers follow the same model as non-wealthy taxpayers. Auerbach and Siegel found the realisations response for wealthy taxpayers to be almost entirely transitory, with the long-run elasticity for this group estimated to be close to nil.

Jacob (2011) examined the elasticity of capital gains realisations using a panel of 230,000 tax returns from Sweden for the years 1971–96. The data set used represented 3.35% of the Swedish population. The years of the panel included a year when there was a substantial change to the taxation of capital gains in Sweden. Specifically, in 1991, a tax reform was introduced that taxed capital gains at a rate of 30%; previously capital gains were taxed at marginal progressive tax rates and these could be as high as 80% (Jacob, 2011). Whereas the previous tax regime was a global system, the new system is a dual income tax, under which capital income is taxed proportionally and separately to labour income, which is taxed progressively. Jacob noted that the previous tax system was said to encourage tax avoidance and tax planning to the point where net revenue from CGT was negative for many years. Jacob found that the 1991 reform in Sweden led to a 60.5% increase in aggregate realised capital gains between the years 1990 and 1991 and that 60% of this increase was attributable to the top 1% of the taxpayer income distribution.

Jacob (2011) restricted his analysis to individuals with information on income and other demographic characteristics for at least five consecutive years, and he excluded any observations where the individual's age was below 18. Income observations that were not within the 0.01 and 99.9 percentiles were excluded, and the regression analysis was restricted to the years 1985–96 (Jacob, 2011).

Jacob (2011) used a life cycle model to analyse how capital gains realisations are affected in a proportional taxation system compared to one that is progressive. The life cycle model referred to differing motives for taxpayers' saving and investment behaviour. The motive for investing in shares, in the case of younger individual taxpayers, is for

34 The first-dollar rate tax refers to the rate applying to the first dollar of capital gains that a taxpayer realises.

precautionary reasons (Jacob, 2011). Individuals have an incentive to save for retirement, which relates to their wanting to maintain an income that is the equivalent to that in their working life; there is also an incentive to cease saving once they are older (Jacob, 2011). One of the impacts of the reform of the Swedish tax system on these incentives is that whereas in the former progressive system, there was an incentive to postpone capital gains realisations to take advantage of a lower post-retirement tax rate, under the new proportional tax system, the benefits of postponing realisation are considerably lower (Jacob, 2011). Jacob found that life cycle savings behaviour is influenced by whether a proportional or progressive tax system is in place.

Jacob (2011) also examined the role of liquidity constraints at the individual level on the propensity to realise capital gains. The general conclusion was that taxpayers are more likely to realise capital gains in years when current income is below average income. Realisation of capital gains in this context may relate to these taxpayers maintaining their expected level of consumption when income is temporarily low (Jacob, 2011). In the contrasting scenario where current income is above average income, the temporarily higher tax rate can act as a lock-in effect.

Jacob (2011) concluded that capital gains realisations behaviour is affected according to whether capital gains are taxed on a progressive or proportional basis. More specifically, Jacob concluded that a proportional tax increased the likelihood of a taxpayer realising capital gains and that this increased realisation of capital gains was more likely to occur among higher-income taxpayers. Jacob noted that there may be substantial effects to observe relating to the capitalisation of tax effects into asset prices, according to the differing behaviour of individual taxpayers under different tax regimes. Another finding of the Jacob study was that after the introduction of the proportional tax system, individuals with temporarily high income significantly increased their capital gains realisations, whereas individuals with lower current income reduced their capital gains realisations following the reform.

Dowd et al. (2012) is one of the more recent capital gains realisations response studies from the United States. The study includes an elasticity point estimate for the entire sample, but it was also concerned with heterogeneity in the capital gains realisations response of taxpayers. The realisations response is expected to vary between taxpayers and for different types of capital gains assets. Dowd et al. used a 10-year panel of tax returns for the years 1999 to 2008; the panel was a stratified random sample of tax returns selected in the 1999 tax year, which oversampled high-income tax returns. Dowd et al. considered that oversampling tax returns of high-income taxpayers addressed the fact that capital asset ownership is highly concentrated within this taxpayer demographic. Specifically, taxpayers in the top income percentile realise more than 50% of total capital gains (Dowd et al., 2012).

Dowd et al. (2012) estimated separate elasticities for long-run and short-run tax changes. Although Dowd et al. adapted a model used in Burman and Randolph (1994), unlike this and other earlier studies Dowd et al. referred to the 'persistent elasticity' rather than permanent elasticity. According to Dowd et al. distinguishing between elasticities that are attributable to permanent and transitory tax rates incorrectly assumes that a permanent tax rate exists. Persistent elasticity considers next year's expected tax rate, the current year tax rate and the previous year's tax rate, and it describes an increase in the tax rate that has persisted over the previous year and is expected to persist into the following year (Dowd et al., 2012).

Dowd et al. (2012) estimated a persistent elasticity of –0.79 and a transitory elasticity of –1.20, and they concluded that these are robust when subjected to a number of sensitivity tests. Part of the Dowd et al. paper is concerned with the variation in persistent and transitory elasticities between taxpayers. Dowd et al. noted that in any given year taxpayers might have different elasticities from each other.

Dowd et al. (2012) referred to some of the demographic differences between the taxpayers in the sample who realised capital gains compared to the entire sample of taxpayers. They noted that the former are, on average, likely to have higher incomes, a higher marginal tax rate, to be approximately ten years older, more likely to be male and married and less likely to have children. Dowd et al. also referred to the different elasticities that apply to different individual taxpayers; they estimated that 75% of taxpayers always have elasticities that are less than 1.00 in absolute value and that these taxpayers realise approximately 45% of all capital gains. Consistent with this, Dowd et al. concluded that the remaining 55% of the taxpayer population have elasticities of more than 1.00, in absolute value, in at least one tax year.

Dowd et al. (2012) found considerable variation in the tax elasticity of taxpayers' capital gains realisations depending on the tax rate that they face, their propensity to realise a capital gain, and the type of assets that they hold. In their conclusion, Dowd et al. found that the decision on the amount of capital gain to realise appears to be much more sensitive to tax rates than does the decision to realise a capital gain. Furthermore, Dowd et al. found that taxpayers with higher realisation responses tend to realise larger amounts of capital gains.

Dowd et al. (2012) referred to some of the limitations of their research including that the consistency of their estimates relied on the distributional assumptions of their parametric model and that their model only examined the average effect of tax changes, whereas there may be substantial variance in effects across different income categories.

In 2015, the authors updated their 2012 study. Dowd, McClelland and Muthitacharoen (2015) reported a preferred persistent elasticity of –0.72, and noted that their estimate is statistically significant and robust to a number of sensitivity tests.

## Summary

The review of the literature on panel data studies revealed that they may be the best alternative for separating the permanent and transitory responses. Panel studies such as Burman and Randolph (1994) have found a large transitory response and a small permanent response. These results imply that the timing of capital gains realisations is very sensitive to changes in the individual taxpayer's tax rate whereas, in the long run, realisations are not sensitive to changes in the statutory tax rate. This finding has implications for why estimates in time series studies tend to be lower in magnitude than cross-sectional studies. Specifically, time series studies are based on aggregate data, and they cannot estimate the timing response of individual taxpayers. The estimates in cross-sectional studies appear to include a measure of timing response, and this cannot be disentangled given the estimate is based on data for one year.

Given that a panel data set is typically for a lesser number of years than a time series, some researchers, including Eichner and Sinai (2000), claimed that panel data are not as useful for separating out the permanent and transitory effects. This implies that the estimates in time series reflect the permanent effect even though these studies do not report separate estimates for the permanent and transitory effects.



## Other studies

This section briefly reviews the literature on capital gains that does not estimate the realisations response by way of regression analysis. Gravelle (1991) and Gravelle (2010) are important contributions to the literature as they provide context to the econometric studies referred to earlier in the chapter. Clarke (2014) provided some useful, albeit general, information on the frequency of capital gains realisations for Australian taxpayers.

In the United States, researchers assessed the reasonableness of the higher magnitude elasticity estimates. One example is the conclusion of Auerbach (1989) that there is an absence of evidence in the historical record of capital gains realisations to accruals to justify an elasticity of 1.00 or more in absolute terms.

Gravelle (1991) hypothesised that the realisations response can only offset a small proportion of the original revenue lost from a CGT rate cut. According to Gravelle, the econometric evidence cannot be relied upon to estimate the realisations response precisely. This was the rationale of Gravelle for presenting an alternative way of estimating the realisations response based on the historical relationship between realisations and the level of accrued capital gains. These data were applied to estimate the upper limit to the realisations response. Unlike the other studies reviewed in this chapter, Gravelle has not statistically inferred the values in her paper from the correlations between tax rates and realisations.

Gravelle (1991) explained that some of the micro data studies current at that time had overestimated the realisations response since these estimates were inconsistent with historical data as well as being in excess of the level of accrued capital gains. Essentially, a very large elasticity may not accurately reflect the year-after-year realisations response given that there would be a point at which there were no capital gains remaining to realise.

Other studies referred to the importance of the stock of accrued gains, with the U.S. CBO (1988) study describing accrued gains as the principal determinant of the level of realisations by individual taxpayers. Eichner and Sinai (2000) found consistent evidence for a dependence of realisation behaviour on the prior sequence of tax rate changes. One example is where previous tax rate changes encouraged a high level of overall capital gains realisations; this would result in a lower stock of accrued capital gains to be realised in future periods.

Gravelle (1991) commented on some of the individual elasticity studies available at that time, noting that the statistical estimates in Gillingham, Greenlees and Zieschang (1989) and in Auten et al. (1989) were inconsistent with historical data on realisations and accruals. Gravelle noted that the results in the U.S. Department of Treasury (1985) study and in Feldstein et al. (1980) were outside the range of plausible responses.

According to Gravelle (1991), time series studies tended to produce results that are lower than and not as variable as the micro data estimates, and these time series estimates have varied between estimates that are close enough to zero so as to have no statistical significance and estimates of around –1.00.

The results of the Gravelle (1991) study indicated that at a 22% CGT rate, the long-run realisations elasticity is between zero and –0.53. Gravelle estimated elasticities at various ratios of realisations to accruals. Although the elasticity of –0.53 is for a hypothetical scenario in which all accrued capital gains are realised in that year, this could be ruled out from actually occurring since in practice there are many CGT assets that are only sold on an infrequent basis (Gravelle, 1991). Gravelle's finding implies that the capital gains realisations response is relatively inelastic and even in a best-case scenario—where all accrued capital gains are realised in a year—it is still significantly less than 1.00 in absolute value. The study by Gravelle is akin to a reality check on some of the high estimates of elasticity that the earlier cross-sectional studies found.

Gravelle (1991) referred to some of the limitations of her study, one of these being that its accuracy depended on the accuracy of estimating accrued capital gains, realised capital gains and taxes, as well as the assumed functional form. According to Burman (1999), models that imply that realisations elasticities that are much higher than –0.5 or –0.6 are inconsistent with observed behaviour. This appears consistent with the findings in the Gravelle study.

Clark (2014) estimated the 'realisation rates' for different types of capital gains assets. Realisation rates are the percentage of the stock of estimated accrued capital gains or losses that are realised in a tax year. According to Clark, the realisation rate for gains from shares is approximately 25%, which equates to an average of four years for which taxpayers hold shares before realising a capital gain. Clark estimated the realisation rate for capital losses on shares separately and found that this is approximately 4%.

Gravelle (2010) has reviewed some of the main elasticity studies conducted in the United States. Gravelle concluded that the results of certain studies were too unreliable to be considered further. Gravelle applied the elasticity estimates from various studies to the scenario of the revenue effect of the expiration of the Bush tax cut provisions in 2019. The expiration of this provision would give effect to an increase in the CGT rate. Gravelle found that in the case of the 11 studies considered, there would be a positive revenue effect.

The studies reviewed in this section suggest that the elasticity estimates in Chapter 5 of this book should be interpreted in a broad context. For example, Gravelle (1991) highlighted the importance of ensuring the estimates are consistent with historical data on realisations. Gravelle (2010) provided a useful overview and critique of the leading realisations response studies completed in the United States at the time.

# 2.6 CONCLUSIONS ON THE REVIEW OF THE CAPITAL GAINS REALISATIONS RESPONSE STUDIES



Analysis of the literature on the capital gains realisations response reveals there is a complete lack of research using Australian taxpayer data. Some of the political commentary from 1999 indicated that the consideration of revenue effects was non-empirical and potentially overly optimistic.[35]

When the 50% CGT discount was introduced, there had been no rate change in previous tax years. At least one CGT rate change is required to effectively estimate the capital gains realisations response. Nevertheless, the tax policy question of the revenue effects of a CGT rate preference has received little attention within Australia from either policy makers or from the broader tax and public finance academic community since 1999.

The broad implication is that if capital gains realisations are not very responsive to preferential rates, the government will have unnecessarily lost large amounts of CGT revenue. This is highly relevant to the Australian context. There have been nominal increases in capital gains realisations since the 50% discount was introduced. However, the Australian Government has lost large amounts of CGT revenue to the extent that capital gains realisations are relatively unresponsive to CGT rates. An elasticity point estimate provides information on the extent to which realisations are dependent on CGT rate changes.

Although capital gains realisations response studies from the United States have produced a wide range of elasticity point estimates using different approaches, time series studies have produced the more stable estimates of elasticity overall. Eichner and Sinai (2000) found that time series studies are the best method of estimating long-run elasticity despite the known problem of aggregation bias. Aggregation bias is a problem with time series studies according to some literature, and the U.S. CBO (1988) explored this issue. In the CBO study, separate estimates were made for the top 1% and bottom 99% of the taxpayer population, and the effect of aggregation was found to be not statistically significant (Gravelle, 1990).

Although aggregation bias is not a characteristic of studies that use micro data, these data approaches—in particular cross-sectional studies—have their own problems. Cross-sectional data tend to produce inflated elasticity estimates, due to the inability of these studies to separate timing effects from the permanent response to rate changes.

The review of the literature suggests that elasticity point estimates may be sensitive to the specification of the equation. Some of the elasticity studies reviewed included a sensitivity analysis as a way of testing the robustness of the results. Where the results are

35 Senator Gibson stated, in reference to his understanding of the U.S. experience on the revenue effect of CGT rate changes, that 'when the capital gains tax was increased, revenue went down; when capital gains tax was decreased, revenue went up' (Commonwealth of Australia, Senate, Monday, 29 November 1999, p. 10,894). This is not a complete or accurate summary of the effects of CGT rate changes on revenue.

sensitive to the inclusion of other variables in the specification, the uncertainty cannot be completely resolved as the correct combination of variables is debatable (U.S. CBO, 1988).

The literature on capital gains realisations response studies also contains references to the problem of choosing an appropriate tax rate to use in time series studies. The choice of tax rate is a compromise given that, although the researcher must decide on a single rate for the purpose of their study, in practice, realisations decisions are made by many personal taxpayers who collectively face a wide range of tax rates on their capital gains realisations. Furthermore, the literature explains that elasticity will not necessarily be constant at all marginal tax rates.

The results of time series studies are more stable across different mathematical formulations in comparison to cross-sectional and panel data studies (U.S. Congress, Joint Committee of Taxation, 1990). This finding is of importance to the capital gains realisations response study in this book, and the use of time series data can be partly justified on this basis. It is difficult to conclude which data type has produced the most credible estimates in the United States. Nonetheless, policy makers in other countries who are of the view that the U.S. studies may have some external validity should focus on the results of time series studies, especially in instances where the loss of tax revenue is of concern.

## The revenue effects of CGT rate cuts in Australia

One of the main applications of capital gains realisations response studies is to inform the question of the revenue effects associated with a change in the CGT rate. The CGT rate change considered in this book is the introduction of the 50% CGT discount for personal taxpayers that resulted in an effective CGT rate reduction.[36] The study in Chapter 5 estimates the elasticity of capital gains realisations in relation to the effective CGT rate cut. Such estimates of the capital gains realisations response may be useful in informing decisions by policy makers on the revenue effects of changing the CGT rate. In the first instance, an elasticity point estimate may provide information about whether revenue is likely to move in the same or opposite direction as a CGT rate change. Higher magnitude estimates imply an inverse relationship between the direction of a rate change and revenue, whereas a lower magnitude estimate implies that a tax rate change will cause revenue to move in the same direction.

As noted above, the question of whether CGT rate cuts have an increasing or decreasing effect on CGT revenue collected in the long run has received limited attention in Australia. This contrasts with the experience in the United States where the revenue effects of CGT rate changes have been debated for decades. During this time there have been several U.S. econometric studies completed on the capital gains realisations response. According to Gravelle (1994), the public debate over the revenue costs of a CGT rate cut, to some extent, has been a debate about how reliable the different econometric approaches in elasticity studies have been. Elasticity estimates that imply CGT rate cuts are likely

36 Not all capital gains by personal taxpayers are eligible for the 50% CGT discount. Furthermore, in some cases where a capital gain is eligible for the discount, the taxpayer may choose to use the indexation method instead where it results in a lower net capital gain. Notwithstanding these qualifications, discount capital gains have clearly comprised the majority of capital gains realisations.

to lead to decreases in revenue over the long run should serve as a compelling case for the Australian Government to tax capital gains at higher rates than those that presently apply.[37] Conversely, if the estimates imply CGT rate cuts are likely to lead to increased revenue then it would support the approach of policy makers responsible for the 50% CGT discount and the predictions made at the time about positive revenue effects.



An important qualification to arguments about revenue and CGT rates is that an increase in revenue might not justify a tax policy change (Cunningham & Schenk, 1993). The merits of an appropriate CGT rate should be considered in terms of economic efficiency and vertical and horizontal equity. Economic efficiency in a tax policy context is partly concerned with the neutrality of the tax system. Where there is a significant difference between the rate of tax on ordinary income and on capital gains, the tax system is not neutral, as taxpayers have an incentive to receive their income in the form that attracts the lowest rate of tax. Cunningham and Schenk (1993) characterised a CGT preference as an aspect of tax policy that may serve as a second-best alternative, but one that will not meet this standard by simply increasing realisations, but by increasing realisations to the point that permits a rate reduction on ordinary income.

The level of capital gains realisations by personal taxpayers, and the resultant increases and decreases in revenue collected, can be affected by the realisations response to changes in CGT rates as well as by other unrelated factors. These include macroeconomic factors such as changes in overall economic growth and factors specific to individual taxpayers such as their age, income and wealth.

One of the motivations for the quantitative study in the book is that the Ralph Review[38] predicted there would be a revenue-positive or revenue-neutral effect of the reform package and a significant capital gains realisations response, which would more than compensate for the static revenue loss from the CGT rate cut. This was a controversial claim challenged by a number of tax experts who appeared before an Australian Senate Committee Inquiry in 1999.[39] For example, Jane Gravelle[40] referred to difficulties associated with adapting data from the United States to the Australian context, but commented that the long-run elasticity for Australia was likely to be about –0.2; Alan Auerbach[41] referred to a likely permanent elasticity of between 0.2 and 0.5.[42] Chris Evans[43] predicted there could be lost

37 If there was evidence of this type of effect at the time that the 50% discount was proposed, there may have been a stronger case for continuing to tax capital gains at the same rates as ordinary income.

38 Which recommended the introduction of the 50% CGT discount.

39 See Australia. Senate Finances and Public Administration References Committee. (1999).

40 Senior Specialist in Economic Policy, Congressional Research Service. Evidence given at: Australia. Senate Finances and Public Administration References Committee. (1999).

41 Robert D. Burch Professor of Economics and Law, UC Berkeley; Director, Burch Center for Tax Policy and Public Finance. Evidence given at: Australia. Senate Finances and Public Administration References Committee. (1999).

42 Although this, in fact, refers to an elasticity of between –0.2 and –0.5, an elasticity is commonly reported without the minus sign.

43 Professor of Taxation, University of New South Wales. Evidence given at: Australia. Senate Finances and Public Administration References Committee. (1999).

CGT revenue of over $1.7 billion in a year in the event that as little as 1% of income was successfully converted into capital gains.

The quantitative research in this book fills an important gap in the literature that originates from the absence of a capital gains realisations response study using Australian data. Data are now available for a sufficient number of years following the enactment of the 50% CGT discount for an empirical capital gains realisations response study to be undertaken. The importance of estimates from an empirical study is that claims of positive revenue effects caused by the 50% CGT discount have been largely untested since the enactment of the policy.

Predictions were made that during the first two years of the 50% CGT discount, there would be a 50% increase in the volume of capital gains asset realisations (Australia. Review of Business Taxation & Ralph, 1999). The estimated realisation responses were a short-term elasticity of −1.7 during the first two years of implementation and an implicit long-term elasticity of −0.9 (Australia. Review of Business Taxation & Ralph, 1999). The high magnitude of the short-term elasticity predicted by the Ralph Review implies a significant lock-in effect in existence at that time and that the 50% CGT discount for personal taxpayers could unlock a significant amount of accrued gains. If the Ralph Review's estimated short-term elasticity of −1.7 were correct, it would follow that the introduction of the 50% CGT discount would have resulted in an increase in revenue for one or two years afterwards as a result of timing behaviour by taxpayers with accrued capital gains. However, the question of whether the 50% CGT discount would increase revenue in the long run is considered in terms of the permanent response. This is consistent with the literature describing any unlocking of capital gains following the lowering of the CGT rate as a temporary phenomenon that is not indicative of the long-term effect on realisations and tax revenues (Minarik, 1984). According to Minarik (1984), because economic theory predicts this transient unlocking of capital gains, it requires that the permanent effect be discounted for the transitory effect.

If the unitary elasticity rule holds, a long-run elasticity of −0.9—as predicted by the Ralph Review—implies a CGT revenue loss rather than a revenue gain.[44] This is notwithstanding the fact that the overall tax revenue loss would be of an even greater magnitude if some taxpayers converted their income into capital gains, as noted in the literature. Furthermore, any increase in realisations in the first year of a CGT rate change is unlikely to lead to the same level of response over time because realisations induced from the rate cut decrease the future stock of realisable gains (Slemrod & Shobe, 1990). In considering the impact of this effect, as well as the loss of overall tax revenue caused by some taxpayers re-characterising income as capital gains, it would appear that the Ralph Review's claim that the 50% CGT discount constituted a revenue-neutral or revenue-gaining reform might be incorrect. The elasticity estimates in Chapter 5 of this book are informative to making a conclusion on whether the predictions of revenue effects prepared by the Ralph Review were correct or not.

44 Specifically, if the unitary elasticity rule holds, an elasticity of −0.9 implies that the static revenue loss from the lower CGT rate will be more than the revenue gain from increased capital gains realisations.

The importance of this type of analysis relates to the fact that if a government has a long-term policy goal of revenue neutrality and a specific tax such as the CGT is losing revenue, there will need to be an increase in other taxes that might be less efficient and more distortionary. It is not the argument of this book that revenue is the primary consideration in the merits or otherwise of a particular CGT rate. Although the results of the quantitative study in Chapter 5 advance the knowledge on the capital gains realisations response and possible revenue effects of CGT rate changes, the study does not attempt to estimate a revenue-maximising tax rate.

It was stated in the Ralph Review that 'the recommendation for capital gains taxation are designed to enliven and invigorate the Australian equities markets, to stimulate greater participation by individuals, and to achieve a better allocation of the nation's capital resources' (Australia. Review of Business Taxation & Ralph, 1999, p. 598). Notwithstanding the merits or otherwise of these stated policy reasons, the Review did not seek to defend the CGT discount in terms of the negative effects it would have on vertical and horizontal equity and on overall tax system integrity.

Table 1 is an extract from the final report of the Ralph Review, which contains the estimates of revenue gains from the enactment of the CGT discount for personal taxpayers.

**Table 1: Ralph Review predicted revenue impact of CGT discount for personal taxpayers, $million**

| | 2000–01 | 2001–02 | 2002–03 | 2003–04 | 2004–05 |
|---|---|---|---|---|---|
| Static cost of CGT discount | –330 | –300 | –290 | –310 | –300 |
| Revenue from increased realisations | +540 | +530 | +500 | +480 | +400 |
| Net revenue increase | +210 | +230 | +210 | +170 | +100 |

*Source:* Australia. Review of Business Taxation and Ralph (1999).

Although there is a lack of empirical support in the literature for the view that a CGT rate cut will lead to an increase in CGT revenue in the long run, there were examples of Australian parliamentarians who spoke in parliament of their confidence in this type of revenue effect.[45] Some parliamentarians deferred to the conclusions in a report commissioned by the Australian Stock Exchange, prepared by Alan Reynolds and submitted to the Review of Business Taxation. This report is not an empirical study of the capital gains realisations response in Australia, and it contains information that is highly questionable. For example, Reynolds (1999, p. 3) states that 'in 1996–97, individuals who realized gains and also had ordinary earnings of more than $50,000 accounted for 28.4% of *individual* capital gains realizations, or $823 million.' A check of *Taxation Statistics* for 1996–97 reveals that, in fact, taxpayers in this income bracket realised a large proportion of capital gains and their tax payable represented the majority of tax payable by personal taxpayers in that tax year. Specifically, of the taxpayer population with taxable capital gains, 60.2% of these gains were realised by taxpayers with taxable incomes of $50,000 and over, with the remaining 39.8% realised by taxpayers with incomes below $50,000. Clearly,

45 One specific example is Senator Gibson: see Chapter 2, footnote 35.

Reynolds (1999, p. 83) was incorrect in his claim that 'only 18 per cent of capital gains tax in 1996–97 was actually collected from individuals in the top tax bracket.'[46]

The two income groups referred to by Reynolds (1999)—taxable income of $50,000 and more and taxable income below $50,000—can be analysed in terms of the proportion of tax payable on capital gains. *Taxation Statistics* reveals that taxpayers with taxable capital gains and taxable incomes of $50,000 and over paid 74.1% of tax on capital gains for individuals, with the remaining 25.9% paid by taxpayers with taxable income of less than $50,000. The data confirm that Reynolds was incorrect in his claim that 'revenues from the Australian tax are most meager where the rate is the highest (individuals in the top two tax brackets)...'

Furthermore, it is clear from the information in Table 2 that as taxable income increases, the proportion of taxpayers with realised capital gains also increases. Specifically, although for the entire population the proportion of taxpayers with capital gains is 7%, for taxpayers with taxable incomes of $50,000 or more, 13.4% had realised capital gains, whereas for taxpayers with taxable income under $50,000, 6.2% had realised net capital gains.

**Table 2: Capital gains subject to tax, by grade of income 1996–97**

| Taxable income ($) | Amount of capital gains ($million) | Tax on capital gains ($million) | Percentage of taxpayers with capital gains |
|---|---|---|---|
| Under 20,700 | 265 | 34 | 5 |
| 20,700–37,999 | 545 | 108 | 6 |
| 38,000–49,999 | 344 | 88 | 8 |
| 50,000–99,999 | 737 | 236 | 12 |
| 100,000–499,999 | 750 | 304 | 22 |
| 500,000–999,999 | 123 | 56 | 32 |
| 1,000,000–4,999,999 | 122 | 57 | 37 |
| 5,000,000 and over | 14 | 6 | 45 |
| **Total** | 2,899 | 888 | 7 |

*Source:* Adapted from *Taxation Statistics* 1996–97 (Australian Taxation Office, 1999).

*Notes.* In addition to the above, there are data on individual taxpayers who had non-taxable capital gains in 1996–97. These taxpayers realised $183,000,000 of capital gains and 6% of these taxpayers had capital gains.

Some of the 1999 arguments about the positive revenue effects of the 50% CGT discount had no empirical basis, and this is part of the justification for the quantitative study in this book. For example, Reynolds (1999, p. 35) made the claim that 'according to two leading revenue-estimating agencies of the U.S. government, a sizable reduction in the highest Australian tax rates on capital gains would clearly *increase* revenue...' It is

46 Perhaps Reynolds was referring to the proportion of capital gains tax paid by individuals facing the top tax rate as a proportion of capital gains tax paid by all taxpayer types. If this is the case, the statement is misleading since corporations were taxed at a flat rate.

obvious that the U.S. revenue-estimating agencies would not have prepared estimates for capital gains realisations response in Australia. Nevertheless, the statement implies that the estimates in U.S. capital gains realisations response studies can be transplanted to the Australian context. However, Reynolds did not justify why the U.S. results might be transferrable to Australia, nor explain what adjustments might be necessary to take into account the institutional differences between the tax systems of the two countries.

One of the purposes of the quantitative study in Chapter 5 of this book is to determine whether the realisations response for the capital gains of personal taxpayers in Australia may be large enough to offset the static revenue loss from the CGT rate cut. The quantitative study provides evidence on the degree to which increases in capital gains realisations are due to taxpayers responding to the tax rate, as distinct from the influence of non-tax factors on realisations.

The recommendations of the Henry Review are considered relevant to the research in this book, given that one of its recommendations was to increase the CGT rate by reducing the CGT discount from 50% to 40% (Henry & Australia, 2010). This was part of one of the broader recommendations of the Henry Review for a savings income discount of 40%, which was to apply to various other forms of passive income (Henry & Australia, 2010). This measure would increase horizontal equity, as capital gains would no longer have preferential status relative to various other forms of non-labour income. Importantly, the Henry Review recommendation for a 40% discount on savings income required that 40% of associated expenses would not be deductible. This recommendation implies that the current mismatch between taxation of capital gains income and deductions for related expenses is an issue in Australian tax policy in need of reform.

*Taxation Statistics* for the years 2006–07 to 2013–14 (Australian Taxation Office, 2016) indicate that the number of personal taxpayers with net capital gains decreased markedly between 2007–08 and 2011–12 (Table 3). The average capital gain per taxpayer was relatively steady over the years included in the table. The data in Tables 3 and 4 may imply that the prevailing preferential rates of CGT in these years were not the only consideration in taxpayers' decisions to realise capital gains.

**Table 3: Capital gains subject to tax (taxable personal taxpayers)**

| Income year | Number with net capital gains ($million) | Amount of net capital gains ($billion) | Average capital gain per taxpayer ($) |
|---|---|---|---|
| 2006–07 | 1.434 | 27.064 | 18,869 |
| 2007–08 | 1.407 | 24.349 | 17,309 |
| 2008–09 | 0.545 | 11.084 | 20,538 |
| 2009–10 | 0.572 | 11.819 | 20,648 |
| 2010–11 | 0.587 | 12.542 | 21,351 |
| 2011–12 | 0.448 | 9.838 | 21,950 |
| 2012–13 | 0.527 | 10.468 | 19,872 |
| 2013–14 | 0.610 | 14.379 | 23,585 |

*Source:* From Individual Table 1, *Taxation Statistics* 2013–14 (Australian Taxation Office, 2016).

The peak year for capital gains realisations was 2006–07. For five of the last six years included in Table 3, realisations of net capital gains have been less than half their peak level in that year. In 2006–07, there was a small reduction in the top marginal tax rate from 47% to 45%. In the same year, there was a significant increase in the level of taxable income at which the top marginal tax rate applied; this increased from $95,000 in 2005–06 to $150,000 in 2006–07. The result of this change is that many taxpayers who accrued capital gains faced a lower tax rate in 2006–07 compared with 2005–06. In 2006–07, the second highest tax bracket rate was reduced from 42% to 40% and the taxable income range for this second highest bracket changed from $63,001–$95,000 in 2005–06 to $75,001–$150,000 in 2006–07. The result of this change is that some taxpayers would have found that their marginal tax rate changed from 47% in 2006–07 to 40% in 2005–06.

Australian CGT data predating the years included in Table 3 reveal a trend of increasing CGT revenue collections from personal taxpayers commencing in the mid-1980s, namely, prior to the introduction of the 50% CGT discount. Some of the reasons revenue may have increased include increased levels of asset ownership among the taxpayer population, increased levels of economic growth, higher levels of share ownership and increases in taxpayer compliance with the CGT provisions.

The Australian pre-1999–2000 CGT data indicate that capital gains realisations reported on tax returns have fluctuated significantly from year to year, during a period of time when there was no statutory CGT rate change. This is consistent with the finding of Minarik (1984) that capital gains realisations have increased in years in which there were no favourable tax rate changes and that these increases could be due to factors such as increases in dividends, economic growth or inflation. The choice to realise capital gains at the personal taxpayer level may be influenced by timing realisations in years when total taxable income is relatively low. Minarik identified that a consideration in capital gains realisations response studies is the counterfactual question; that is, in the case of a CGT rate cut, rather than comparing realisations between two sequential years, it may be more important to consider what would have occurred in the one year in the absence of the CGT rate cut. According to Gravelle (1994), elasticity is not necessarily constant at all levels of taxable income, and it may be expected to increase as income increases.

**Table 4: Capital gains subject to tax, by grade of taxable income 2013–14**

| Taxable income ($) | Number of taxpayers with net capital gains | Amount of capital gains ($million) | Percentage of total net capital gains | Percentage of taxpayers in the income band |
|---|---|---|---|---|
| Up to 18,200 | 82,347 | 439 | 3.0 | 19.2 |
| 18,201–37,000 | 120,874 | 666 | 4.6 | 24.0 |
| 37,001–80,000 | 186,469 | 1,734 | 12.1 | 37.3 |
| 80,001–180,000 | 158,470 | 3,166 | 22.0 | 16.6 |
| 180,001 and over | 61,518 | 8,372 | 58.2 | 2.9 |
| **Total** | **609,678** | **14,379** | | |

*Source:* Adapted from *Taxation Statistics* 2013–14 (Australian Taxation Office, 2016).

Set out in Table 4 are 2013–14 data on the number of taxpayers within each income tax bracket, as well as the number of taxpayers with net capital gains in each income bracket and the amount of net capital gains. The data confirm that taxpayers in the highest income bracket realise the greatest proportion of total net capital gains. Although there are no data available on accrued capital gains, it is expected that the largest proportion of accrued capital gains are held by taxpayers in the highest income bracket.



## 2.7 RESEARCH QUESTIONS AND HYPOTHESES

The review of the literature in this chapter initially established that there is an ongoing and unresolved debate about whether preferential treatment of capital gains is appropriate, and has considered how responsive individual investors are to changes in the rate at which capital gains are taxed. It identified there is some uncertainty about the most appropriate means by which responsiveness to rate changes can or should be measured, and has established that little empirical research has been conducted in this area in Australia.

The first of these points gives rise to the general research question identified in this book: are CGT rate preferences a necessary feature of CGT systems? One of the motivations for this research question is that much of the tax literature, as outlined in this chapter, considers a CGT regime without rate preferences to be a better alternative.

Despite this view in the literature, CGT rate preferences are part of the Australian tax system and a common feature of the tax systems of several comparable jurisdictions. The literature review has highlighted the conflict between the tax literature on the topic of CGT rate preferences and the practice of policy makers on this tax system feature. In considering this research question, the literature review has explored the arguments for and against the preferential taxation of capital gains.

This book uses a mixed methods approach, which is outlined in detail in Chapter 3. The first component of the research in this book is a qualitative in-depth, semi-structured study drawing on responses from a series of interviews. Specifically, Chapter 4 presents and analyses the interview responses of CGT experts. Although the qualitative study does not commence with a series of hypotheses, it is concerned with the exploration of broad themes. These are (1) the role of CGT preferences and (2) whether and how to reform the CGT system as it applies to personal taxpayers. These two themes give rise to six secondary research questions that are considered by way of interviews with experts. The secondary research questions are:

i) What are the main benefits and disadvantages of CGT preferences?
ii) How have policy makers sought to justify changes to CGT for individual taxpayers?
iii) Do the benefits of deferral for capital gains diminish the case for a CGT preference?
iv) Is the case for a CGT preference due mostly to economic efficiency considerations, political considerations or to a combination of both?
v) Have CGT preferences been successful in achieving the economic objectives that they were intended to?
vi) How can the CGT system in Australia be reformed?

The quantitative research in this book is concerned with another secondary research question: what is the magnitude of the capital gains realisations response? This secondary research question is related to the broader research question—whether rate preferences for capital gains are a necessary feature of tax systems—given that one of the possible benefits of a lowering of the CGT rate is an increase in revenue through a sufficient realisations response. If the realisations response is found to be high in magnitude, it may be that CGT revenue has increased as a result of the halving of the tax rate that effectively occurred with the introduction of the 50% CGT discount in 1999. However, in the event that the realisations response is moderate or insignificant, the CGT discount is likely to have led to reduced tax revenue.

The secondary research question gives rise to the following two alternative hypotheses, which are tested by way of the quantitative study in Chapter 5 of this book:

- H1: The 50% CGT discount for personal taxpayers, introduced in the 1999–2000 tax year, is likely to have caused a decrease in CGT revenue over the long run.
- H1alt: The 50% CGT discount for personal taxpayers, introduced in the 1999–2000 tax year, is likely to have caused an increase in CGT revenue over the long run.

The following chapter outlines the methodology and research design of the book.

# CHAPTER 3

# Methodology and Research Design

## 3.1 INTRODUCTION

The previous chapter reviewed the literature on the taxation of capital gains. The literature review identified arguments for and against taxation of capital gains at preferential rates. Chapter 2 included a review of the literature on capital gains realisations response studies, and detailed the research question and hypotheses that this book addresses. The focus of this chapter is on identifying and explaining the methodological framework suitable for addressing this broad research question and the hypotheses.

This section outlines the main features associated with qualitative, quantitative and mixed methods research. The research paradigm and research questions are determinative in deciding which research method is best suited to the study—a quantitative, qualitative or mixed methods approach. After assessing the strengths and weaknesses of the three approaches, consideration turns to which of the three is most appropriate for this research. The conclusion is that a mixed methods approach comprising two components is best suited. The final section of this chapter details the qualitative and quantitative components of the research in this book.

## 3.2 RESEARCH FRAMEWORKS AND APPROACHES

### Different research approaches

According to McKerchar (2010), the two core research frameworks can be described as 'positivism' and 'non-positivism'. These two frameworks are at opposite ends of a continuum, between which there are a number of possible frameworks including critical realism and pragmatism (McKerchar, 2010). The research in this book originates from a pragmatist framework; underlying this is the philosophy that the research questions should drive the research methods used.

The choice of research framework is viewed as an influence on research methodology. McKerchar (2010) characterised research methodology as the middle ground between philosophical discussion about theoretical frameworks and discussion on research methods. The choice of research methodology is between quantitative and qualitative. According to

Thomas (2003), although there has been debate about which of these two approaches is superior, many researchers see qualitative and quantitative approaches as complementary rather than competing. One of these two approaches may be better suited to a particular type of research question and, in some cases, a mixed methods approach may be most suitable.

## Qualitative research approach

Cresswell (2009) explained that qualitative research is suitable for exploring and understanding the meaning that individuals or groups ascribe to a social or human problem. The qualitative research methodology is interpretative in nature, and it is concerned with a subjective rather than objective reality (McKerchar, 2010). In contrast with quantitative research, qualitative research relies on inductive logic. Where a qualitative methodology is used, knowledge is usually created inductively and there is no expectation that the research can be replicated (McKerchar, 2010). Another feature of qualitative research is that it builds theories using inductive reasoning, as opposed to proving or disproving theories by deductive reasoning and empiricism (McKerchar, 2010).

An advantage of using a qualitative methodology is that it can be useful for describing complex phenomena in depth. Another advantage is that the researcher can be more adaptive to changes that may occur during the course of the research and the enquiry can be modified accordingly.

A weakness of qualitative research is the inability to generalise the results of the study. Another limitation is that collecting data can be time consuming, and it may also be limited by budget constraints.

## Quantitative research approach

Quantitative research is used to test objective theories by examining the relationship between variables (Cresswell, 2009). McKerchar (2010) noted that a quantitative research methodology is underpinned by positivism and its emphasis is on an empirical approach as a means of ascertaining truth. Typically, when the quantitative approach is used, the hypotheses are determined before the data are collected.

A principal advantage of the quantitative research paradigm is that the results of a particular study are considered capable of being replicated. Another main advantage of a quantitative approach is that it is more likely that the research findings can be generalised, in comparison with a qualitative study. Quantitative research is also useful where the population of interest is large in magnitude.

However, there are also a number of limitations to the quantitative approach. One of those limitations is the assumption that there is a known relationship that exists between variables. An example that may apply in the case of the quantitative study in this book is the relationship between the CGT rate and capital gains realisations. Most previous studies have found an inverse relationship between these two variables, and it may be that, partly because of these findings, this inverse relationship is now assumed.[1]

1 Nevertheless, the fact that the tax rate coefficients from the Chapter 5 equations have a minus sign indicates that the assumed inverse relationship is most likely to be correct.

The literature review in Chapter 2 of this book has outlined a number of further limitations applying to a quantitative capital gains realisations response study using time series data. These include the fact that some of the existing studies may not be robust to minor specification changes. A limitation of capital gains realisations response studies per se is the fact that the decision to realise gains is likely to reflect a complex life cycle model, and a complete understanding of this model is usually outside the scope of a capital gains realisations response equation. For example, according to Gravelle (1990), some of the specifications used in realisations response studies do not appear to account for the fact that taxpayers sometimes realise capital gains for consumption and that to include consumption decisions correctly would require a complex life cycle model overlapping generations.



## Mixed methods approach

A mixed methodology describes one that draws from more than one research approach in the overall research design (McKerchar, 2010). According to Ivankova, Cresswell and Stick (2006), the rationale for mixing quantitative and qualitative research within the one study is based on the theory that neither of these methods is sufficient, by itself, to capture the trends and details of a given situation. A mixed methods design may be appropriate where the researcher needs to both explore and explain (Cresswell, 2009). A potential benefit of mixed methods is the possibility of triangulation of results, which may neutralise any bias that exists.

There are a number of reasons that a researcher might adopt a mixed methods approach. According to Johnson and Onwuegbuzie (2004, p. 17), the mixed methods approach is an expansive rather than limiting form of research that attempts to 'legitimate the use of multiple approaches in answering research questions'. Patton (2002) identified that studies relying on only one method are potentially more vulnerable to errors associated with the particular method. According to McKerchar (2010), mixed methods may be appropriate for researchers who adopt a single methodological approach. For example, where an empiricist uses a survey and an experiment, they are using mixed methods rather than a mixed methodological approach.

According to Hesse-Biber and Leavy (2011), one motivation for a mixed methods research design is that it can result in a more complete understanding of the research problem for the researcher. Furthermore, mixed methods research can be motivated by reasons related to development; specifically, the results from one method can help to develop or inform the other method (Greene, Caracelli & Graham, 1989).

According to Morgan (2014), one of the advantages of mixed methods research is the number of purposes that the researcher can pursue. However, there may be a greater complexity of procedures when the quantitative and qualitative approaches are combined (Morgan, 2014). According to Johnson and Onwuegbuzie (2004), an advantage of mixed methods research is that the research can use the strengths of one method to overcome some of the weaknesses of another method. Furthermore, the use of mixed methods can add insights and understanding that may be absent when only a single method is used.

In their paper that argued in favour of using a mixed methods approach, Johnson and Onwuegbuzie (2004, p. 21) identified that 'methodological purists' may contend that one should choose either a qualitative or quantitative paradigm. Despite such views, it would appear that the mixed methods approach is a widely accepted research framework.

# 3.3 APPLICATION OF RESEARCH PARADIGMS TO THE RESEARCH QUESTION AND THE HYPOTHESES

## The choice of research approach

A mixed methods approach has been adopted for the research in this book. One of the justifications for the mixed methods approach is that it is most suitable means of addressing the research question, and it is an original way of doing so. Previously, much of the research on the effect of tax rate changes on capital gains realisations has used a quantitative research methodology. While the quantitative study in Chapter 5 addresses the issue of the realisations response, there remain several other issues related to CGT preferences that are better addressed by way of a qualitative research approach.

The first component of the research in this book consists of a qualitative study using interviews with experts on CGT in Australia, Canada and the United States. The second component consists of a quantitative empirical capital gains realisations response study using time series data. The two methods used in the book are sequential. The qualitative chapter precedes and informs the quantitative chapter, although the results of the latter are not dependent on the former. Rather, the outcomes of the Chapter 4 study are considered to have informed the study in Chapter 5. Chapter 4 is concerned with broader questions on the taxation of capital gains in comparison to Chapter 5, which is concerned with a more specific question—the capital gains realisations response for personal taxpayers in Australia.

The alternative hypotheses for the book were outlined in Chapter 2. They relate to the underlying research question: should capital gains be taxed at preferential rates? There are several views on this question. The qualitative study in Chapter 4 demonstrates there is not necessarily a consensus among experts on CGT in relation to this question. Notwithstanding this, the literature review highlighted the absence of empirical evidence for the argument that a CGT rate preference can increase the rate of saving or investment. The importance of the studies in this book relate partly to the questionable case for such claimed benefits of preferential CGT rates as well as the fact that a moderate or low realisations response would lose tax revenue for the government. The importance of preferential CGT rates is analysed as part of the general research question explored in the qualitative study in Chapter 4, while the specific hypotheses related to the elasticity of capital gains realisations are explored in the quantitative study in Chapter 5.

## Qualitative phase—interviews with CGT experts

### Interview design

The first component of the research in this book is a qualitative study drawing on responses from a series of interviews. The interviews were semi-structured and in-depth, and these two characteristics are compatible with one another. According to Leech (2002, p. 668), semi-structured interviews 'allow respondents the chance to be experts and to inform the research'. According to Hesse-Biber and Leavy (2011), in-depth interviews are useful when the researcher has a particular topic of interest, and the goal of in-depth interviews is to gain rich qualitative data from the perspective of selected individuals. According to Minichiello, Aroni and Hays (2008), the main purpose of an in-depth interview is to understand the significance of human experiences from the respondent's perspective, as interpreted by the interviewer. Ideally, a good interview should resemble a conversation and to this end possess the following characteristics: a two-way flow of dialogue, active listening on the part of the interviewer, as well as encouragement for the respondent to share more of their experiences (Liamputtong & Ezzy, 2005).



The focus of Chapter 4 is a series of semi-structured interviews conducted with CGT experts in Australia, Canada and the United States. The interviewees were tax academics, tax practitioners and tax economists. The interview participants are not identified by name, as one of the conditions of their participation was that they would be anonymous in any subsequent published research. In order to allow for the reader to identify quotes that are attributed to the same interview, a unique letter code has been assigned to the respondents quoted in Chapter 4. Table 5 shows the distribution of interviewees by letter code.

**Table 5: Distribution of interviewees by letter code**

| | Academic | Tax practitioner | Tax economist | Total |
|---|---|---|---|---|
| Australia | G, M, N, P, Q, S, T, U, V, Y | Z | – | **11** |
| Canada | E, H, I, J, K, O | F, L | – | **8** |
| United States | – | R | A, B, C, D | **5** |
| **Total** | **16** | **4** | **4** | **24** |

One of the purposes of the qualitative study is to identify areas of CGT policy that require reform. Another objective is to acquire an understanding of the features of the Canadian and U.S. CGT systems, given that these systems pre-date the Australian CGT system and Canada and the United States have experienced a greater number of CGT rate changes.

The qualitative study in this book is exploratory in nature. Saunders, Lewis and Thornhill (2003) warned of the possibility of interviewee or response bias and cautioned that interviews should be standardised to avoid the potential for reliability issues. The responses to the interview questions from Chapter 4 are not considered to suffer from the problem of non-standardisation. Specifically, a series of standard questions formed the basis of each interview. In some cases, follow-up questions were asked in the context of individual interviews, and in some cases, the order of the questions was changed to suit the flow of a particular interview.

According to Thomas (2003), interviews may be a superior form of data collection than surveys and questionnaires, as they allow for more flexibility and personal control. Furthermore, interviews allow the respondent more scope to elaborate on their answers. A disadvantage of interviews is that they take more time to complete, since the researcher is required to meet with each respondent individually. The qualitative study in Chapter 4 benefited from the use of interviews as opposed to alternatives such as surveys and questionnaires.

As well as being semi-structured and in-depth, the interviews with CGT experts, which took place in 2011, were exploratory in nature. As previously noted, the purpose of the interviews was to explore two broad themes. The first theme related to CGT rate preferences and the second theme was how to reform the CGT system as it applies to personal taxpayers.

It would be incorrect to characterise the interviews as structured, given that they were not limited to an identical set of questions and the order of the questions was changed, in some instances, according to the flow of the conversation. The aim of the interviews from the outset was to identify themes, and semi-structured interviews were conducive to achieving this aim. Each interviewee received a list of indicative questions prior to each interview, and an audio recording was made of each interview.

The interview questions were open-ended rather than closed questions. According to Grindsted (2005), open-ended questions are a typical feature of qualitative interviewing. According to Aberbach and Rockman (2002), an open-ended interview approach is a way of maximising response validity, since there is a greater opportunity for respondents to organise their responses within their own framework. In deciding on an interview method, informal conversational interviews were also considered; these are, according to Patton (2002), the most open-ended approach to interviewing. The informal conversational interview style was ultimately rejected as it was considered important for all the interviews to cover the same issues. There was no requirement for the interviews to follow a standardised format.

There are several well documented tax policy reasons for taxing capital gains at the same rate as ordinary income as outlined by Krever and Brooks (1990), Evans (1998), Kenny (2005), Clark and OECD (2006) and Minas (2011). Notwithstanding this, Australia, Canada and the United States all currently tax capital gains at preferential rates. One of the questions the interviews explored is whether the fact that each of the three countries operates CGT preferences is due to political considerations or concerns about economic efficiency or a combination of both factors.

## CGT preferences in the three jurisdictions

Australia, Canada and the United States each provide a rate preference for CGT payable by personal taxpayers. The three tax jurisdictions are broadly comparable, and they have all experienced at least one CGT rate change. These common features of the CGT systems of Australia, Canada and the United States influenced the inclusion of these three countries in the qualitative interview study.

A notable difference between Australia and the North American jurisdictions is the experience each has had with full-rate CGT regimes. The Australian CGT regime is one that initially (from 1985) taxed capital gains at full marginal rates, and did so through to 1999.[2] Indeed, Australia has taxed capital gains at full marginal tax rates in more income years than the United States and Canada, even though the Australian CGT regime has been in place for fewer years. From the time it enacted its CGT (in 1971), Canada has always had a tax on capital gains that is lower than the tax rate on ordinary income. In the United States, capital gains were taxed at ordinary income rates between 1988 and 1990, with preferential rates in place during the remainder of the time that CGT has operated there (from 1913 until the present day).



Of the three jurisdictions in the qualitative interview study, the United States has experienced the highest number of CGT rate changes in the last 40 or so years, with maximum rates on capital gains varying between roughly 15% and 40%. Specifically, in 1978, the rate decreased from 39.875% to 33.85%. In 1979, the maximum CGT rate decreased to 28%, and in 1981, it decreased to 20%. In 1987, the rate increased to 28%. There were moderate increases in the CGT rate in later years—the maximum rate was 28.93% in 1991 and 29.19% in 1993. The maximum rate decreased in 1997 to 21.19%. The next significant change in the rate was in 2003 when the maximum rate decreased to 16.05%. The maximum rate decreased to 15.7% in 2006 and 15.35% in 2008. In 2013, the maximum rate increased to 25.012% (U.S. Department of Treasury, Office of the Secretary of the Treasury, Office of Tax Analysis, 2016).

Canada has had, at various times, a CGT inclusion rate of one-half, two-thirds and three-quarters.[3] Although the Carter Commission had recommended the taxation of capital gains at full ordinary income tax rates, the inclusion rate of the CGT (as originally enacted) was 50%. In 1990, the inclusion rate was increased to 75%, and in February 2000, the rate decreased to two-thirds. In October 2000, the inclusion rate further decreased to 50%, and it has been at that level until the present day.

The Canada Revenue Agency website (Canada Revenue Agency, 2017) provides historical personal tax rate data for the 1985 tax year onwards. This information was used, in combination with the information on changes in the inclusion rate, to summarise the top marginal tax rate on personal capital gains from 1985 to 2017.[4] From 1985 to 1987 inclusive, the top marginal tax rate on capital gains was 17%. In 1988 and 1989, the top marginal tax rate on capital gains was 14.5%. In 1990, when the inclusion rate was increased to 75%, the top marginal tax rate on capital gains was 21.75%. The 21.75% rate continued to apply until February 2000, when the rate became 19.33% due to the inclusion rate being dropped to two-thirds. In October 2000, when the inclusion rate was lowered again, to 50%, the top marginal tax rate on capital gains was 14.5%. This rate increased to 16.5% for the 2016 and 2017 tax years.

2 From September 1985 until September 1999, with the indexation of cost base allowed where the asset had been held for 12 months.

3 Inclusion in this context refers to the inclusion in taxable income of net capital gains.

4 That is, the real marginal tax rate on the amount of capital gains realised, rather than the marginal tax rate on the amount of capital gains included in income.

Australia has experienced several changes to statutory tax rates since the enactment of its CGT in 1985. However, there has been one specific change to the taxation of capital gains—the enactment of the CGT discount in 1999—that resulted in a change to the real rate of tax on capital gains for personal taxpayers. The main CGT rate reduction was achieved by changing from the previous system of including the entire net capital gain in assessable income, with an indexed cost base, to the current system of including 50% of the net capital gain in ordinary income, without an indexed cost base.[5] The latter is the basic operation of the 50% CGT discount, a provision that became operational in September 1999. As per s 115-25 of the *ITAA1997*, one of the requirements for a taxpayer to qualify for the CGT discount is that they have held the asset subject to the CGT event for at least 12 months.

Canada seemingly has more in common with Australia than the United States in its approach to the taxation of capital gains realised by personal taxpayers. A historical similarity between Canada and Australia is the fact that, in both systems, capital gains were not part of the initial tax base.[6] A similarity in the current systems is that in Canada, taxpayers are only required to include half of a capital gain in their taxable income, as per s 38 of the *Income Tax Act*, RSC 1985, c. 1 (5th Supp.). The Canadian system differs from Australia's in that a taxpayer is eligible for the 50% CGT inclusion irrespective of the amount of time that they have held the asset prior to its disposal. A minimum holding period requirement for a preferential, or more preferential, CGT rate can be somewhat arbitrary in terms of where to set the definitional boundary. Nevertheless, the absence of one, as in the case of the Canadian CGT system, might extend the availability of the preference to gains that are arguably closer in character to ordinary income rather than capital.

Slemrod and Bakija (2008) noted that, in the American context, the Republicans have generally wanted to reduce CGT rates, whereas the Democrats have wanted to keep the rates closer to those on other income. Musgrave (1968) is one of several economists who are of the view that the preferential treatment of capital gains in the United States has reduced the overall progressivity of the American tax system. In the Australian context, the current rate of preferential CGT, achieved by way of the 50% CGT discount, appeared to have bipartisan support until recent years. This is evidenced by the fact that in 1999, the then Howard Coalition Government introduced a CGT rate preference[7] and the fact that in 2010, the then Rudd Labor Government ruled out adopting a recommendation of the Henry Review to change the rate of CGT discount for personal taxpayers from 50% to 40% (Swan & Rudd, 2010, 2 May). More recently, the Coalition Government has ruled out reducing the rate of the CGT discount (effectively increasing the rate of CGT) as way of gaining tax revenue (Murphy & Hutchens, 2017). This is despite the fact that the

5 The indexation of cost base is, however, still available in the case of pre-21 September 1999 CGT assets. The taxpayer can elect to use either the discount or the indexation method, where they qualify for both.

6 This is in contrast with the United States where capital gains were taxable as income from when the taxation system commenced there.

7 The 50% CGT discount.

budget is currently in deficit. By contrast, the Labor opposition proposed the reduction of the CGT discount from 50% to 25% (Taylor, 2016).

Although CGT rate preferences can prevent the inflationary component of a taxable capital gain being subject to tax, they are clearly an imprecise way of achieving this.[8] However, the case for indexation applying to cost base is an unsteady one as noted by Minarik (1992), who identified that inequity results when only one part of a tax system is subject to inflation adjustments. Furthermore, it is apparent that Australia is currently experiencing significantly lower rates of inflation today compared with the mid-1980s, the time of the original enactment of the CGT regime.



The specific design features of a particular tax system can also be an influence on the rationale for the preferential treatment of capital gains. For example, Australia operates an imputation credit system, which prevents the economic double taxation of dividends.[9] By contrast, the modified classical system used in the United States fails to prevent double taxation, and some of the U.S. interviewees referred to the double taxation in the United States tax system due to the lack of an income tax provision that integrates the corporate and personal tax system. A preferential rate of CGT may appear to be an appropriate way of providing an adjustment for this lack of integration. However, according to Minarik (1992), a CGT rate preference fails to eliminate the problem caused by the double taxation in the classical system; instead, it only reduces its impact. In the event that policy makers consider a CGT rate preference a necessary tax policy to reduce the double taxation of corporate stock, it should apply to this specific capital asset only (Minarik, 1992).

## Research questions

The focus of the qualitative interview study is on two thematic areas: first, CGT rate preferences and, in particular, their advantages and disadvantages; and second, the broad question of how to reform the individual CGT in each country. The Appendix contains a full list of all 22 interview questions; however, the study in this chapter focuses on five of these questions.[10] The first of these themes is considered according to the responses provided to the following three interview questions:

- Q1. What do you consider to be the main benefits and disadvantages of CGT preferences?
- Q2. On what basis have previous changes to the taxation of individual capital gains in (Australia/Canada/the United States) been justified by policy makers? In your view, what are the merits or otherwise of these justifications?
- Q3. Given the benefits of deferral that apply to capital gains and the ability of the taxpayer to effectively choose when and if they will realise a capital gain, are preferential rates for capital gains considered appropriate?

8 The indexation system used in Australia prior to the CGT discount and still available in some circumstances is a more precise way of achieving an inflation adjustment.

9 The imputation credit system does not apply to dividends from shares in foreign companies.

10 The Appendix lists the questions in the order that they were asked in the interviews. Nevertheless, for ease of identification, this chapter labels the six selected questions 1 to 6.

The overarching purpose of Question One was to compare the thinking of CGT experts on CGT preferences and the specific rate preferences offered in their country. Although the focus of this question was on CGT rate preferences, respondents were able to discuss other types of CGT preferences.

One of the motivations for Question Two was the apparent lack of a clear policy rationale for the 50% CGT discount in Australia. The responses of the Australian interviewees to this question are highly relevant to the research question. The responses from interviewees in Canada and the United States are also of relevance given that a rate preference for capital gains appears to be an entrenched feature of tax policy in those jurisdictions. Burman (1999) noted that low CGT rates are the historical norm in the United States and that this was an influence on U.S. Congress increasing the magnitude of the capital gains preference in 1997. The views from the experts on the rationale for CGT rate changes may be informative to future tax policy on CGT.

Question Three was designed to complement Question One and Question Two. Most of the responses provided to this question gave a clear indication as to whether the interviewee was in favour of CGT rate preferences or not. In total, 14 of the 24 respondents indicated that rate preferences for capital gains were inappropriate in light of the deferral benefits that applied. Four respondents argued that there was some justification for CGT preferences, while a further six either did not provide a conclusive answer to the question or referred to arguments both for and against CGT preferences.

As part of the interviews, two other questions related to CGT rate preferences were asked:

- Q4. Is the case for retaining capital gains preferences due mostly to economic efficiency considerations, political considerations or a combination of both?
- Q5. How successful do you think CGT rate preferences have been in achieving the economic objectives that they were intended to?

The response to Question Four may be dependent on the responses to the previous questions. It may be the case that an interviewee who was of the view that preferential rates for capital gains do not have a strong tax policy foundation might conclude that it is more likely that the reasons for them being a feature of the respective tax systems of each country are more related to political rather than economic efficiency considerations. The interview responses, discussed in Chapter 4, indicate that all of the respondents were of the view that political considerations were part of the reason for CGT rate preferences.

Question Five was intended to be an open-ended and unbiased question. Although the wording of the question is such that it may be perceived as confirming a link between CGT rate preferences and the attainment of certain economic benefits, it allows the respondent to comment on whether there is such a link or simply to state what they understand is the policy justification for the CGT rate preference in their country. It also allows for an exploration of, and comparison between, how a rate preference for CGT has been explained or justified in each of the three jurisdictions (Minas & Lim, 2013).

The second theme of the interviews was explored by way of the following question:

- Q6. How do you think that the capital gains tax system in (Australia/Canada/the United States) can best be reformed?

Question Six was designed to allow the respondents the opportunity to summarise the main points discussed in their interview and speak about any other CGT issues that had not been covered by the previous questions. At the end of each interview, respondents were able to add any further comments or discuss areas that the earlier part of the interview had not covered. One of the justifications for Question Six was that asking a final open-ended question is an approach consistent with inductive reasoning; it is considered that this approach has the potential to uncover ideas that might inform the research (McKerchar, 2010).

Although Question Six can be considered a broad question, capable of generating a wide range of possible responses, it is nevertheless considered valuable to the study as a whole. Question Six enabled the interviewees to talk specifically about what they saw as the priorities for reform of CGT in their jurisdiction. One of the advantages of the question is that it is free from bias and does not limit what respondents can address in their answers (Minas & Lim, 2013).



Question Six was intended to be the most open-ended question asked in the interviews; this was reflected in the diversity of interview responses as a number of new themes emerged.

## Interview conduct

The methodology for the study was individual, in-depth interviews with experts on CGT. As all the interviews were conducted in person, there were budgetary constraints on the number of locations where these could take place. For practical reasons, the interviews were restricted to one or two locations in each of Australia, Canada and the United States where several CGT experts were located. Consequently, the selection of interviewees was limited to the extent that there were locations where a lesser number of experts were located that were excluded from this study. The interviews were transcribed in full, shortly after the interviews took place. An initial reading of the transcripts was then followed by a second reading, during which areas of convergence and divergence within the themes for the study were identified. The individual quotes included in Chapter 4 are those that are best aligned with the themes as well as those that are representative of arguments for and against topics within these themes. The use of direct quotes is considered 'quite helpful in demonstrating the diversity of opinion in this controversial area' (Mcnaughton, 2014, p. 924).

The selection of interviewees for the research resulted in 24 interview participants in total: 11 from Australia, 8 from Canada and 5 from the United States. The interviewees were a mixture of tax academics, tax practitioners and tax economists. The distribution of interviewees by country and broad demographic group is shown in Table 6.

**Table 6: Distribution of interviewees**

| | Academic | Tax practitioner | Tax economist | Total |
|---|---|---|---|---|
| Australia | 10 | 1 | 0 | **11** |
| Canada | 6 | 2 | 0 | **8** |
| United States | 0 | 1 | 4 | **5** |
| **Total** | **16** | **4** | **4** | **24** |

The breadth of the interview sample might have been improved had some interviewees from all three demographic groups been interviewed in each individual country, although this is not essential for a qualitative study. Ideally, interviewees would have included academics in the United States and tax economists in Australia and Canada. This would have increased the overall representativeness of the sample in each individual country and allowed for comparisons between the demographic groups by country. Nevertheless, the interviewees comprise a good sample of CGT experts (Minas & Lim, 2013). In the case of the 10 Australian academics interviewed, more than half were either professors or associate professors, and the majority of these interviewees had publications on CGT. The tax practitioners and tax economists were all identified as having a high level of CGT expertise and were selected for interview based on their credentials. Some of these interviewees had publications on CGT, and others had been identified as CGT experts for other reasons.

## Quantitative phase—capital gains realisations response study

### The relevance of capital gains realisations response to Australia

Australia has had two markedly different CGT rate regimes for personal taxpayers. From the introduction of CGT on 20 September 1985 to 21 September 1999, taxation of capital gains was at ordinary income tax rates, with the indexation of cost base. From 21 September 1999 onwards, a taxpayer with a net capital gain calculated using the discount method[11] only included half of that net capital gain in assessable income. This has resulted in taxation of capital gains at effectively half the taxpayer's marginal tax rate.

There are two counteracting revenue effects arising from a CGT rate reduction. First, there is the static cost to the revenue resulting from the lowering of the CGT rate. Second, there is the expected increase in realisations in response to the lower CGT rate. The second of these effects may lead to increased tax revenue if it is large in magnitude.

The lack of empirical work that informed the decision in Australia to enact the CGT discount is in contrast with the United States, where proposed CGT rate changes require the analysis and forecast of revenue effects. Although it is not the argument of this book that revenue effects are the primary concern in deciding the CGT rate, it is arguable that they have not received requisite attention in the Australian tax policy setting.

CGT for personal taxpayers in Australia originally applied at full marginal income tax rates from its introduction on 20 September 1985. The enactment of the CGT discount in the 1999–2000 income tax year saw the introduction of a generous preference for capital gains. The 1975 Asprey Report, which recommended a CGT 10 years before its actual introduction, considered the inclusion of only half the capital gain in assessable income as well as taxation of capital gains at a fixed rate. The Committee explained in its report that it rejected the latter approach because it would make the tax system less progressive; it instead recommended partial inclusion of capital gains in assessable income (Commonwealth Taxation Review Committee & Asprey, 1975). The Committee did not indicate in its report that there should be a preference for capital gains per se; rather,

11 This refers to (a) capital gain(s) eligible for the 50% CGT discount.

partial inclusion was intended to be a proxy for an inflation adjustment of cost base, given that at the time this was considered to be too complex (Commonwealth Taxation Review Committee & Asprey, 1975). The Hawke Government, however, opted to introduce a CGT with inflation of cost base rather than inclusion of a proportion of the gain.[12]

Partial inclusion of capital gains became a policy issue again in 1999 when the Ralph Review proposed—and the Howard Government enacted—the CGT discount, although there was an absence of a rationale for moving from indexation of cost base to the CGT discount. Nevertheless, the government at the time appears to have attempted to justify the policy, in part, based on a forecast of revenue gains it would provide.[13]



In reducing the CGT rate by way of the CGT discount, some policy makers in Australia appear to have undertaken a largely superficial consideration of the realisations response and the related revenue effects.[14] As highlighted in Chapter 2, in at least one case, there was the incorrect assumption that increased capital gains realisations would necessarily result in increased tax revenue.[15] The flaws of such an assumption were highlighted by Mehrota and Ott (2016, p. 2,536) who noted that 'many advocates of the capital gains tax preference have contended that lower tax rates on capital gains would always and everywhere lead to increased tax revenue, even though there was little objective, empirical evidence to support that theory.'

It is a reasonable assumption that a CGT rate reduction is likely to engender some increase in capital gains realisations. However, whether a CGT rate cut is revenue gaining or revenue losing depends on the magnitude of this realisations response. The study in Chapter 5 fills an important gap in the knowledge about the capital gains realisations response for personal taxpayers in Australia.

Although Feldstein et al. (1980) estimated a capital gains realisations response of a high magnitude, they noted that their simulations were measures of the quantum of sales and realised gains, ceteris paribus, under different tax rules in the tax year in question. That is, the elasticity point estimates were not forecasts, because changes in tax rules involve transitional adjustments that can be difficult to predict and that could last several years (Feldstein et al., 1980). It follows that an elasticity point estimate from a U.S. capital gains realisations response study cannot be directly applied to the Australian context. The need for empirical evidence on the Australian capital gains realisations response is one of the motivations for this book and, in particular, the study in this chapter.

## Issues informing the equation specification

The focus of the quantitative research in this book is a capital gains realisations response study. The study estimates the responsiveness of capital gains realisations of personal taxpayers in Australia to tax rates. Chapter 5 outlines the estimating equation used. The

12 Specifically, the Hawke Government enacted s 160ZJ of the *ITAA1936*, the purpose of which was to provide an inflation adjustment based on 'movements in the weighted average in the All Groups Consumer Price Index in the eight capital cities' (*Income Tax Assessment Amendment (Capital Gains) Bill* 1986 (Cth)).

13 See Table 1 in Chapter 2.

14 See, for example, the statement of Senator Gibson, Chapter 2, footnote 35.

15 See Chapter 2, footnote 32.

equation includes a tax rate variable and a number of other independent variables that influence capital gains realisations. As discussed in Chapter 2, there is a choice of data types for use in a capital gains realisations response study, and the benefits and disadvantages of each have been outlined in that chapter. Essentially, the choice for this study lies between three possible data types: panel data, cross-sectional data and time series data.[16]

The unavailability of panel data, for a sufficient number of years, immediately eliminated the choice of this type of study.[17] The remaining choices of data type were time series, cross-sectional or pooled data.[18] A cross-sectional study is not preferred for the quantitative study as, although this was the approach taken in some of the earlier studies, there are a number of significant problems with this data type. One of the main problems is that cross-sectional studies only take into account a single year and the results can vary widely depending on the influence of non-tax variables in the year chosen. For example, if 1986 was the chosen year for a U.S. elasticity study, it is likely that an overstated elasticity estimate would be the result. Such an estimate would be misleading given the exceptional circumstances of that particular year. Specifically, a large amount of capital gains were realised in advance of a pre-announced CGT rate increase, reflecting a timing effect rather than a permanent effect. Although this timing behaviour is not reflective of the long-run realisations response, it is an inherent characteristic of the results reported in cross-sectional elasticity studies.

Given the unavailability of panel and pooled data, and the unsuitability of cross-sectional data, time series data were used for the quantitative study in this book. Although time series data may be considered to be 'best second best,' these data are suitable, and they have been used to good effect by U.S. researchers to produce credible estimates of the capital gains realisations response. The literature review in Chapter 2 concluded that time series studies produced elasticity point estimates that are lower in magnitude than cross-sectional studies. This is consistent with apparent propensity for cross-sectional studies to overestimate the realisations response.

Following this data choice, a key design aspect was to determine the variables (dependent and independent) to include in the regression model. Chapter 2 concluded that the elasticity estimates in time series studies can be sensitive to the regression equation specification. One of the benefits of a time series study is that, since these studies span several years, the effect on the elasticity point estimate of a particular year that is unusual can be observed.[19] In some cases it may be necessary to control for the effects of an unusual tax year; this may include running regressions with and without the year in question and comparing the results of the two regressions.

16 A fourth alternative is a time series of cross-sectional data; this is commonly referred to as pooled data.

17 The ATO is the only organisation in Australia that holds the taxpayer data required. Although these panel data, in de-identified form, were formally requested from the ATO, the request was refused due to ATO resource constraints and, surprisingly, concerns about taxpayer confidentiality.

18 The ATO has made a random sample of tax return data for individual tax years from 2003–04 onwards available to researchers in recent years. Data for years before and after the rate change would be required for a pooled data study.

19 Discussion of 1986 as an unusual year for capital gains realisations and the implications of this for studies conducted in the United States are discussed in Chapter 2.

Given the difference between the operation of the Australian and U.S. tax systems, there is a further definitional issue to consider in relation to the dependent variable in the capital gains realisations response study. Whereas in the United States capital gains are taxed at a separate rate to ordinary income, in Australia the 50% CGT discount is not, by strict definition, a rate preference. Net capital gains in the Australian time series data are net capital gains after the CGT discount has been applied. Although these capital gains are then taxed at ordinary marginal tax rates for individuals, the real CGT rate can be seen as approximately half the marginal tax rate that applies. Because of this treatment of capital gains in the Australian system, it is appropriate to include a measure of net capital gains, adjusted to represent the amount of capital gains before the discount has been applied. Consistent with this, a CGT rate should be chosen that approximates the real CGT tax rate. Consequently, the regressions do not use the statutory marginal rate on discounted capital gains for the years following the introduction of the CGT discount. 3

Although the main research hypotheses are concerned with the capital gains realisations response, the revenue implications of a CGT rate change are closely related and are of the most concern to tax policy makers. Although an empirical realisations response study is not intended to be predictive, it is a first and important step in understanding more about the revenue effects of a CGT rate change.

The revenue effects of a CGT rate change are not the sole focus of CGT policy. The background to the introduction of Australia's 50% CGT discount indicates that, at that time, policy makers were concerned about the revenue effects of the effective rate reduction to the CGT. Specifically, there were arguments advanced about a strong taxpayer response to the 50% CGT discount, which would 'unlock' capital gains and lead to an overall increase in revenue.

There are several issues to consider in the design of the regression specification in Chapter 5. The regression equation includes a dependent variable, being a measure of net capital gains realisations, and a number of independent—or explanatory—variables. The independent variable of interest is the CGT rate; the other independent variables in the equation are for a number of non-tax factors that potentially influence the level of capital gains realisations.

There are various functional forms for estimating the elasticity of capital gains realisations to tax rates. Gravelle (2010) explained that one of the most common examples is the following semi-log equation, where *G* is capital gains, *t* is the tax rate and *b* is the tax rate coefficient that the equation estimates:

$$\log G = bt$$

In practice, the complete specification would also include non-tax variables.

Given the expected inverse relationship between capital gains realisations and CGT rates, *b* will be negative. Much of the capital gains realisations response literature reports it as an absolute value.[20] In a semi-logarithmic equation, the elasticity point estimate is the coefficient (*b*) multiplied by the tax rate. In a log-log equation, the elasticity point estimate

20 That is, reports elasticity without the minus sign. Effectively, this assumes that the inverse relationship is a given.

is equal to the tax rate coefficient (Gravelle, 2010). Where a semi-logarithmic equation is used, another consideration is the tax rate at which to estimate elasticity.[21] The approach in many of the U.S. realisations response studies has been to measure realisations response at the midpoint between the CGT rates applying before and after a proposed CGT rate change. Gravelle (1990) noted that this is the most appropriate value to use for a given proposed tax rate change. The estimates in this chapter include a measure of elasticity based on a midpoint of the current CGT rate and the CGT rate that would exist if the 50% CGT discount were abolished.

## The estimating equation and its variables

This section outlines the equation developed for estimating the capital gains realisations response for personal taxpayers in Australia. One of the purposes of the literature review in Chapter 2 was to analyse the previous capital gains realisations response research and consider the estimating equations used in that research and the potential relevance of these to the study in this chapter. After carefully considering the equations used in the U.S. time series studies, the study by Eichner and Sinai (2000) was identified as one that could inform the development of the estimating equations in this chapter. The study in this chapter does not replicate the Eichner and Sinai (2000) estimating specifications.

### Model specification

The main regression equation used in this study is:

$$Ln(Discount\ capital\ gains)_t = a_1 + a_2\ Top\ marginal\ CGT\ rate_t + a_3\ Ln(ASX\ 200)_t + a_4\ Ln(Real\ GDP)_t + a_5\ Ln(GDP\ deflator)_t + u_t \quad (1)$$

Where *Ln(Discount capital gains)*, *Top marginal CGT rate*, *Ln(ASX 200)*, *Ln(Real GDP)* and *Ln(GDP deflator)* are detrended variables, respectively.

### The variables in the regression equation

The regression equations in this chapter consist of a dependent variable and several independent (explanatory) variables. The tax rate coefficient from a regression equation provides information on the effect of a change in the CGT rate on capital gains realisations. In a semi-log specification, the coefficient multiplied by the tax rate is the elasticity point estimate.

The dependent variable in the regression equation is a measure of capital gains realisations; this variable is dependent on the explanatory variables on the right-hand side of the equation. The main equation includes several independent variables—a marginal tax rate variable and the following non-tax variables:[22] the ASX 200 index, real GDP and a GDP deflator (Minas, Lim & Evans, 2018).

21 This is a separate consideration to which tax rate to use in the estimating equation.

22 Which together with the tax rate are seen as influencing capital gains realisations.

The aggregate time series data used in the regression analysis are predominantly from two sources. The first is tax return data for the years 1989–90 to 2014–15, sourced from *Taxation Statistics* (Australian Taxation Office, 2016). These data form the basis for the calculation of the dependent variable, which is a measure of the capital gains realisations in each of the years. The same taxpayer data are the source of one of the independent variables: the top marginal CGT rate.

The data on the other independent variables in the regression equation— the ASX 200 index, gross domestic product (GDP) and a GDP deflator—are from the second source of data: data sets published by the ABS. The ABS previously used a third-party source for the ASX 200 index data set that it no longer produces. For the missing years in the ABS time series, the data were sourced from the Standard and Poor's website (http://us.spindices.com/indices/equity/sp-asx-200), and it has been confirmed that for the years in which both agencies published the ASX 200 data, the reported amounts were identical (Minas et al., 2018). Table 7 reports the descriptive statistics for the data used in the analysis.



**Table 7: Descriptive statistics of the variables used in the analysis**

| | Number of observations | Mean | Median | Standard deviation | Min. | Max. |
|---|---|---|---|---|---|---|
| *rLn(Discount capital gains)* | 27 | 23.135 | 23.624 | 1.184 | 21.019 | 24.834 |
| *rTop marginal CGT rate* | 27 | 0.339 | 0.243 | 0.125 | 0.2325 | 0.5025 |
| *rLn(ASX 200)* | 27 | 8.05 | 8.105 | 0.447 | 7.314 | 8.744 |
| *rLn(Real GDP)* | 27 | 27.724 | 27.740 | 0.260 | 27.32 | 28.114 |
| *rLn(GDP deflator)* | 27 | 4.259 | 4.212 | 0.228 | 3.912 | 4.605 |
| *fdLn(Discount capital gains)* | 27 | 0.1140 | 0.1430 | 0.357 | –0.846 | 0.935 |
| *fdTop marginal CGT rate* | 27 | –0.010 | 0.000 | 0.047 | –0.2425 | 0.0125 |
| *fdLn(ASX 200)* | 27 | 0.047 | 0.069 | 0.119 | –0.277 | 0.212 |
| *fdLn(Real GDP)* | 27 | –0.111 | 0.035 | 0.738 | –3.802 | 0.489 |
| *fdLn(GDP deflator)* | 27 | 0.030 | 0.026 | 0.025 | –0.006 | 0.112 |
| *Ln(Discount capital gains)* | 27 | 0 | –0.038 | 0.706 | –1.094 | 0.973 |
| *Top marginal CGT rate* | 27 | 0 | 0.035 | 0.737 | –0.154 | 0.117 |
| *Ln(ASX 200)* | 27 | 0 | –0.047 | 0.206 | –0.306 | 0.374 |
| *Ln(Real GDP)* | 27 | 0 | 0.014 | 0.716 | –0.135 | 0.100 |
| *Ln(GDP deflator)* | 27 | 0 | 0.006 | 0.434 | –0.130 | 0.086 |

*Notes. rLn(Discount capital gains), rTop marginal CGT rate, rLn(ASX 200), rLn(Real GDP)* and *rLn(GDP deflator)* are variables with raw data. *fdLn(Discount capital gains), fdTop marginal CGT rate, fdLn(ASX 200), fdLn(Real GDP)* and *fdLn(GDP deflator)* are first-differenced variables. *Ln(Discount capital gains), Top marginal CGT rate, Ln(ASX 200), Ln(Real GDP)* and *Ln(GDP deflator)* are detrended variables.

The data used in the analysis are summarised in Table 8.

Table 8: Data used in the analysis

| Income year | Real discount capital gains ($billions) | Top marginal CGT rate | ASX 200 | Real GDP ($trillions) | GDP deflator |
|---|---|---|---|---|---|
| 1988–89 | 1.940 | 0.5025 | 1,521 | 0.735 | 50.0 |
| 1989–90 | 1.791 | 0.4925 | 1,501 | 0.761 | 53.1 |
| 1990–91 | 1.344 | 0.4825 | 1,506 | 0.758 | 54.7 |
| 1991–92 | 1.651 | 0.4825 | 1,645 | 0.761 | 55.6 |
| 1992–93 | 2.016 | 0.4825 | 1,738 | 0.792 | 56.1 |
| 1993–94 | 4.311 | 0.4840 | 1,989 | 0.824 | 56.6 |
| 1994–95 | 2.860 | 0.4840 | 2,017 | 0.856 | 57.9 |
| 1995–96 | 3.892 | 0.4850 | 2,242 | 0.890 | 59.4 |
| 1996–97 | 5.453 | 0.4870 | 2,726 | 0.925 | 60.2 |
| 1997–98 | 8.452 | 0.4850 | 2,668 | 0.966 | 60.9 |
| 1998–99 | 10.101 | 0.4850 | 2,969 | 1.014 | 61.1 |
| 1999–2000 | 17.211 | 0.2425 | 3,311 | 1.054 | 62.7 |
| 2000–01 | 15.921 | 0.2425 | 3,490 | 1.074 | 65.7 |
| 2001–02 | 18.193 | 0.2425 | 3,216 | 1.115 | 67.5 |
| 2002–03 | 19.278 | 0.2425 | 3,027 | 1.150 | 69.7 |
| 2003–04 | 28.194 | 0.2425 | 3,533 | 1.197 | 71.9 |
| 2004–05 | 32.544 | 0.2425 | 4,278 | 1.236 | 74.6 |
| 2005–06 | 40.862 | 0.2425 | 5,074 | 1.273 | 78.4 |
| 2006–07 | 60.969 | 0.2325 | 6,275 | 1.320 | 82.3 |
| 2007–08 | 53.397 | 0.2325 | 5,215 | 1.369 | 86.0 |
| 2008–09 | 22.905 | 0.2325 | 3,955 | 1.394 | 90.3 |
| 2009–10 | 23.716 | 0.2325 | 4,302 | 1.422 | 91.2 |
| 2010–11 | 24.151 | 0.2325 | 4,608 | 1.456 | 96.8 |
| 2011–12 | 18.760 | 0.2325 | 4,095 | 1.509 | 98.8 |
| 2012–13 | 20.827 | 0.2330 | 4,803 | 1.546 | 98.6 |
| 2013–14 | 28.926 | 0.2330 | 5,396 | 1.585 | 100.0 |
| 2014–15 | 33.349 | 0.2450 | 5,459 | 1.620 | 99.4 |

*Notes.* Discount capital gains have been converted from nominal to real dollars using the GDP deflator in this table.

Some of the notable trends in the data are now considered. First, in the years from 1989 to 1999, there was a significant increase in real GDP, a significant increase in real discount capital gains realised and only a minor decrease in the top marginal tax rate. Specifically, real GDP increased by more than 37% between 1989 and 1999. During this time, real capital gains increased by more than 500%. The top statutory rate of tax decreased from 50.25% to 48.5%. It is unlikely that a tax decrease of this magnitude could explain the more than fivefold increase in capital gains realisations. The Chapter 5 study considers the effect of tax rate changes on realisations in more detail.

Another notable trend is an increase in capital gains realisations between the years 2000–01 and 2006–07, at which point capital gains realisations were at their peak level for all years in the time series. Although the ASX 200 index did not increase in all the years between 2000–01 and 2006–07, it increased significantly between 2002–03 and 2006–07. More specifically, the ASX 200 index more than doubled during these years. Since 2006–07, the trend in realisations of capital gains has been one of decline. The decline was moderate between the years 2006–07 and 2007–08 and pronounced between 2007–08 and 2008–09. Capital gains realisations (in nominal terms) in 2008–09 were less than half the level they had been in the previous year and at their lowest level since 2003–04. In the second latest year of the time series, 2012–13, realisations were even lower than in 2008–09 and lower than in 2003–04. The CGT discount has been in operation for all the years referred to, and this suggests that tax rates may not be the only determinant of capital gains realisations. For example, it may be that the global financial crisis (GFC) in the later years of the twenty-first century had a negative effect on the propensity of taxpayers to realise capital gains (Minas et al., 2018).



A review of *Taxation Statistics* indicates there were a number of taxpayers who had a large amount of capital gains for which no tax was payable (Australian Taxation Office, 2016). For example, in 2013–14, there were approximately $641,000,000 of non-taxable net capital gains realised by personal taxpayers (Australian Taxation Office, 2016). *Taxation Statistics* contains aggregate time series data for all taxpayers in the population; the reason why these capital gains escape taxation in each individual case cannot be ascertained from the available data. Where the taxpayer has a taxable income above the tax-free threshold, a possible reason is that they had a large amount of deductions or current or prior year income losses.[23] Taxpayers' realisations of these non-taxable capital gains appear to be unrelated to the realisations response to the 50% CGT discount. Rather, these realisations may be an example of a timing effect pertaining to the effective CGT rate faced by the taxpayer—a rate of zero given the gains are non-taxable—rather than the prevailing statutory marginal tax rate on net capital gains. In the time series study that is the subject of Chapter 5, there are no data available on the taxable incomes of those taxpayers who realise non-taxable capital gains. It follows that it is not possible to observe the extent to which taxpayers realise capital gains in years where their taxable income is temporarily low.

The capital gains realisations variable used in a time series study should be a measure of capital gains net of aggregate capital losses. The realisation of capital losses in prior years may create an incentive to realise capital gains that is not completely dependent on the prevailing CGT rate. Consequently, the study in this chapter uses a capital gains realisations variable that is net of all capital losses applied, both prior year and current year losses.

23 Given that the ATO data are for 'net capital gains' it is assumed that current and prior year capital losses have already been applied in the calculation of the net capital gain.

According to Burman and Randolph (1994), when taxpayers make a decision on whether to sell specific assets in their portfolio, realising a capital gain is merely incidental, and it follows that taxpayers do not make the decision to realise capital gains directly. That is, realising a capital gain is necessarily a consequence of the primary decision to sell assets with an accrued capital gain. This point confirms the difficulty in determining how to model the capital gains realisations response. The issue is further confounded by the fact that although CGT is largely a discretionary tax, taxpayers regularly decide to sell assets with accrued capital gains and, in doing so, they voluntarily incur a CGT liability.

Prior to the study in this book, there have been no previous comprehensive empirical studies on the capital gains realisations response for Australian taxpayers. Consequently, there is no previous research from Australia to compare to the elasticity point estimates in this chapter. The estimates can be discussed with reference to similar studies completed in other tax jurisdictions.

**The dependent variable**

In the years 1988–89 to 1998–99, discount capital gains are net capital gains for individual taxpayers as reported in *Taxation Statistics* (Australian Taxation Office, 2016). In the years 1999–2000 to 2014–15, discount capital gains are the amount of net capital gains as reported in *Taxation Statistics* (Australian Taxation Office, 2016) adjusted by an appropriate gross-up factor.[24] The discount capital gains for all years have been converted from nominal to real amounts using the GDP deflator prepared by the Australian Bureau of Statistics.

**Independent variables**

In the years 1988–89 to 1998–99, the top marginal CGT rate is the highest marginal tax rate for individual taxpayers. In the years 1999–2000 to 2014–15, the top marginal CGT rate is half the marginal tax rate for individual taxpayers. The ASX 200 data are from the ABS publication *Australian Economic Indicators* (Australian Bureau of Statistics, 2012). The source of the real GDP data is the amounts reported by the ABS in *Australian National Accounts: National Income, Expenditure and Product* (Australian Bureau of Statistics, 2016a). This publication reports gross domestic product using 'chain volume measures'. Broadly, under this approach, index numbers are applied to the nominal GDP amounts in each year so that the effects of inflation are removed from the time series. The data on the GDP deflator are from a data set published by the Australian Bureau of Statistics.

The main equation specification is in semi-log form, for which all variables, except for the tax rate variable, are in log form. Guiding the decision to use a semi-log form equation was the fact that previous time series studies (Auerbach, 1988; Auerbach, 1989; Auten & Clotfelter, 1982; Burman et al., 1994) used this same functional form to good effect. According to Zodrow (1992), a log-log specification is preferable as it avoids the problem of a tax rate coefficient that is biased towards zero. As outlined in Chapter 2, the semi-logarithmic specification has a number of advantages in comparison to the alternatives (Burman & Randolph, 1994).

24 The gross-up factor and adjustment required is detailed in this chapter.

As explained earlier in this chapter, the rationale for using discount capital gains is that the realisations variable should be a measure of the capital gains that taxpayers have decided to realise. Because of the change to the CGT legislation in 1999, this is not the same amount as net capital gains that are included in assessable income.[25] In the years prior to 1999–2000, this variable is net capital gains as reported by Australian Taxation Office (2016). In the years from 1999–2000 to 2014–15, this variable is the amount of net capital gains reported by Australian Taxation Office (2016), multiplied by the appropriate gross-up factor.

The choice of variables is guided by theory and existing literature on the factors that may influence capital gains realisations, although the equations used in the Chapter 5 study do not replicate any one previous study. Examples of previous studies that have included a stock market index as an explanatory variable are Minarik (1984) and Auerbach (1989). An independent variable for gross domestic product has been a feature of many previous capital gains realisations response studies.

3

The number of years (observations) in the time series is consistent with the Gravelle (2010) definition of the long-run response. OLS regressions have been used to produce the elasticity point estimates in this chapter.

The capital gains realisations response study in this chapter uses aggregate data on net capital gains for personal taxpayers sourced from *Taxation Statistics* (Australian Taxation Office, 2016); the data for the other variables in the specification are predominantly from the Australian Bureau of Statistics (ABS). Because the study uses aggregate time series data, it necessitates using a single tax rate for the entire taxpayer population. The tax rate chosen for the study is a measure of the top marginal tax rate on capital gains.

The tax rate used in the study in this chapter is half of the top statutory marginal tax rate. In each case, the Medicare levy has been added to the top marginal tax rate (before reducing the total of statutory tax rate and Medicare levy by 50%), since this liability will occur for most personal taxpayers who face the top marginal tax rate.[26]

The use of the top marginal tax rate is, arguably, an assumption that the taxpayer's taxable income is in the top marginal tax bracket. Previous capital gains realisations response studies have used the top marginal tax rate (Bogart & Gentry, 1995). A possible implication is that the elasticity point estimate will be at the upper bound of possible responses. This is because it is likely that taxpayers facing a higher marginal tax rate will be more responsive to CGT rate changes.

The remainder of this section sets out some considerations in determining the non-tax explanatory variables to include in an estimating equation.

In the design of the regression equation in this chapter, careful consideration has been given to which non-tax variables to include in the specification. The choice of variables is limited because of the fact that the time series study uses aggregate data rather than micro data and the regression equation is a reduced form representation of capital

25 The net capital gains amounts that are reported in *Taxation Statistics*.

26 There are some exemptions from the Medicare levy for a small proportion of taxpayers, but there is no exemption from the Medicare levy on the basis of income for taxpayers who face the top marginal tax rate.

gains realisations decisions. As noted in Chapter 2, a complex life cycle model would be required to more accurately reflect the fact that some capital gains realisation decisions are motivated by consumption.

Based on the previous research on capital gains realisations response, reviewed in Chapter 2, there are several non-tax variables to consider for inclusion in the regression equation. These include measures of income from capital (other than capital gains), gross domestic product, the performance of the stock market and a GDP deflator.

Given that the literature and a number of capital gains realisations response studies have identified a correlation between growth in GDP and stock market performance and capital gains realisations, it is important to include these types of non-tax variables in the estimating equation. Notably, although Eichner and Sinai (2000) found that higher levels of GDP result in more capital gains realisations, they found that this effect was not statistically significant. The importance of these variables provides an insight into the weakness of cross-sectional studies, since a study that is only concerned with a single tax year cannot adequately measure the impact of macroeconomic variables. This is especially the case given that some of these non-tax variables may have a lagged effect.

According to Shobe (1991), there are several factors that are determinative to an individual's capital gains realisations response that are not observable. One example is risk aversion, and it is the view of Shobe that in interpreting variables that are used in regressions, there is a need to make some assumptions about risk aversion. For example, one theory on how risk aversion may apply to the independent variables is that a taxpayer in receipt of a high amount of dividend income may be one who is risk averse (Shobe, 1991). The assumption in this case is that more risk-averse taxpayers will prefer income receipts rather than receipts in the form of riskier capital gains (Shobe, 1991). In a time series study that uses aggregate taxpayer data, the amount of dividends received at the individual taxpayer level is unobservable.

**Capital gains realisations**

The theory that guides the choice of variables used in this study is from the U.S. literature on capital gains realisations. Nevertheless, the taxation of capital gains in Australia is different to the CGT in the United States. One of the main differences is that whereas the United States taxes capital gains under a separate rate schedule, Australia does not. Instead, Australian taxpayers who are eligible for the 50% CGT discount only include half of their capital gains, net of capital losses, in assessable income. It follows that only half of the capital gains that these taxpayers have decided to realise are taxed at the statutory tax rates that apply to personal taxpayers.

This difference in the tax treatment of capital gains between the two tax jurisdictions requires an adjustment to the ATO-reported amount of net capital gains in the years 1999–2000 to 2014–15 (the CGT discount years). The approach to the required adjustment was to first use the ATO data to calculate the percentage of capital gains realised in the CGT discount years that were not discount capital gains. Once this percentage was known, an appropriate factor by which to gross-up capital gains in each of the CGT discount years could be determined. In the event that 100% of capital gains realised were discount capital gains, the appropriate gross-up factor would be 2.00. If 95% of the capital gains realised in a discount year were discount capital gains, the appropriate gross-up factor would be 1.90 (i.e. 2 multiplied by 0.95). Using this approach to the gross-up of net capital gains results in an amount that approximates discount capital gains net of losses in each year. It effectively excludes the small proportion of non-discount capital gains in each of the discount years.

The benefit of this approach is twofold. First, the only adjustment required to the statutory tax rate (including the Medicare levy) is to multiply it by a factor of 0.5. Second, the realisations of capital gains that are subject to tax at full marginal rates are excluded from the years in which the CGT discount was available. This is justified on the basis that the realisation of these gains does not represent the realisations response to the lower tax rate, given that this rate only applies to discount capital gains.



The percentage of non-discount capital gains, gross-up factors, net capital gains (as reported by the ATO) and real discount capital gains for the years 1999–2000 to 2014–15 are set out in Table 9.

**Table 9: Gross-up factors and real discount capital gains (1999–2000 to 2014–15)**

| Year | Percentage of capital gains that are not discount capital gains | Gross-up factor | Net capital gains ($billions) | Real discount capital gains ($billions) |
|---|---|---|---|---|
| 1999–2000 | 0.147 | 1.706 | 6.3253 | 17.2105 |
| 2000–01 | 0.147 | 1.706 | 6.1313 | 15.9208 |
| 2001–02 | 0.102 | 1.796 | 6.8375 | 18.1928 |
| 2002–03 | 0.073 | 1.854 | 7.2479 | 19.2778 |
| 2003–04 | 0.077 | 1.846 | 10.9815 | 28.1944 |
| 2004–05 | 0.081 | 1.838 | 13.2089 | 32.5444 |
| 2005–06 | 0.074 | 1.852 | 17.2978 | 40.8617 |
| 2006–07 | 0.073 | 1.854 | 27.0645 | 60.9691 |
| 2007–08 | 0.057 | 1.886 | 24.3485 | 53.3968 |
| 2008–09 | 0.067 | 1.866 | 11.0845 | 22.9055 |
| 2009–10 | 0.085 | 1.830 | 11.8190 | 23.7159 |
| 2010–11 | 0.068 | 1.866 | 12.5418 | 24.1508 |
| 2011–12 | 0.058 | 1.884 | 9.8378 | 18.7596 |
| 2012–13 | 0.047 | 1.906 | 10.7740 | 20.8267 |
| 2013–14 | 0.044 | 1.912 | 15.1287 | 28.9260 |
| 2014–15 | 0.050 | 1.900 | 17.4469 | 33.3493 |

*Notes.* Discount capital gains have been converted from nominal to real dollars using the GDP deflator in Table 8.

## CGT rate

One of the issues to be considered in the design of a time series study is the choice of an appropriate tax rate. A serious econometric problem identified by Gravelle (2010) is the fact that while the effective tax rate could be used as an exogenous variable, it is an endogenous variable given that it is influenced by the amount of capital gains realisations.

Using maximum statutory tax rates, predicted gains or instrumental variables are some ways of overcoming this problem (Gravelle, 2010). According to Gravelle (2010), the endogeneity of the tax rate variable is less important in a time series study.

Given that CGT in Australia is not a separate tax, it is assumed in the quantitative study that a CGT rate that is half of the top marginal rate applies for the post-CGT discount years. Consistent with this, a grossed-up amount of net capital gains reported by the Australian Taxation Office (2016) is used as a measure of capital gains realisations. The study is concerned with an approximation of the real marginal tax rate on capital gains rather than the statutory rate of CGT. Net capital gains reported in *Taxation Statistics* for the post-CGT discount years do not reflect the amount of capital gains that the taxpayer has decided to realise, whereas the net capital gains in the pre-CGT discount years do represent this amount. The adjustment to the post-CGT discount years' net capital gains allows for a meaningful comparison of the pre- and post-CGT discount year realisations (Minas et al., 2018).

Although some previous studies have used a constructed last-dollar marginal tax rate, according to Zodrow (1992) there are significant simultaneity problems with this approach. Although using the top marginal tax rate counteracts the simultaneity problem, it can potentially underestimate the responsiveness of realisations to CGT rate changes (Zodrow, 1992). The approach taken in the quantitative study is to use the top marginal tax rate on capital gains in the data set and to estimate elasticity at the midpoint between the current rate of CGT and the rate if CGT were restored to full marginal tax rates for individuals.

**Stock market index**

The independent variable ASX 200 has been included in the equations as a measure of the performance of the Australian stock market (Australian Securities Exchange). In theory, improvement in the ASX 200 indicator should correlate with increased capital gains realisations. Therefore, the coefficient for this variable is expected to have a positive sign.

The literature review in Chapter 2 referred to the finding of Seltzer (1951) that the fluctuation in the realisation of capital gains and losses was more closely aligned with changes in share prices rather than tax rates. This finding appears to be supported in some of the recent literature. For example, Clark (2014, p. 38) explained that the largest movements in capital gains realisations have been related to changes in the stock market—in particular, there was a decline in realisations in the early 2000s, seemingly related to the 'dot-com crash' and a decline related to the GFC following the peak of the ASX 200 index in October 2007. Jacob (2011) made a similar finding—that the aggregate capital gains of taxpayers in Sweden were strongly correlated with stock market returns, whereas such a correlation was not present between aggregate capital gains and the house price index.

In summary, the findings of Seltzer (1951), Clark (2014) and Jacob (2011) indicate that there is a compelling case for including a variable for a stock market index in the estimating equations. Furthermore, several U.S. capital gains realisations response studies have included a stock market index variable. For these reasons, such a variable has been included.

### GDP

The GDP variable has been included in the equations as a measure of the overall level of economic activity. Theory suggests that CGT realisations will increase as GDP increases. It is expected, therefore, that the coefficient for this variable will have a positive sign. The U.S. CBO (1988) referred to the effects that a GDP variable captures. First, GDP is a comprehensive measure of total spending, which captures the incentive for taxpayers to sell assets for consumption. Second, GDP, as a measure of aggregate economic activity, can capture some of the influences on total wealth that are missing in the stock market variable (U.S. CBO, 1988). The GDP variable, together with a variable for the value of the stock market, better explains capital gains realisations than a measure of household wealth other than corporate shares (U.S. CBO, 1988).

The justification for the inclusion of a real GDP variable is that it provides a measure of economic conditions over the years of the time series. Changes in these economic conditions will influence taxpayers' decisions to realise capital gains. The literature reviewed in Chapter 2 noted the use of such a variable in previous studies. Although an unemployment rate variable is an alternative measure of economic conditions, it is not appropriate to include a variable for GDP and the unemployment rate in the same equation. Hence, only the GDP variable has been included.

### GDP deflator

The GDP deflator is included in the equations as a measure of the price level. Several capital gains realisations response studies have included a GDP deflator in the estimating equations (Auerbach, 1989; Eichner & Sinai, 2000; Gillingham & Greenlees, 1992). The coefficient on the GDP deflator variable is expected to have a minus sign.[27]

## Other considerations for the estimating equation variables

Maddala (2001) identified that the problem of omitted variables has implications for the accuracy of the estimates. Specifically, where important explanatory variables are omitted, the result is likely to be an estimate of the coefficient of the tax rate variable that is overstated. One explanation in the literature of a more specific omitted variable problem is that where the omitted variable is positively correlated with an included variable, the result is an upward bias in the estimated coefficient of the included variable, since the effect the omitted variable would have caused, had it been included, is attributed to the included variable (Maddala, 2001). Although additional control variables can be used as a means of addressing the problem of omitted variable bias, there is a risk that such an approach might, in fact, worsen the bias in the coefficient of interest (Clarke, 2005).

In designing the capital gains realisations response study in Chapter 5, the possibility that some of the variables are non-stationary has been considered. Where an estimating equation includes non-stationary variables, one approach to addressing this problem is to take first differences of the data for the variable. However, taking first differences of data to make a variable stationary has two potential problems. First, it necessarily changes the

27 As per the coefficient of 'log of GDP deflator' having a negative sign in Gillingham and Greenlees (1992). Nevertheless, in some other studies, the coefficient on the GDP deflator variable has a positive sign.

meaning of the variable, which may make the interpretation of the results more difficult. Second, first-differenced data result in lost information on how the variable changes over time.

## 3.4 CONCLUSIONS ON METHODOLOGY AND RESEARCH DESIGN

This chapter justified the use of a mixed methods approach for the research in this book. One of the advantages of conducting the research in two distinct phases is that the results of the qualitative research are informative to the quantitative research. The qualitative study examines broader issues in the taxation of capital gains, whereas the focus of the quantitative study is on the more specific issue of the realisations response of capital gains for personal taxpayers in Australia. The conclusions in Chapter 6 include recommendations for reforming the current system of taxing capital gains in Australia. Each component of the mixed methods approach has informed and contributed to these recommendations.

The following chapter reports the results of the qualitative research component; specifically, it explores and analyses responses from interviews with CGT experts in three jurisdictions in order to inform the approach of the ensuing quantitative study. Chapter 5 then explores a more specific issue in the taxation of capital gains—the capital gains realisations response for personal taxpayers, together with the consequent revenue effect.

# CHAPTER 4

# Qualitative Results—the Voice of the Experts

## 4.1 INTRODUCTION

This chapter presents the results of a qualitative interview study designed to consider rate preferences in three CGT regimes. The interviews took place in 2011 with an interview population of CGT experts based in Australia, Canada and the United States. Chapter 3 outlined the research framework for the qualitative interview study. The primary focus of this chapter is the research findings of the study.

The rationale for the interview study was to compare the views of the experts with the existing literature and to gain additional insights that may have not been available from existing sources. A brief comparison of CGT preferences in Australia, Canada and the United States was set out in Section 3.3 of Chapter 3. Section 4.2 of this chapter presents the research findings and Section 4.3 provides key conclusions.

The interview responses analysed in this chapter indicate that some of the claimed benefits of CGT preferences may be overstated. Several respondents were unconvinced as to some of the rationales advanced by proponents of preferential rate CGT. The results of the interview study in this chapter confirm the need for the capital gains realisations response study in Chapter 5. Specifically, a study that empirically tests the purported revenue-raising benefits of the 50% CGT discount advanced by Australian policy makers is required. This is due to the lack of support in the literature for some of the other possible benefits of CGT preferences.

## 4.2 RESEARCH FINDINGS

As outlined in Chapter 3, the interviews explored two themes: (1) the role of CGT preferences and (2) whether and how to reform the CGT system as it applies to personal taxpayers. This section explores these themes by way of the interview responses. A full coded list of interviewees, including their jurisdictional and demographic characteristics, was contained in Table 5 and Table 6 in Chapter 3. This chapter initially explores the first interview theme—CGT preferences—and subsequently the second interview theme—reforming CGT. The material derived from the interviewee responses feeds into the analysis of the results of the second, quantitative phase of the research contained in Chapter 5.

## Theme One: CGT preferences

Theme One was explored through six interview questions.[1] Question One was designed to elicit what the interviewees considered to be the main benefits and disadvantages of CGT preferences. Question Two sought comments on the appropriateness of preferential CGT rates. The interview data may provide a useful comparison between the views of the experts selected for the study and the literature on CGT preferences, and may lead to further insights into the taxation of capital gains. Such insights are important in light of what Burman (1999, p. 2) described as the 'shibboleths about capital gains,' which appear to have their basis in anecdotal evidence rather than in facts and empirical evidence.

Questions Three, Four and Five explored some of the issues related to the policy justifications for CGT preferences. More particularly, Question Three asked whether CGT rate preferences remain appropriate in light of the benefits of deferral. Question Four sought views on whether the policy justifications for capital gains preferences are due mostly to economic efficiency considerations, political considerations or a combination of the two.

Question Five was concerned with how successful CGT rate preferences have been in achieving their policy objectives.

Question Six, which is addressed in a later section in this chapter dealing with the second theme (reforming CGT), was an open-ended question that sought the respondents' views on how they would reform the CGT system in their country.

### Responses to Questions One, Two and Three

The remainder of this section presents selected responses from the interview population to these six questions. Where appropriate, quotations from the interviews are included to minimise the risk of misinterpretation of the responses. Also, where possible, there is a reference to the literature on the same topic and a comparison made between the responses to questions and the relevant literature.

#### Responses to Question One[2]

The experts from the three countries could identify more disadvantages related to CGT preferences than benefits. In answering Question One, respondents referred to issues such as vertical equity, economic efficiency, the distortions that may be caused by preferential CGT rates, and the incentive to characterise income as capital gains. In some instances, issues such as the benefits of deferral and the 'bunching' of capital gains were also referred to.

Respondent M (Australia) stated:

> The main disadvantages are ... there are clear equity implications and ... since capital gains form an increasing percentage of income as incomes rise ... the effect of it is quite

1 As detailed in Section 3.3 of Chapter 3.

2 Q1. What do you consider to be the main benefits and disadvantages of CGT preferences?

> regressive. The benefit accrues more and more ... as your income rises, but perhaps a more important disadvantage is the economic distortions it causes by altering the efficient allocation of capital ... [A]ncillary to that is to take advantage of the distortions requires a lot of reorganisation of transactions, which means there's a lot of deadweight losses ...

M's response is consistent with a view in the literature about the importance of horizontal and vertical equity in a tax system. Not taxing capital gains at full rates can lead to mismeasurements of income and, in turn, horizontal inequity (Krever & Brooks, 1990). In Australia, as well as in other jurisdictions, capital gains are more highly concentrated at higher income levels, which allows for a lower effective tax rate among higher-income taxpayers with more capital gains (Minas & Lim, 2013).

Respondent N (Australia) also disagreed with the need for preferential CGT rates:

> [I]t is inappropriate to have a CGT discount or an exclusion or a lower rate of capital gains than you have for other forms of income because ... investors can choose when to realise their assets ... so you do potentially get some game-playing going on ...



The views of Respondents M and N on the distortions caused by reorganising transactions to take advantage of the lower tax rates on capital gains are consistent with the literature discussed in Chapter 2.

Respondent B (United States) referred to only one benefit of preferential CGT rates:

> About the only possible benefit ... of preferential rates on capital gains is ... to deal with the fact that the corporate income tax and the individual income tax in the U.S. are not integrated particularly well ... [W]e have a situation where some income is taxed once, some income is taxed twice (at both the corporate and the individual level) and then there is some income that's not taxed at all.

Respondent B also stated that they did not think any of the rationales for a preferential rate CGT were justified. Specifically, Respondent B was not of the view that a reduced CGT rate would increase savings. They referred to the fact that although U.S. CGT rates had decreased since 1986, the savings rate had actually decreased during this time. Respondent B also rejected arguments about CGT rate cuts spurring short-term and long-term economic growth.

In answering Question One, Respondent C (United States) referred to two possible benefits of preferential CGT rates:

> I think that the two [benefits] I can see as having some justification are, one, the problem ... with people being locked in to assets and so ... the relief of lock-in, particularly if individual income tax rates are very high, is some justification for having the [capital] gains rate lower. Essentially, you've got unrealised gains that are going untaxed and ordinary income that's going taxed, and so probably the least distorting thing to do with the realised gains is to tax it somewhere in between ... To the extent that some gains come from corporate profits and some of those corporate profits have previously been taxed at the enterprise level ... that would produce a second level of tax which might lead to over-taxation of corporate enterprises relative to other businesses.

The response of Respondent C is consistent with the literature on the lock-in effect. The lock-in effect describes taxpayers choosing to hold their capital assets that have appreciated in value, so that the CGT on the accrued capital gain can be deferred or altogether avoided (Auerbach, 1991). Lindsey (1987b) described lock-in as an impediment to selling one asset and replacing it with another that has a higher pre-tax return. The existence of a strong lock-in effect implies that taxpayers will be responsive to a lowering of the CGT rate, and will choose to realise accrued capital gains once they consider the CGT rate to be acceptably low (Minas & Lim, 2013).

On Question One, Respondent F (Canada) stated:

> [P]referential [CGT is] ... intended to deal with the integration of taxation ... at a corporate level together with the taxation of the shareholders ... [I]t doesn't seem appropriate that the full amount of the gain should be taxed when the shareholder disposes of the shares, because the same income has effectively been taxed twice ... I think the primary disadvantage ... is there's an incentive for taxpayers to ... characterise one type of income as a capital gain rather than as the income it should be characterised [as].

Respondent S (Australia) was also clear about their opposition to preferential CGT rates:

> I think that deferral is a big advantage and that preferential treatments in fact exacerbate lock-in factors ... I think the deferral aspects on the whole outweigh the case for any sort of concessional treatment. Tax on a realisation basis is in itself a concessional treatment.

The statement on the benefits of deferral by Respondent S is consistent with the view of Burman (1999), who argued that the benefit of deferral compounds over time and it is a justification for taxing capital gains at the same rate as ordinary income.

Respondent N (Australia) also referred to the bunching of capital gains as one of the major problems with a realisation-based CGT regime. According to Krever and Brooks (1990), bunching is an overstated problem as most capital gains are derived by high-income taxpayers whose income is at the top marginal rate of tax regardless of whether they realise capital gains in a particular year. Furthermore, in the case of capital gains realised several years after the asset was acquired, the benefits of deferral can be seen as counteracting the bunching problem. In some cases, the deferral benefits may completely offset the bunching effect (Cunningham & Schenk, 1993).

According to Respondent I (Canada), the disadvantages outweighed the benefits of preferential rate CGT:

> I'm not persuaded there are lots of benefits but [I] see lots of disadvantages. I'm not convinced ... that [it] encourages entrepreneurialism ... There are other things that drive ... entrepreneurial motivations that are much more significant than the prospect of low rate on a gain at the end of it all, when they sell out ... The disadvantages ... there are vertical equity disadvantages ... and the complexity and the games that are played around the borderline ... As soon as you've got those discrepancies between one kind of income or another, one thing or another, people will fight over those battles and that creates a need for anti-avoidance rules ... so those are the huge disadvantages.

Respondent I also referred to the previous cumulative lifetime exemption for small businesses for certain types of capital gains that used to operate in Canada. One of the remaining lifetime exemptions that still operate in Canada is the exemption for shares in a Canadian-controlled private corporation. Respondent I stated that the justification for this exemption appears to be to encourage the growth of Canadian small businesses. A criticism the respondent provided for this justification was that it is not logical in policy terms, given that the exemption applies at the time of the shares being sold. It was the respondent's view that this policy creates an incentive to sell small businesses rather than grow them (Minas & Lim, 2013).

Respondent J (Canada) was clearly opposed to preferential rate CGT:

> All the evidence is clear in Canada and other countries that capital gains are realised disproportionately by higher-wealth, higher-income individuals. Any sort of preference is [from a distributional perspective] somewhat odd ... [There are] administrative compliance costs associated with re-characterisation of capital income as capital gain, which is another negative. And the benefits ... [the] behavioural response ... savings decision, lock-in effect, inflation adjustment ... risk-taking, those are supposed benefits.

Respondent K (Canada) expressed similar views to Respondent J:

> The main disadvantages are that it's unfair and that it creates inefficiencies and it creates administrative problems and it makes the tax system a less effective instrument for redistributing income ... The alleged benefits are that it reduces lock-in, reduces the bunching effect and compensates for inflation and encourages risk-taking.

4

Respondent K (Canada) went on to say that, in giving capital gains preferences, governments have argued that these preferences are necessary for encouraging risk-taking and entrepreneurship, but in the interviewee's personal view these arguments did not have any merits:

> No, indeed the fact that you get ... to defer it is an additional tax benefit. I mean it's an argument for taxing them at full rates. You've already given them preferential treatment by allowing people to defer the gain and you know, all that does is exacerbates ... the lock-in effect.

A theme that emerged from the Canadian interviews was that many interviewees—including Respondents F, I and J—referred to problems with the borderline between income and capital, and the incentives created for taxpayers to convert ordinary income into capital gains where preferential rates were provided for the latter. According to Avi-Yonah et al. (2011), taxpayers can achieve an arbitrary conversion of income into capital through complex financial instruments designed to provide a cash flow similar to dividends or interest while classifying the receipts as something other than dividends or interest.

Some of the Canadian respondents also considered inequity and unfairness to be disadvantages of CGT preferences. One of the Canadian respondents described a benefit of preferential CGT as moving the tax base towards a consumption-type base. As Cunningham and Schenk (1993) noted, if a consumption tax applied, income from capital would only be subject to tax when it was consumed, and it therefore follows that excluding a proportion of capital gains moves a tax system closer to a consumption tax base.

The fact that Respondents J (Canada) and K (Canada) respectively referred to inflation adjustment as an 'alleged' and 'supposed' benefit of a CGT preference implies that they were unconvinced as to the need for an inflation adjustment. Interestingly, the Carter Commission argued that an inflation adjustment was not required, as increases in stock market indexes were substantially higher than increases in inflation (Canada & Carter, 1966).

Respondent P (Australia) referred specifically to the problem of few capital gains made by non-residents being subject to Australian tax. The respondent referred to this as an inequitable approach to CGT, in that foreign residents receive a 'capital gain holiday' in Australia whereas resident taxpayers are subject to CGT on the same type of gains. Respondent P did not comment on the likelihood or otherwise of such taxpayers being subject to tax on these capital gains in their jurisdictions of residence.

As was the case for a number of Canadian respondents (including Respondents J and L), several of the Australian respondents (including Respondents N and Y) referred to the incentives to re-characterise income into capital as a specific disadvantage of preferential CGT (Minas & Lim, 2013). In response to an interview question not utilised in this chapter (Question 12 in the Appendix), some respondents provided examples of ways in which taxpayers had achieved such re-characterisation.

In response to Question One, Respondent A (United States) stated:

> I think the big benefit is probably in ... not interfering with the realisations of capital gains, so the realisations response. The disadvantages ... once you have a differential between capital gains and other assets, you start all this game-playing ... to turn one kind into another to transform income into a capital gains form. I think it leads to distortions in the kinds of assets you hold, and it leads to a lot of gaming of the system ...

Respondent A was of the view that there were better forms of saving and investment incentives than a CGT rate preference. This respondent also referred to previous CGT rate reductions in the United States being justified by policy makers on the basis of revenue gains. However, the respondent believed that the literature that estimates a large revenue gain as a result of a CGT rate cut is not persuasive due to flaws in the econometric techniques. Respondent A referred to the potential for politicians to confuse increased CGT revenue from economic growth with that from taxpayers' response to CGT rate reductions. This comment from Respondent A is of relevance to the Chapter 5 study given that there was a period of economic growth in the years following the enactment of the CGT discount. Typically, a realisations response study includes an independent variable for GDP as a control for economic growth.

In summary, the responses in all three countries as to the benefits and disadvantages of CGT rate preferences indicate that not all respondents were convinced as to the claimed benefits of such preferences. As Respondent A noted, although a lower tax rate on capital gains may enhance efficiency, any such benefit is reduced by the inefficiency associated with the distortions induced by a lower rate on capital gains relative to other forms of income. Although Question One sought comment on the advantages and disadvantages of CGT rate preferences, several of the respondents focused their response on disadvantages. In particular, respondents highlighted the negative effects on horizontal and vertical equity and the fact that tax policy that causes such effects is counter to the principles of good tax system design. Respondent S referred to the benefits of deferral outweighing the need for a CGT preference. Notably this point received little attention in the debate that preceded the enactment of the CGT discount.

### Responses to Question Two[3]

Question Two was designed to identify the rationalisations to justify the introduction of the CGT rate preferences in the three jurisdictions where the interviews took place, given there is a CGT rate preference currently in operation in each. The question sought the views on the rationale for changes to the taxation of capital gains. In the case of Australia, the most notable change was the introduction of the 50% CGT discount for individuals. In the other two jurisdictions, there have been changes to the CGT rate and/or the inclusion rate for capital gains. Of particular interest was that several respondents summarised their understanding of the policy justifications for a CGT preference and proceeded to outline their objections.

Respondent V (Australia) stated that, although they did not know the actual policy justification for the CGT discount, it achieved simplicity despite lacking fairness.

It is not surprising that Respondent V could not refer to the policy justification for the CGT discount, despite their expertise on CGT. It appears there was a lack of coherent policy justification for the CGT discount at the time of its introduction. This is in stark contrast with the discussion of CGT in the Asprey Report, which preceded the enactment of the CGT in Australia in 1985. The Asprey Report was clear about the case for a CGT resting upon equity and the misallocation of resources that is likely to occur in the absence of a CGT (Commonwealth Taxation Review Committee & Asprey, 1975).

It was also the view of Respondent Z (Australia) that the policy justification for the CGT discount was simplicity. Nevertheless, they referred to the 'ludicrous situation' whereby a taxpayer who had 'held an asset for one year and two days gets a 50% discount,' while a taxpayer who had held an asset for 20 years would receive the same CGT discount.

Consistent with the response of Respondent Z, Lochan (2002) commented on the arbitrary and inequitable nature of the CGT inclusion preference in Canada. According to Lochan, where there is no established process for the policy review and adjustment of the inclusion rate, there is a danger it will become entrenched at an inappropriate level and fail to meet its policy objectives.

Although Respondents V and Z identified a CGT rate preference as being simpler than calculating the indexation of cost base, there are complexities that arise from a tax rate differential between capital gains and other types of assessable income. One prominent example is the need for legal line-drawing, given that CGT preferences typically apply to certain types of gains (Bradford, 1986). This type of differentiation applies in the case of the CGT discount. Cunningham and Schenk (1993) identified that rate differences between ordinary income and capital gains increase the likelihood of disputes between taxpayers and the revenue authority, cause everyday transactions to become more complex and costlier, and lead to inefficiency and uncertainty.

According to Respondent S (Australia), at the time the CGT discount was introduced, there was concern about trying to promote investment in Australian equities, and this was 'the principal argument'. Respondent S referred to 'concern about the treatment of

3 Q2. On what basis have previous changes to the taxation of individual capital gains in (Australia/Canada/the United States) been justified by policy makers? In your view, what are the merits or otherwise of these justifications?

U.S. pension fund investors in particular' and that 'indexation was probably regarded as complex and not well understood by foreign investors'.

It is unclear whether Respondent S agrees with the concerns they referred to. It would appear, however, that such concerns were misguided. The current treatment of CGT for foreign residents is such that only a limited range of CGT assets are subject to taxation in Australia. Furthermore, the merit in promoting investment in Australian equities to non-resident personal taxpayers through a preference in the tax system is questionable.

Respondent B (United States) stated that although there had been 'a lot of rationales,' they did not believe the arguments. The respondent identified three arguments used to justify CGT preferences. The first is that the preference increases saving and investment. Second, in a recession, a preference is a way to stimulate the economy in the short run. Third, if the economy is on an upswing, the justification is that the preference 'boosts long-term economic growth'.

Respondent C (United States) stated that while 'proponents say it's economic growth ... they never advance any particular line of evidence that connects growth rates to the levels of capital gains tax.' Respondent C explained that 'there was a growth in financing through venture capital firms following the CGT rate cut in 1978' and that 'a lot of the financing of these venture capital firms was from ... corporations that were not subject to individual capital gains rates ...' Respondent C added that entrepreneurs making large pre-tax returns did not need help by way of a lower CGT rate.

Respondent E (Canada) explained that the government at the time of the Carter Commission originally proposed 'full taxation of capital gains except for tradeable financial assets and ... public shares and bonds and so on'. Respondent E stated that, according to the proposal, such tradeable financial assets would be subject to a modified accrual and taxed every five years at half rates. Respondent E noted that 'these proposals went over like lead balloons' and that when the Bill was passed they went with 'the half-taxation of capital gains'. Respondent E added, 'I don't remember whether there was an intelligent rationale at the time or whether it was just [because] there was a lot of backlash because you're going from a system with no capital gains tax.'

Respondent I (Canada) was of the view that changes in the inclusion rate for capital gains in Canada had been 'to a large extent [because] we've tended to track what the U.S. does'. Respondent I provided the example that when Canada introduced its CGT in 1972, the 50% inclusion rate was the same as in the United States, and that subsequently the inclusion rate in Canada increased from 50% to 75% (in 1988–89), soon after the United States taxed capital gains at ordinary income rates (in 1987).

Respondent I presented a unique perspective by suggesting that CGT rate changes in the United States influenced the changes in the CGT inclusion rate in Canada. None of the other Canadian respondents referred to the same phenomenon.

It was the view of Respondent J (Canada) that the primary justification for CGT preferences had been 'as a stimulus to risk-taking'. They added that 'to a lesser extent' the justification had been 'as a proxy for inflation adjustment' and 'savings, but as a secondary matter'.

Respondent K (Canada) explained that governments have argued that a CGT preference is 'necessary to encourage risk-taking and entrepreneurship'. The respondent added that 'I don't think those arguments have any merits.' This appears consistent with the view in the literature that although CGT preferences have attained 'an air of economic determinacy and logical inevitability, there is hardly anything natural, neutral, or necessary about [them]' (Mehrota & Ott, 2016, pp. 2,535–36).

In response to Question Two, Respondent H (Canada) referred to the incentives to re-characterise income as capital.

> [T]here's a view that the tax rate on capital gains needs to be almost the same as the tax rate on dividends. The rationale is that there is ... a set of corporate reorganisations you can do to convert dividends into capital gains or vice versa within a private, closely held corporation ... and the government's view has been that they couldn't do much about it. The argument was that, if you found that capital gains were getting too lightly taxed relative to dividends, people would convert what would otherwise be dividends in a private corporation setting into capital gains or ... if dividends were more lightly taxed they would try and create a situation where it would be for tax purposes a dividend.



Respondent D (United States) referred to specific examples of justifications for particular tax policy changes. First, they explained that the policy reason for the rate cut in 1978 was to increase revenue, as in the 1970s 'capital gains realisations were drying up'. Second, they referred to the 1986 rate cut by the Reagan Administration as 'automatic, there was no thinking about it; it was part of his across-the-board rate cut.' Third, they stated that the 1986 CGT rate increase was justified by the principle of 'taxing all income the same' and gaining extra revenue to fund a reduction in the tax rate on ordinary income.

Respondent R (United States) stated that the CGT preferences had been justified based on 'emotion' and the decision to introduce rate preferences was 'not analytical'. Respondent R added they were in favour of 'the broadest possible tax and the lowest possible rate'. Tran-Nam, Addison, Andrew, Drum and Evans (2006) identified that the introduction of CGT in Australia was, in itself, a form of base broadening. Freebairn (2005) presented a case for base broadening to fund lower rates and, in doing so, he referred to some of the large tax expenditures in the current Australian tax system, including the 50% CGT discount.

In summary, the responses to Question Two highlighted doubts as to the merits of some of the policy justifications for preferential CGT. There were several respondents (C, K and R) who, in answering the question, stated they did not agree with the justification for preferential CGT that they had identified. The responses to Question Two indicate that perhaps the views of CGT experts on the appropriateness or otherwise of CGT preferences are not in accord with those of policy makers in the three countries.

### Responses to Question Three[4]

Table 10 sets out a summary of responses to Question Three by country. It indicates that a significant majority of interviewees—overall and in each of the three countries—are of the

4 Q3. Given the benefits of deferral that apply to capital gains and the ability of the taxpayer to effectively choose when and if they will realise a capital gain, are preferential rates for capital gains considered appropriate?

view that preferences for capital gains are not appropriate in light of the benefits of deferral and the discretion that taxpayers have in choosing when to realise their capital gains.

**Table 10: Interview responses to Question Three by country**

| Q3. Given the benefits of deferral that apply to capital gains and the ability of the taxpayer to effectively choose when and if they will realise a capital gain, are preferential rates for capital gains considered appropriate? | | | | |
|---|---|---|---|---|
| | Yes | No | Inconclusive | Total |
| Australia | 1 | 7 | 3 | **11** |
| Canada | 2 | 4 | 2 | **8** |
| United States | 1 | 3 | 1 | **5** |
| **Total** | **4** | **14** | **6** | **24** |

A summary of responses to Question Three by demographic is shown in Table 11. This suggests that the opposition to preferential CGT rates is strongest among the interviewees from academia. Five times as many academics answered 'no' to this question, compared to those who answered 'yes'. For the other two demographics—'tax economist' and 'tax practice'—there were two negative responses compared to one positive response in each case. In comparing the ratio of negative to positive responses, the inconclusive responses have been disregarded. Nevertheless, if they were to be included, the majority of the interview population would still be unconvinced as to the appropriateness of CGT preferences.

**Table 11: Interview responses to Question Three by demographic**

| Q3. Given the benefits of deferral that apply to capital gains and the ability of the taxpayer to effectively choose when and if they will realise a capital gain, are preferential rates for capital gains considered appropriate? | | | | |
|---|---|---|---|---|
| | Yes | No | Inconclusive | Total |
| Academic | 2 | 10 | 4 | **16** |
| Tax practitioner | 1 | 2 | 1 | **4** |
| Tax economist | 1 | 2 | 1 | **4** |
| **Total** | **4** | **14** | **6** | **24** |

The predominantly negative response is now elaborated upon by reference to particular quotes from the interviewees. Respondent A (United States) indicated that they did not think preferential CGT rates were appropriate:

> Probably not, I think they're pretty favoured as is. Relative to dividends they're favoured already because of deferral and exclusion at death ... [I]f you hold on to them until death you don't pay any tax. So, exclusion cuts it by about half, exclusion and deferral itself cuts the rate by about half all by itself. I think there are other more efficient ways to give up revenue than the capital gains cuts.

According to Respondent A, CGT rate preferences lead to lost tax revenue. They noted that the recent evidence on the capital gains realisations response show that the response is quite modest. Respondent A also referred to the flaws in the earlier realisations response studies that reported very large estimates.

Another aspect of the U.S. CGT that leads to lost revenue is the highly preferential treatment of capital gains at death. On this point, Respondent A stated that attempting to reform the effective CGT exclusion at death would be too difficult to deal with politically. According to Gravelle (1994), the failure to tax capital gains at death is a large impediment to the sale of assets, which increases with a taxpayer's age. This implies that there is a tax policy rationale for the reform of the current CGT rules at death, despite any political impediments to reform.

Respondent C (United States) noted that:

> The deferral provides a preference even without a special rate, so in that sense, you're adding on to the favourable treatment of capital gains when you give a preference ... It is the deferral or it is the voluntary nature of realisations which means that you ... get into the situation where if you have high individual rates and you don't have a preference, you're likely to have a lot of gains that might have been realised that aren't, then you sacrifice revenue and you keep people from keeping their portfolios in the form which is most beneficial to them, so you do produce deadweight losses when you do that.

As a follow-up question, Respondent C (United States) was asked whether something less than full-rate CGT is the ideal. Their response was:

> [I]t really depends on the kind of system you have. If you insist on having very high top individual rates I think you have to have some preferential treatment of capital gains. I can imagine a situation where you can get the top individual rate low enough that you don't need that. In fact, we did that here [in the United States] in 1986.

Respondent C did not state whether they were of the view that the CGT rate preference in the United States was set at an appropriate rate or at a rate that was too low relative to the rates on ordinary income.

As was the case for Respondent B, Respondent C also referred to the absence of corporate integration in the U.S. tax system as being a benefit of and reason for preferential CGT. Respondent C argued that the optimal rate for CGT, in terms of maximising revenue, is a rate lower than that which applies to ordinary income.

Respondent D (United States) referred to what they identified as two conflicting principles. First, Respondent D noted 'that all income should be taxed the same'. Second, they described an inverse elasticity rule, which requires lower tax rates for items with a more elastic response and higher tax rates for items with a less elastic response. None of the other respondents referred to the inverse elasticity rule.

A theme to emerge from the American interviews was that of the need to consider CGT in the context of the budget deficit that the United States was experiencing. A recurring suggestion was that CGT should be reformed as part of an overall tax reform package under which CGT rates were either increased or capital gains were taxed as ordinary income and ordinary income tax rates were lowered. The purpose of this type of reform would be to increase overall tax revenue (Minas & Lim, 2013).

Some of the responses to Question One were of relevance to Question Three. Specifically, although Question One did not include a reference to deferral, several respondents highlighted deferral in their response. Some of the respondents were of the view that deferral lessens the case for CGT rate preferences, and they spoke about this in their answers.

In summary, a theme from Questions One and Three was that the rate of tax on capital gains should be increased while the rates on ordinary income should be decreased. Several respondents were of the view that the tax rates on ordinary income and capital gains should be the same. Some respondents did not think that the rates of tax on capital gains should be increased. The responses to Question Three confirm the influence of political considerations on setting CGT rates (Minas & Lim, 2013).

## Responses to Question Four[5]

The focus of Question Four was on whether the case for retaining CGT preferences is due mostly to economic efficiency considerations, political considerations or a combination of the two. This question relates to the identification of a rhetorical gap in the conversation between academic economists and political leaders (Cordes, Klamer & Leonard, 1993). Cordes et al. (1993) highlighted three negative consequences of this gap: (1) waste, given that much of what academic economists produce is not used in politics; (2) ignorance, given that the economic knowledge of politicians is often superficial; and (3) ineffectiveness, given that political arguments tend to crowd out economic arguments. The answers to Question Four revealed an area in which there was a degree of consensus across all countries and all types of respondent. Specifically, none of the respondents said that the case for retaining CGT preferences was due mostly to economic efficiency considerations. A distribution of the answers to Question Four is shown in Table 12. Australia had the highest proportion of respondents who said that CGT preferences were due mostly to political considerations, while the lowest proportion of respondents who said the same was in the United States (Minas & Lim, 2013).

**Table 12: Interview responses to Question Four**

| | Political | Both | Economic efficiency | Unanswered | Total |
|---|---|---|---|---|---|
| Australia | 9 | 2 | 0 | 0 | **11** |
| Canada | 4 | 3 | 0 | 1 | **8** |
| United States | 2 | 3 | 0 | 0 | **5** |
| **Total** | **15** | **8** | **0** | **1** | **24** |

As indicated in Table 12, none of the 24 respondents were of the view that the case for retaining CGT preferences was due to economic efficiency considerations alone. Most respondents were of the view that political considerations were the most important consideration, while a third of the interviewees were of the view that the case for retaining preferences for capital gains was due to a combination of political and economic efficiency considerations.

5 Q4. Is the case for retaining capital gains preferences due mostly to economic efficiency considerations, political considerations or a combination of both?

According to Respondent A (United States), both economic efficiency and political considerations contributed to the retention of CGT preferences:

> I think it's a combination ... [A] lot of politicians have been searching ... for the magic bullet ... something we can do to cut taxes and not [lose] a lot of money ... so they readily listen to these arguments that you can't really raise revenues with capital gains or you don't lose much when you cut them because of these realisation responses.

Several of the Canadian interviews discussed the influence of political considerations in setting the original rate of CGT when it was first enacted in 1972. Some Canadian respondents explained that policy makers, at that time, perceived that there would be difficulties in going from a zero rate of CGT to 100% inclusion of capital gains in ordinary income. In this sense, the 50% inclusion rate might have been a necessary political compromise. One interviewee suggested that the CGT preference in the United States at the time might also have contributed to the decision by Canada not to tax capital gains at full rates (Minas & Lim, 2013).



According to Respondent Q (Australia), both political and economic efficiency considerations are an influence on retaining a preferential rate CGT regime; they also noted that 'more often than not, it's to do with the power of lobby groups'.

Respondent D (United States) was of the view that both political and economic efficiency considerations had a role in the retention of CGT preferences, and they noted: 'I don't think you can separate the two.'

Respondent K (Canada) was of the view that political considerations were more influential, and they added '[W]hen I say political considerations, I don't mean there's a sentiment in the country ... I just mean the political clout of wealthy taxpayers.'

It was noted that of the three demographic groups, academics had the highest proportion of respondents who answered that the use of CGT preferences was due mostly to political considerations. In comparison, interviewees in the tax economist demographic had the highest proportion that answered that CGT preferences were due to a combination of political and economic efficiency considerations (see also Minas & Lim, 2013).

According to Shaviro (1993), there is a danger in setting CGT rates too low that has more to do with politics than with estimating error in determining the revenue-maximising CGT rate. Shaviro believed that once Congress is on a path of setting preferential CGT rates, pressure from interest groups and the popularity of tax cuts act as incentives for it to enact a rate cut that is too large.

Aside from the influence of political considerations in the decision to retain rate preferences, it is apparent that these factors can also act as a barrier to the original implementation of a CGT and can influence the design features of the CGT, as was the case for Australia. Sandford (2000, p. 175) referred to the 1984 Australian election campaign where the Liberal Party was campaigning on a platform of 'no wealth taxes, no estate duties and no capital gains tax'. Head (1987) identified one prominent example of political compromise in the decision to allow 'carry-over of basis' for the heir of a deceased taxpayer after fierce opposition from small business and the farm sector to the original proposal for a deemed realisation at death.

## Responses to Question Five[6]

Question Five was concerned with the respondents' views on how successful CGT preferences had been in achieving their economic objectives. This question was motivated by the view that, as well as evaluating a tax system with CGT preferences against the traditional characteristics of a good tax system, there should be some consideration of the success or otherwise of CGT preferences in achieving their economic objectives. Question Five did not include any suggestions as to what the economic objectives of CGT preferences might be so as to avoid bias in the question. Furthermore, the economic objectives articulated by policy makers in each jurisdiction may not necessarily be the same.

Respondent M (Australia) was clearly of the view that CGT preferences were not required to achieve objectives such as increasing investment:

> The greatest investments have always happened in the times of the highest capital gains tax rates; the best example ... is the United States—[they] eliminated all preferences for capital gains tax under the Reagan Administration and that ... directly affected investment ... Silicon Valley and the American computer industry and electronics industry took off [once there was] the full inclusion of capital gains and the full recognition of losses. Most of the studies of that period suggested [the level of investment] has nothing to do with tax.
>
> There's no evidence in any country that [CGT preferences have] led to increases in investment. There is evidence of ... a capital gains discount [causing] more re-characterisation of transactions and more distortionary activity.

Respondent P (Australia) did not conclude that the CGT discount led to increased investment. They noted that the interaction of negative gearing and the CGT discount might have influenced or distorted the decisions of some taxpayers:

> The timing of the [CGT discount was when] Australia was moving into its big boom ... so the difficulty ... is that ... the discount is only one element of the tax picture ... If you can get access to people's financial plans on things like rental properties ... a lot of it will be driven by negative gearing and the perceived gains that arise from that process ... [A]t the end of the exercise they will have a calculation methodology that sets out how much extra [they will gain] because of the 50% discount. But the initial driver is all on the conversion of income into capital and having a present value ... calculation on the deduction for interest upfront.

Respondent Z (Australia) referred to the incentive for taxpayers to convert ordinary income into capital gains:

> I think the CGT discount may well have encouraged people to try and turn income into capital. I don't know that it really has made a huge difference to people's decisions. The only area where I can think it probably has had an impact is on bank deposits where owning shares in the bank and getting franked dividends together with capital growth has been a much more attractive investment ... I think a lot of [people], who perhaps in the past would have just had term deposits, have looked at the attractiveness

6 Q5. How successful do you think CGT rate preferences have been in achieving the economic objectives that they were intended to?

> of discounted capital gains and perhaps been more willing to go into the stock market or managed funds.

According to Respondent Q (Australia), it is widely accepted that there are economic efficiency costs associated with a CGT preference, given that any preference is a departure from neutrality and an invitation for taxpayers to devise schemes. Respondent M (Australia), as quoted earlier in this chapter, expressed a similar view about the deadweight losses that occur from taxpayers reorganising their transactions; essentially, this is what a revenue authority might define as a 'scheme'.

Respondent K (Canada) was not convinced that the rate preference for CGT had achieved its policy objectives:

> I think the objectives were to increase entrepreneurship and risk-taking ... I just don't think it has any effect on entrepreneurship and risk-taking ... [I]t's enormously target inefficient. In Canada, about one-half of the capital gains are realised on real estate for which the argument wouldn't apply. Another real large percentage of capital gains are realised on shares on secondary exchanges for which again the argument really wouldn't apply.



Respondent K's views are consistent with literature on the topic. For example, according to Auerbach (2012) the argument that low CGT rates encourage the formation of new enterprises is weak since only a small proportion of capital gains are associated with new ventures. Furthermore, even if such arguments are accepted, the general rate of CGT is irrelevant to encouraging entrepreneurship, which would require a highly targeted preference (Auerbach, 2012).

Respondent L (Canada) was also of the view that CGT rate preferences have not been successful in spurring entrepreneurship:

> In terms of ... the objective of trying to increase investment in entrepreneurial activity, I think they've been relatively poor. In terms of increasing home ownership, they've probably been relatively good, in the sense that if you wanted to promote home ownership [by exempting] the gain from tax, I think Canada has been relatively successful in increasing the rate of home ownership in this country.

By contrast, Respondent H (Canada) perceived that the CGT rate preference had been somewhat successful:

> A lot of this was about the dividend question and, yes, I think it has been quite successful. We don't have a lot of people trying to do these transactions to move dividends into capital gains and vice versa. Yes, I think there's probably some effect and my best bet is there's some effect in higher economic growth from not having a 100% inclusion rate and there's some effect of not having a lock-in effect, hard to know how much.

Respondent H referred to a point that was raised by several other Canadian interviewees about a perceived need to have the rate of tax on capital gains and dividends aligned. Having a preferential CGT rate has prevented arbitrage transactions that would have taken advantage of the lower rate on dividends from occurring had the CGT rate been higher than the rate achieved by way of the current 50% exclusion. Nevertheless, the assertion made by Respondent H that there might be higher economic growth as a result of a CGT preference is counter to the literature on this topic. For example, according to Slemrod (2003), there is no evidence linking aggregate economic performance to lower CGT rates. Cunningham and Schenk (1993) rejected the claim that a CGT preference stimulates economic growth as a stand-alone argument, and Burman (1999) found that numerous changes in U.S. CGT rates between 1954 and 1996 had no perceptible effect on economic growth.

Respondent E (Canada) expressed a view that there may be some justification for a preferential rate on capital gains:

> I'm giving an opinion here ... I think if we didn't have a lower rate of capital gains tax then it would be a deterrent for people investing in equities and other assets where a large part of the yield is ... future capital gains ... I'm uncertain about it, although ... I would certainly encourage people to hold more equities than they otherwise would.

The opinion of Respondent E seems to imply that a high CGT rate may be responsible for a lock-in effect for personal taxpayers who invest in corporate equities. The lock-in effect for this type of taxpayer may not be of great importance. According to Burman (1999), the argument that lock-in can trap capital in inefficient investments is of more relevance to a small privately held business than to the stock market investments of personal taxpayers.

Respondent J (Canada) noted that in their view there was little empirical evidence in support of a capital gains preference, in terms of inducing a higher level of risk-taking and savings and reducing the lock-in effect.

Respondent A (United States) was of the view that the CGT rate preference had failed to achieve its policy objectives:

> The objectives varied at different times ... [T]he original objective was just averaging a progressive tax system and I'm sure that it dealt with the one-time huge gain from being taxed at high rate, but I think it was a blunt instrument to achieve that objective. More recently it's been about growth and I really don't think the savings rate [is] much affected by any kind of capital income tax rate so I don't think it's achieved any sort of growth objective ... so I don't think the policy objectives have been achieved.

Respondent D (United States) referred to the difficulty in disentangling the effects of the CGT rate cut in 1978 and other events that occurred around the same time, including the tax exemptions that were allowed to certain pension funds.

The responses to Question Five from the U.S. interviews (particularly Respondents A and D) reveal there is some doubt as to the success of CGT preferences in achieving their intended objectives. The view of Respondent A on the failure of CGT preferences to achieve economic growth is consistent with the literature. According to Burman (1999), a large CGT preference is likely to depress the economy only slightly. For example, Burman (1999) found that the correlation between the percentage change in real GDP and the maximum tax rate on capital gains was –0.01.

The majority of respondents from all three countries did not favour CGT rate preferences. This was apparent in many of the answers provided to the question about the advantages and disadvantages of CGT preferences, where most of the interviewees focused on the disadvantages and some did not refer to any advantages of CGT preferences. Respondent S (Australia) referred to the case for taxing capital gains more heavily than ordinary income, rather than preferentially, given the benefits of deferral. Several interviewees mentioned the vertical equity disadvantages of CGT preferences and the fact that capital gains are realised disproportionately by higher-income taxpayers. Kenny (2005) described vertical equity as taxation based on ability to pay, which may be achieved by progressive rates of tax. Several interviewees referred to the administrative and compliance problems caused by CGT rate preferences.

Some respondents stated that a reduction in the magnitude of the lock-in effect was an advantage of preferential rates. One interviewee described reduced lock-in as of some relevance to an individual seeking to balance their portfolio, but as not necessarily more efficient for the whole economy. This is consistent with the view of Johnson (2008) who argued that lock-in does not require a remedy in the form of a CGT rate preference. One of the reasons given for this is that lock-in at the individual investor level is unlikely to have a significant effect on the overall allocation of capital, since there is enough capital that is not subject to lock-in (Johnson, 2008). Another interviewee said that, in their view, the lock-in of financial assets was overblown as there are 'major players' in the market who move the capital around. Respondent N (Australia) stated that, in their opinion, lock-in might be an overstated problem. Respondent N noted that capital gains realisations can be motivated by good commercial reasons or for the purpose of consumption. According to Ingles (2015), the removal of the CGT discount in a realisation-based CGT system would exacerbate the lock-in effect.

4

Although a reduced tax rate on capital gains is likely to reduce lock-in, there are other factors referred to in the literature that may be more important in causing lock-in than CGT rates. One such example is the treatment of capital gains at death in the United States, which is the primary cause of lock-in in that country (Johnson, 2008). The fact that a taxable capital gain does not arise at death also contributes to lock-in in Australia (Minas & Lim, 2013). However, the preference for capital gains at death in Australia is less pronounced than in the United States, given that the cost base of a 'post-CGT' asset in Australia is not 'stepped-up' at death.[7]

Several interviewees referred to an incentive to characterise income as capital gains where the CGT rates are lower. According to one of the interviewees, in a self-assessment tax system, such as Australia's, taxpayers who have the means to engage in this arbitrage are effectively choosing their rate of tax. Clearly, there is a vertical equity problem associated with this, as such a choice is not available to all taxpayers. Furthermore, it is most unlikely that the policy intent of a preferential CGT rate includes the facilitation of arbitrage and

7 The effect of s 128-10 of the *ITAA1997* is that in most cases, a capital gain or loss arising from the death of a taxpayer will be disregarded. A more important CGT implication in the event of death will be the treatment of the cost base of the inherited asset. Unlike the United States, which allows for a 'stepped-up' basis, in Australia, the cost base of the asset for the inheriting taxpayer is the same as the cost base of that asset for the deceased, as per s 128-15(4) of the *ITAA1997*. The exception to this rule, under s 128-15(4) of the *ITAA1997*, is in the case of an inherited asset that was 'pre-CGT' when held by the deceased. In that case, the cost base for the inherited asset will be its market value, meaning that it effectively loses its CGT-free status on the event of death.

allowing taxpayers to choose a lower rate on income that would be taxed at ordinary rates in the absence of preferential CGT (Minas & Lim, 2013).

Several interviewees referred to the distributional impact of preferential rate capital gains as one of its disadvantages. That is, since there is a skewed distribution of realised capital gains towards higher-income earners, this same taxpayer demographic group enjoys the benefits of preferential rates at a disproportionately higher level than lower-income taxpayers do (Minas & Lim, 2013).

The responses of the interviewees to the five Theme One questions—when considered collectively—confirm the view that capital gains rate preferences operating in each of the three countries are at odds with much of the literature on taxing capital gains (Minas & Lim, 2013). It appears that some of the claimed benefits of CGT rate preferences are overstated or difficult to prove empirically, such as the argument that CGT rate cuts have a positive effect on economic growth and savings. By contrast, some of the disadvantages of CGT rate preferences are apparent. In particular, the vertical inequity of a rate preference is reflected in the individual taxpayer data in *Taxation Statistics*. The taxpayer data for 2013–14 indicate that more than 58% of total net capital gains were realised by taxpayers with taxable incomes of more than $180,000 and that this group of taxpayers comprised less than 3% of the taxpayer population (Australian Taxation Office, 2016).[8]

Furthermore, it appears that the benefits of deferral in a realisation-based CGT system, although emphasised by some of the interview population, may not have been given due consideration by policy makers.

## Theme Two: Reforming CGT

The second theme of the interview study was concerned with whether the CGT system for personal taxpayers in each country required reform and, if it did, how it could be reformed. This theme was addressed entirely by Question Six.[9]

Question Six was an open-ended question that gave each respondent an opportunity to speak about their ideas for the reform of CGT systems, rather than addressing the more specific earlier questions. It was the final question asked in each interview.

According to Respondent N (Australia), reform could be achieved by:

> The removal of as many preferences as it is possible to sensibly remove without impacting on business creativity and growth and by the introduction of the tax-free threshold and ... I would also get rid of the pre-85 exemption ...

Some interviewees from Australia referred to the need to reduce the complexity of the CGT system. It was suggested by one respondent that more input from tax practitioners should be allowed in formulating CGT policy and tax policy more generally, and this would achieve a reduction in the complexity of the CGT provisions. The respondent was of the view that tax practitioners had a thorough understanding of the effect of proposed

8 A similarly skewed distribution of net capital gains among the highest-income taxpayers can also be seen in earlier tax years.

9 Q6. How do you think that the capital gains tax system in (Australia/Canada/the United States) can best be reformed?

tax policy changes and their input was not being given due consideration before the introduction of some of these changes. The respondent argued that parts of the CGT legislation had become unnecessarily complex and that complex tax law changes could have been avoided if practitioners were allowed more involvement in the reform process and the drafting of legislation (Minas & Lim, 2013).

The issue of 'grandfathering' of pre-20 September 1985 CGT assets[10] was considered to be problematic by several of the Australian interviewees. Respondents N and U were among those who proposed that the issue of grandfathered pre-20 September 1985 CGT assets be addressed. Their concerns are consistent with the view of Cooper and Evans (2014) that grandfathering is a uniquely Australian CGT characteristic that has bedevilled the CGT since its inception. The problem of grandfathering could have been avoided if Australia had followed the example of the Canadian CGT, and the approach used in several other jurisdictions, and implemented a valuation date system for CGT assets. Under such a system, the market value of the CGT asset on the nominated valuation day is its cost base or basis. The introduction of a valuation date system in Australia would eliminate the current grandfathered status of pre-20 September 1985 CGT assets from the valuation day onwards. Taxpayers with pre-20 September 1985 CGT assets may argue that implementing a valuation date system for these assets would constitute a type of retrospective tax reform. However, any gain on a pre-20 September 1985 CGT asset that had accrued prior to enactment of a valuation day rule would escape tax, and this proportion of the post-19 September 1985[11] gain that is untaxed is effectively a CGT preference. It is therefore difficult to support the view that this type of valuation date system would be retrospective in its application (Minas & Lim, 2013).

Respondent A (United States) argued that an exclusion of a set percentage of capital gains from taxable income is a superior form of CGT in comparison to a separate rate schedule that operated in the United States at the time of the interview. If such a reform were adopted, the individual American CGT system would bear a closer resemblance to those currently operating in Australia and Canada. It is clear that Respondent A was of the view that CGT rates in the United States should be increased as a means of increasing tax revenue:

> [G]etting rid of this rate structure and [implementing] an exclusion ... I think we could afford to raise the capital gains tax rate, given our revenue needs, without doing much harm to anything, and we could raise some revenue ... [G]o back to the pre-Bush tax cut level of 20% and maybe higher or its equivalent in proportional rates ... Raise [CGT rates], make an exclusion and get rid of it entirely for owner-occupied housing ... The foremost policy [factor] that I think should drive tax policy of any kind right now, at least in this country, is dealing with the deficit, and I think raising taxes needs to be a part of that because it's just too hard to do it on the spending side.

10 In Australia, a pre-20 September 1985 CGT asset (pre-CGT asset) is one that the taxpayer themselves had acquired before 20 September 1985. Once the asset is subject to a CGT event, it loses its pre-CGT status.

11 Capital gains on pre-20 September 1985 capital gains assets are not subject to CGT in Australia because of the grandfathering rules that accompanied the introduction of CGT.

Respondent B (United States) described simplicity benefits that would result from the removal of the CGT rate preference in the United States. They also referred to lower overall tax rates that could be enacted in the event that all income was to be taxed at the same rate:

> Just tax it as ordinary income and ... [get] rid of a lot of other tax preferences and ... [go] back to the kind of reform we had in 1986. You can have lower tax rates on all income ... With capital gains, you have to fill out this whole schedule and ... if you got rid of a lot of tax preferences, you might get rid of a whole bunch of schedules.

Respondent C was also clear in their support for one tax rate for all types of assessable income:

> Moving toward more accrual taxation, equalising rates on gains and ordinary income and bringing in the corporate rate I think are the kind of three-legged stool of better taxation of capital income.

According to Respondent D (United States), the CGT rate could be reduced without any loss of revenue; in their view, a CGT rate reduction 'wouldn't be the end of the world'. Respondent D did not refer to the specific rate reduction they were contemplating in relation to a proposed CGT rate reduction.

These four responses to Question Six from the United States respondents demonstrated a divergence of opinion, particularly in the case of Respondents A and D, who appear to have differing views on the revenue effects of CGT rate changes. Respondent B suggested that a reform similar to the *TRA86* is required. In summary, the *TRA86* reduced the top marginal tax rate on ordinary income from 50% to 28% and increased the tax rate on capital gains from 20% to 28%. Respondent C also suggested the same kind of reform without specifically referring to the *TRA86*.

Respondent C suggested the taxation of gains at death; in doing so, they referred to it as a form of accrual taxation. The term 'accrual taxation' in this context accurately describes the interviewee's reform proposal given that, in the event of a taxpayer's death, no sale or exchange of the asset has taken place, as is generally required for a capital gain or loss to occur under U.S. CGT law. The effect of such a reform would be to reduce the incentive to hold assets until death. An alternative would be to remove the stepped-up basis preference, which currently exists in the American system, and replace it with the capital gains treatment at death in the Australian system, in which the cost base of the post-19 September 1985 asset stays the same when the taxpayer's heir inherits it.[12] Respondent L (Canada) noted:

> I think we ought to be eliminating the general preference for capital gains and ... at the same time, eliminating the poor treatment of capital losses in the sense that only half of them are subject to tax, and to the extent that we want to justify particular types of investment, we should have targeted rules but they do have to be appropriately targeted ...

12 Under s 128-15(4) of the *ITAA1997*, the cost base of a post-19 September 1985 asset is 'the cost base of the asset on the day (the deceased) died'.

Respondent L's comment on the inappropriately targeted CGT rules is consistent with the view in the literature that attempting to encourage risk-taking by way of a CGT rate preference is target-inefficient (Krever & Brooks, 1990). One of the specific objections to such a preference is that it benefits investments that do not involve risk as well as assets that are non-productive and those assets that have an inelastic supply (Krever & Brooks, 1990). Respondent L's comment about the poor treatment of capital losses is similar to the view of Halperin (1993, p. 389) that 'greater allowance of capital losses would be possible with permanent equal treatment for capital gain and ordinary income.'

Respondent K (Canada) stated that although they would like to see full inclusion of capital gains in assessable income, 75% inclusion would be politically feasible. Furthermore, Respondent K supported the abolition of the $500,000 capital gains exemption for small businesses and farms.

4

Unlike several of the other Canadian interviewees, Respondent F did not object to CGT rate preferences per se. Nevertheless, they did not support any further reduction of the CGT rate or the introduction of other forms of CGT preferences. This suggests that if policy makers consider a preferential CGT rate necessary, they should also consider the appropriate rate to apply. This is especially important in the context of the capital gains realisations response literature, much of which has concluded that CGT rate reductions lead to revenue losses in the long run (Minas & Lim, 2013).

Of the three countries that were the subject of the study in this chapter, Canada is the only one that has not taxed capital gains for individuals at the same rate as ordinary income. The proportion of a capital gain that is to be included in a taxpayer's income has, at various times that the Canadian CGT regime has been in operation, varied between half, two-thirds and three-quarters. The fact that capital gains have been taxed at preferential rates in Canada might have contributed to the perception among some of the Canadian interviewees that taxing capital gains at ordinary income rates could be difficult to achieve in practice. That is, it might be that Canadian taxpayers have an expectation of preferential CGT rates due to Canada's taxing of capital gains at less than full rates over the last four decades.

The responses from Canada indicate a diversity of opinion on the appropriate rate at which to tax capital gains. Whereas Respondent I argued for full-rate CGT, Respondent K stated that although, in their view, full rates are the ideal, 75% inclusion may be more politically achievable. Respondent F was of the view that the current system of 50% inclusion worked well. One of the Canadian interviewees referred to problems in defining realisations, citing corporate reorganisations as an example of situations in which definitional issues arise. There was an absence of responses in favour of CGT preferences based on arguments about increased fairness as a result of preferences. This is consistent with the view of Minarik (1992) that such arguments are baseless, whereas fairness arguments against a CGT preference carry considerable weight.

Most respondents spoke at length about their suggestions for the reform of CGT, in response to the final open-ended question. However, a small number of interviewees chose not to answer the final question as they were of the view that their ideas for reform had been covered in responses to the preceding questions.

It is evident that several Australian interviewees who spoke about the issue of grandfathering of 'pre-CGT' assets did not support this policy. Although the introduction of a valuation day would address the grandfathering problem and improve the CGT regime, the prospects of achieving this type of reform in practice are unclear (Minas & Lim, 2013).

It is arguable that borrowing against an asset is the equivalent to realising a capital gain and that it should therefore give rise to a taxable CGT event. If this view is considered correct, it diminishes the case for negative gearing. Respondents in all three countries referred to negative gearing as another problem related to CGT rate preferences.[13] Negative gearing is an issue closely related to preferential CGT rates insofar as it creates an incentive for capital gains over other returns regardless of the economic efficiency of the investment (Burman, 1999). The concerns of some of the interviewees about negative gearing in a preferential rate CGT regime were consistent with the literature on this topic (Minas & Lim, 2013).

Although taxation of capital gains on an accrual basis—for particular types of assets—was a reform suggested by some respondents, several interviewees were strongly opposed to accruals taxation of capital gains in any form. These respondents cited unfairness, liquidity problems and valuation problems as some of the reasons they did not support such a reform. According to Schenk (2004), liquidity problems alone do not explain the realisation-basis system of CGT. The liquidity argument is essentially one based on cash flow being such a serious concern that monetisation should be required for an imposition of tax. Schenk highlighted the inadequacy of this argument and noted that monetisation is an insufficient trigger for taxation since there would be no CGT if there were an exemption for a swap of properties. Schenk noted that for most assets the need to provide cash to pay an annual tax on the change in value is akin to any other cost of owning an asset and is one that should be borne by the taxpayer. In the Australian context, monetisation is not required to trigger a CGT liability. For example, the market value substitution rule in s 116-30 of the *ITAA1997* ensures that a CGT disposal event can occur where the taxpayer has not received capital proceeds in respect of an asset disposal.

One of the respondents stated that they disagreed with proposals to use an accrual-basis CGT for certain types of assets, such as publicly traded shares. It was their view that this would skew investment towards other types of capital gains assets that were taxed on a realisation basis and it would be difficult to see the benefits of this type of distortion to investment incentives (Minas & Lim, 2013).

Several interviewees questioned whether a CGT rate preference was the best means of achieving the associated tax policy objectives.[14] Some argued that, if such incentives

---

13 Although the term 'negative gearing' is not in common use outside Australia, several respondents in Canada and the United States spoke about what would be considered the equivalent of negative gearing. In Australia, negative gearing allows taxpayers who have borrowed to purchase a CGT asset to deduct from their non-investment assessable income the excess of interest payments over taxable receipts, net of other deductible expenses.

14 These might include objectives such as encouraging investment in new capital, increasing entrepreneurship and reducing the extent of the 'lock-in' effect in relation to capital gains realisations.

were considered necessary, a better-targeted measure should replace a rate preference (see also Minas & Lim, 2013).

## 4.3 CONCLUSIONS ON THE INTERVIEW STUDY

The qualitative interview study in this chapter canvassed the opinions of CGT experts in three countries. One of the purposes of the study was to ascertain the main areas of convergence and divergence on issues associated with CGT for individuals, particularly those related to CGT preferences. The interview data have provided a source of comparison with the CGT literature, and these responses are informative to the quantitative study in Chapter 5.

Some differences of opinion arose in the interview responses, and these may reflect the difficulties and controversy associated with the taxation of capital gains. Nevertheless, the research revealed several areas in which the interviewee population agreed. For example, the Australian interviewees who spoke about grandfathering were unanimous about how problematic it was.



It is noteworthy that despite the fact that each of Australia, Canada and the United States offers a CGT rate preference for the taxable capital gains of individual taxpayers, a significant proportion of the CGT experts interviewed were not supportive of such CGT rate preferences and were unconvinced as to their claimed benefits (Minas & Lim, 2013). This is consistent with a large proportion of the interviewees referring to the influence of politics on the retention of CGT rate preferences.

Respondent A suggested that U.S. policy makers abolish the separate CGT rate schedule in the United States and replace it with a CGT exclusion. 'Exclusion' in this context refers to a system whereby a taxpayer is required to include a proportion of net capital gains with ordinary income (the proportion remaining after the exclusion is applied) and the aggregate amount is subject to tax. Respondent A argued that the use of an exclusion method would be a superior means of providing a CGT rate preference. The enactment of such a change would bring the American system of taxing capital gains of individuals closer to those operating in Australia and Canada. This would be considered a worthwhile reform for the U.S. CGT system given the simplicity benefits it would afford as well as the fact that it would diminish the rate differential between the taxpayer's tax rate on their ordinary income and their CGT rate, especially at the highest marginal tax rate (Minas & Lim, 2013).

As noted in the literature review, some of the distortions caused by preferential rate CGT originate from the tax rate differential between that on ordinary income compared with capital gains. The mechanism for the rate difference can be a separate CGT rate schedule, as in the case of the United States, or a provision that requires taxpayers to include less than the full capital gain in taxable income,[15] as in the cases of Australia and Canada. Notably, none of the Australian or Canadian interviewees suggested that a separate CGT rate schedule should replace the current CGT rate preference systems in those countries.

---

15 This can also be a provision that excludes a percentage of the net capital gain from income subject to assessment.

Several Australian respondents were critical of the grandfathered status of pre-20 September 1985 CGT assets. Grandfathering of CGT assets is a feature unique to the Australian CGT, and it did not occur in Canada or the United States when each country started taxing capital gains. Although the original intention for the Australian CGT system was that it would use a valuation date system, grandfathering was introduced by way of a late and unexpected policy change. Australia's grandfathering of pre-20 September 1985 assets provided a windfall, in the form of preferential tax treatment, to taxpayers who held these assets at the time of the tax law change.

In this context, it is unclear why Australia's 50% CGT discount was designed to apply to capital gains from assets that were acquired prior to the introduction of this reform. Preferences afforded to capital gains that had accrued before the introduction of the CGT discount are a form of windfall gain for taxpayers holding assets before the tax law change (Minas & Lim, 2013). Furthermore, extending the preference to accrued gains conflicts with one of the more common justifications for CGT preferences: that of encouraging new investment in capital. The date of the introduction of the CGT discount would have been a logical point in time to introduce a valuation day for capital gains assets, which could have also applied to pre-CGT assets.

Many interviewees referred to the influence of politics in decisions by governments to retain CGT rate preferences.[16] An analysis of the interview data suggests that, ideally, the tax policy advantages, disadvantages and implications of CGT preferences warrant consideration on their own merits. Nevertheless, the cases for and against CGT rate preferences are politically charged issues, and the interviews with the experts highlighted the extent to which, in 1999, policy makers in Australia focused on the arguments for a preference without adequately addressing the concerns of those who argued against the CGT discount.

Graetz (1977) highlighted the misunderstanding among some policy makers as to the meaning and importance of retroactivity as it applies to tax policy. Such misunderstanding has led to anomalous outcomes such as Australia's decision to keep pre-20 September 1985 assets out of the 'CGT net'. According to Graetz, grandfathering rules do not guarantee fairness for taxpayers affected by a change in the law. Although the broader intention of grandfathering rules may be to preserve fairness, a requirement for enacted laws to remain unchanged can lead to unfairness and expectations for preserving the status quo, and these are inconsistent with a system of lawmaking within a representative democracy (Graetz, 1977). Even if such arguments are not accepted, it is clear that a valuation date system for capital gains assets would not constitute a retroactive tax policy change, as it would only bring into the CGT net the capital gains or losses accruing from the valuation date. Furthermore, it is difficult to characterise such a tax law change as retrospective in its effect.[17]

16 As previously explained, this was in response to a specific interview question about the relative importance of political and economic considerations in such decisions.

17 Broadly, the difference between a tax law change that is retroactive and one that is retrospective is that the former is enacted to take effect at an earlier date than the date of enactment, whereas the latter is seen as imposing new results in respect of past events.

The collective views of the experts in the interview sample suggest that there is a tax policy case for taxing capital gains at ordinary income rates. Nevertheless, some of the respondents outlined the case in favour of preferential CGT rates. Ideally, policy makers should set out objective and transparent reasons justifying the enactment of a preferential CGT rate. Although some policy makers have relied on the argument that a rate cut will necessarily lead to increased revenue, this is unconvincing in the absence of empirical evidence.

According to some respondents, an accrual-based CGT would be feasible. However, a larger proportion strongly opposed a CGT on an accruals basis, with their main objection being practical considerations.[18] The views of the experts on an accrual CGT are consistent with current practice, given that a completely accrual-based CGT is not a feature of Australia, Canada or the United States or other comparable tax systems. Nonetheless, this relatively untested approach to taxing capital gains is not without its benefits. As outlined in Chapter 2, an accrual-based CGT would eliminate the lock-in effect, and it would allow taxpayers to offset their capital losses against ordinary income.[19]



If the recommendations of the majority of the interviewees are to be balanced with the political considerations that restrain tax reform generally, CGT rate reform for personal taxpayers should be concerned with increasing the effective CGT rate in each country so that more than 50% of capital gains are taxable at all levels of income (Minas & Lim, 2013). Increasing the rate of CGT, while maintaining a rate preference relative to ordinary income, may constitute a second-best type of improvement to the current respective CGT systems. It would address the concerns expressed by the majority of the interviewees about current CGT rates being too low (Minas & Lim, 2013). One of the main conclusions of the interview study for CGT policy in Australia is that the 50% discount should not remain in its current form. Chapter 6 sets out the options for reform of the Australian CGT regime for personal taxpayers.

Based on the interview responses, there is an absence of an overarching tax policy case to justify CGT rate preferences. Furthermore, there is an absence of a convincing economic argument in favour of CGT rate preferences.

Another perspective from which CGT rate preferences can be considered is according to whether or not the lower CGT rates that the preferences give effect to are likely to increase tax revenue through an increase in capital gains realisations. The results of an empirical study, which estimates the capital gains realisations response for personal taxpayers in Australia, are reported in Chapter 5. The realisations response estimates

18 It was noted in Australia by the Commonwealth Taxation Review Committee and Asprey (1975, p. 415) that 'the impracticability of taxing capital gains as they accrue is universally recognised: the tax can only attempt to deal with realised gains.'

19 It would also counteract a significant asymmetry problem in the Australian tax system resulting from the interaction of the negative gearing rules and the CGT discount. Essentially, the problem is a mismatch between deductible losses on negatively geared investments and income from the same. Although the Australian tax system does not contemplate or require an exact matching of income and deductions, the fact that a significant proportion of income from negatively geared assets is in the form of capital gains results in a high volume of revenue leakage from the government's perspective. Given the practical problems with accruals CGT, Australian policy makers should address the problem through other types of tax law reform. The potential revenue gains are one of several compelling policy reasons for doing so.

provide information that can be used to impute the revenue effects of a change in the CGT rate.

The following chapter presents the results of the quantitative component of this book. This is an empirical study on a more specific topic in the taxation of capital gains. Given that the three jurisdictions chosen for the qualitative study in Chapter 4 all tax capital gains at preferential rates—as do a number of other tax jurisdictions worldwide—there is a case for testing one of the possible benefits of preferential rate CGT: that is, whether the capital gains realisations response is large enough to cause a tax rate reduction to increase revenue collected. Although much research on this topic has been conducted in the United States, this is a largely unanswered question in the Australian context.

The results of the qualitative study in this chapter inform the quantitative study in Chapter 5. In summary, the literature reviewed in Chapter 2 appears to indicate that the case for a large capital gains preference is built on weak empirical foundations. Nonetheless, taxing capital gains preferentially is a practice that is currently applied in Australia, as well as in Canada and the United States. The disconnect between theory and practice on the taxation of capital gains, reinforced by the interviews in this chapter, provides a strong justification for an empirical study on the capital gains realisations response in Australia.

# CHAPTER 5

# Quantitative Results—Capital Gains Realisations Response Study

## 5.1 PURPOSE OF THE QUANTITATIVE STUDY

The qualitative study in Chapter 4 detailed the results of interviews that explored the views of CGT experts in Australia, Canada and the United States on the taxation of capital gains. A particular focus of the qualitative study was CGT rate preferences. The views of the experts indicate that the current system of taxing capital gains in Australia falls short of the ideal. According to the literature reviewed in Chapter 2—including Burman (1999), Cunningham and Schenk (1993), and Krever and Brooks (1990)—several of the supposed benefits of preferential rate CGT may be overstated. Many of the respondents interviewed in Chapter 4 were unconvinced as to the overall benefits of CGT rate preferences.

The results of the qualitative study in Chapter 4 inform the study in this chapter, which is focused on a more specific aspect of the taxation of capital gains—the capital gains realisations response for personal taxpayers in Australia. The fact that several interviewees questioned some of the claimed benefits of CGT rate preferences is sufficient motivation to revisit the predictions made by policy makers in 1999 about the benefits of the 50% CGT discount, including that the CGT discount would be self-financing.[1]

The quantitative study in this chapter is concerned with estimating the magnitude of the capital gains realisations response to changes in CGT rates for Australian personal taxpayers.[2] Australia has operated a preferential CGT regime in the form of the CGT discount since 21 September 1999. The enactment of this preferential CGT regime is the main rate change considered by the study.[3]

1 Senator Julian McGauran highlighted this point in parliament on 29 November 1999 (Commonwealth of Australia. Senate, 1999, p. 10,886) when he stated: 'importantly, the review was also requested to look at the business tax system in a revenue neutral context. We believe we have achieved this.'

2 This chapter draws on a previously published journal article. See Minas et al. (2018).

3 In addition to this major rate change, there have been some changes to the statutory tax rates applying to all forms of taxable income during the years of the study.

According to Burman and Randolph (1994), when taxpayers decide whether to sell specific assets in their portfolio, realising a capital gain is merely incidental, and it follows that taxpayers do not make the decision to realise capital gains directly. Realising a capital gain is necessarily a consequence of the primary decision to sell assets with an accrued capital gain. This point confirms the difficulty in determining how to model the capital gains realisations response. The issue is further confounded by the fact that although CGT is largely a discretionary tax, taxpayers regularly decide to sell assets with accrued capital gains and, in doing so, they voluntarily incur a CGT liability.

The majority of U.S. studies completed since 1980 indicate a lack of empirical support for a capital gains realisations response that is large enough to compensate for the static revenue loss from a CGT rate cut. One of the conclusions of the literature review in Chapter 2 was that the estimates from cross-sectional studies are inaccurate and unreliable and that, therefore, they should not inform estimates of revenue effects. Only a small proportion of time series and panel data studies report elasticity point estimates that imply a revenue increase from a CGT rate cut. Most of the realisations response literature concludes that a reduction in CGT rates will induce an increase in capital gains realisations. However, the debate on the capital gains realisations response is concerned with the magnitude of this response.

Previous research on the capital gains realisations response has used regression analysis to estimate the elasticity of tax rate changes on realisations while controlling for a number of non-tax factors. The study in this chapter uses the same approach to estimating the realisations response.

This chapter presents the results of an empirical study on the capital gains realisations response in Australia. The main aim of the study is to provide estimates of the capital gains realisations response that identify the revenue effect of the 1999 rate change and inform future tax policy in Australia. These estimates address a previously unanswered policy question: the extent to which tax rates influence the realisation of capital gains by personal taxpayers in Australia. The elasticity point estimates for the capital gains realisations response may be useful in forecasting the possible revenue effects of CGT rate changes. According to Clark (2014), the revenue estimates for CGT in Australia are difficult to predict, and the volatility of CGT has been a major contributor to revenue forecasting errors over the past 10 years.

In line with previous research in this area,[4] the quantitative study includes elasticity point estimates for various specifications. Each specification uses the available aggregate time series data. The estimates are useful in determining whether enactment of the 50% CGT discount led to revenue losses or gains. This information is of particular importance to policy makers who are contemplating changes to the CGT rate.

The structure of this chapter is as follows. Section 5.1 sets out background issues that confirm the importance of the capital gains realisations response to Australia. Section 5.2 presents the estimation results, and Section 5.3 presents the results for two sub-periods from the entire time series. The regressions using fewer observations are to confirm the robustness of the estimates. Regression results using the capital gains realisations of

4 Conducted outside of Australia.

companies are then set out in Section 5.4 as an additional robustness check. Finally, the conclusions on the quantitative study are set out in Section 5.5.

## 5.2 ESTIMATION RESULTS

This section sets out the results of the regression equations. The focus is on the main equation and the elasticity point estimates derived from that specification. This section includes an explanation of the preliminary steps involved in determining the preferred equation. The discussion now turns to the estimation results.

Table 13 presents the results for an initial regression. This regression is preliminary and non-preferred, so the table does not report elasticity point estimates.

**Table 13: Coefficients for initial regression (1988–89 to 2014–15)**

| | Expected sign | Coefficient | *t*-statistic |
|---|---|---|---|
| Constant | | –65.98** | –2.21 |
| *rTop marginal CGT rate* | – | –2.25*** | –3.29 |
| *rLn(ASX 200)* | + | 2.04*** | 6.42 |
| *rLn(Real GDP)* | + | 3.26** | 2.56 |
| *rLn(GDP deflator)* | – | –1.07*** | –4.10 |
| Adjusted $R^2$ | | 0.97 | |
| *F*-statistic *F*(4, 22) | | 243.42*** | |
| Durbin–Watson | | 1.38 | |
| Number of observations | | 27 | |

*Notes.* Asterisks denote significance at the 1% (***), 5% (**) and 10% (*) levels. The 'r' prefix for each variable refers to the raw data used in the level equation.

The dependent variable in the regression equation is discount capital gains. In the years after the CGT discount was introduced, this is the net capital gains reported by the Australian Taxation Office (2016), multiplied by the gross-up factor reported in Table 9.

The adjusted $R^2$ of 0.97 reported in Table 13 appears to indicate a spurious regression. Table 14 reports the calculations of pairwise correlation coefficients for the variables included in the initial regression, and Table 15 reports the variance inflation factors (VIFs) for the same variables.

**Table 14: Pairwise correlation coefficients—raw data**

| | *rLn(Discount capital gains)* | *rTop marginal CGT rate* | *rLn(ASX200)* | *rLn(Real GDP)* | *rLn(GDP deflator)* |
|---|---|---|---|---|---|
| *rLn(Discount capital gains)* | 1 | | | | |
| *rTop marginal CGT rate* | –0.9965*** | 1 | | | |
| *rLn(ASX 200)* | 1.0000*** | –0.9964*** | 1 | | |
| *rLn(Real GDP)* | 1.0000*** | –0.9971*** | 1.0000*** | 1 | |
| *rLn(GDP deflator)* | 0.8194*** | –0.8321*** | 0.8957*** | 0.9783*** | 1 |

*Notes.* Asterisks denote significance at the 1% (***), 5% (**) and 10% (*) levels.

**Table 15: Variance inflation factors (VIFs)—raw data**

| Variable | VIF |
|---|---|
| *rTop marginal CGT rate* | 5.16 |
| *rLn(ASX 200)* | 14.27 |
| *rLn(Real GDP)* | 77.96 |
| *rLn(GDP deflator)* | 34.83 |
| Mean VIF | 33.05 |

The correlation coefficients in Table 14 are high, which suggests that multicollinearity could be an issue. The VIFs for all variables, except the top marginal CGT rate, are greater than 10 and the mean VIF is 33.05, which suggests that the influence of multicollinearity is of a significant magnitude.

Differences of the variables were taken, and the pairwise correlation coefficients for the differenced variables, as reported in Table 16, are lower in magnitude in comparison with the raw data.[5] Table 17 reports the VIFs for the variables in first differences.

**Table 16: Pairwise correlation coefficients—data in first differences (1989–90 to 2014–15)**

| | *fdLn(Discount capital gains)* | *fdTop marginal CGT rate* | *fdLn(ASX 200)* | *fdLn(Real GDP)* | *fdLn(GDP deflator)* |
|---|---|---|---|---|---|
| *fdLn(Discount capital gains)* | 1 | | | | |
| *fdTop marginal CGT rate* | –0.2083 | 1 | | | |
| *fdLn(ASX 200)* | 0.5756*** | –0.1079 | 1 | | |
| *fdLn(Real GDP)* | 0.0052 | –0.0958 | 0.0604 | 1 | |
| *fdLn(GDP deflator)* | 0.0715 | –0.0021 | –0.2311 | 0.2885 | 1 |

*Notes.* Asterisks denote significance at the 1% (***), 5% (**) and 10% (*) levels.

**Table 17: Variance inflation factors (VIFs)—data in first differences**

| Variable | VIF |
|---|---|
| *fdTop marginal CGT rate* | 1.02 |
| *fdLn(ASX 200)* | 1.09 |
| *fdLn(Real GDP)* | 1.12 |
| *fdLn(GDP deflator)* | 1.17 |
| Mean VIF | 1.10 |

Although taking first differences of the data appears to have addressed the multicollinearity problem, it introduces another problem in relation to the time series data

5 The data were transformed into first differences by subtracting the value of the variable in the previous year from the value of the variable in the current year.

set used in the regressions. Specifically, any equation that is estimated in first-differences data is dependent on the main CGT rate change that occurred in the 1999–2000 tax year. The value in this type of estimate is questionable given there does not appear to be enough exploitable variation in the tax rates. Particularly, in the years 1999–2000 to 2014–15, there is little variation in tax rates from year to year in an equation estimated in first differences. The specific problem is that the capital gains realisations response study is concerned with the effects of a preferential CGT rate in all of these years. Although there was no change in the CGT rate for several of the post-CGT discount years, the CGT rate was considerably lower in the post-CGT discount years in comparison to the pre-CGT discount years. The latter phenomenon is of greater importance to the study than the former. Figure 1 illustrates the lack of variation in the CGT rate and confirms that this makes differencing the data problematic.

Figure 1: *fdLn(Discount capital gains)* plotted against the *fdTop marginal CGT rate*

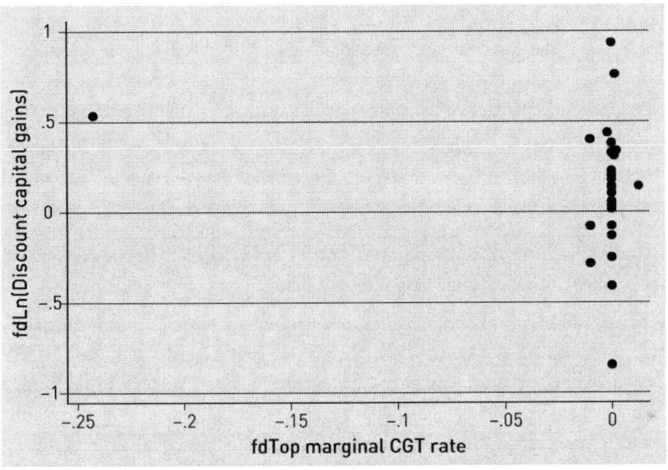


A solution to the multicollinearity problem, which does not result in the loss of variation in tax rates, is to detrend the data. As noted by Baum (2006), detrending removes the trend component from a time series by regressing the series on a time trend. According to Gujarati (2003), the problem of a spurious correlation can be avoided by introducing a time trend variable into the equation or by detrending the variables in the equation and running the regression on these detrended variables. The latter approach has been adopted for the equations in this chapter that use detrended data. As indicated in Figure 2, there is variation in the detrended data for *Ln(Discount capital gains)* and the top marginal CGT rate.

Figure 2: *Ln(Discount capital gains)* plotted against the *Top marginal CGT rate* (both detrended)

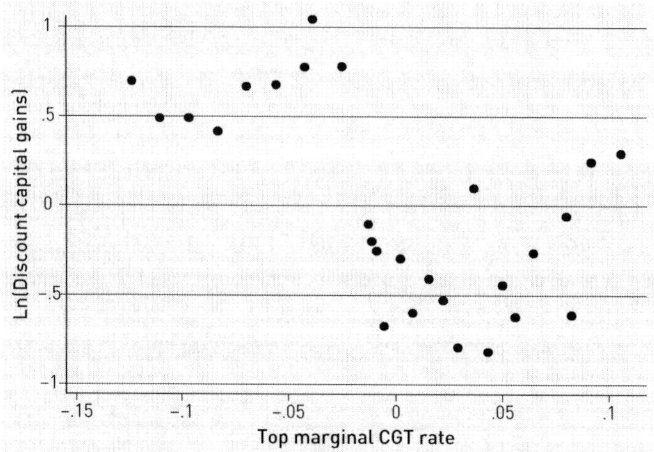


The pairwise correlation coefficients using detrended data are reported in Table 18 and the VIFs are reported in Table 19. It appears that multicollinearity is less of a problem in the detrended data in comparison with the pairwise correlation coefficients reported in Table 14. Consequently, the results of an equation using detrended data are less likely to be spurious compared to the results of the initial level equation.

**Table 18: Pairwise correlation coefficients—detrended data**

| | *Ln(Discount capital gains)* | *Top marginal CGT rate* | *Ln(ASX 200)* | *Ln(Real GDP)* | *Ln(GDP deflator)* |
|---|---|---|---|---|---|
| *Ln(Discount capital gains)* | 1 | | | | |
| *Top marginal CGT rate* | –0.5857*** | 1 | | | |
| *Ln(ASX 200)* | 0.8677*** | –0.3397* | 1 | | |
| *Ln(Real GDP)* | 0.7697*** | –0.5813*** | 0.5751*** | 1 | |
| *Ln(GDP deflator)* | –0.7328*** | 0.3466* | –0.5962*** | –0.4288** | 1 |

*Notes.* Asterisks denote significance at the 1% (***), 5% (**) and 10% (*) levels.

**Table 19: Variance inflation factors (VIFs)—detrended data**

| Variable | VIF |
|---|---|
| *Top marginal CGT rate* | 1.84 |
| *Ln(ASX 200)* | 3.08 |
| *Ln(Real GDP)* | 5.92 |
| *Ln(GDP deflator)* | 2.28 |
| Mean VIF | 3.28 |

All the equations in the remainder of this chapter use detrended data. The elasticity point estimates evaluated at two different tax rates are reported in Table 20. First, elasticity is estimated at a tax rate of 33.9%, being the average tax rate for all years of the time series. Second, elasticity is estimated at a 36.75% tax rate, which is the midpoint between the top marginal CGT rate and the statutory top marginal tax rate in 2014–15. The coefficients for all variables have their expected sign.

**Table 20: Capital gains realisations elasticity (1988–89 to 2014–15)**

| | | Coefficient | *t*-statistic |
|---|---|---|---|
| Constant | | –0.00<br>(0.036) | –0.00 |
| *Top marginal CGT rate* | | –2.15***<br>(0.668) | –3.19 |
| CG realisations elasticity | (at 33.9%): –0.73<br>(at 36.75%): –0.79 | | |
| *Ln(ASX 200)* | | 2.08***<br>(0.212) | 6.66 |
| *Ln(Real GDP)* | | 3.25*<br>(1.245) | 2.61 |
| *Ln(GDP deflator)* | | –3.13**<br>(1.261) | –2.48 |
| Adjusted $R^2$ | | 0.93 | |
| *F*-statistic $F(4, 22)$ | | 87.18*** | |
| Durbin–Watson | | 1.44 | |
| Number of observations | | 27 | |

*Notes.* Asterisks denote significance at the 1% (***), 5% (**) and 10% (*) levels. Standard errors are in parentheses.

The results in Table 20 indicate that at a 36.75% tax rate, the elasticity point estimate is –0.79. This implies that a 1% increase in the tax rate would result in a 0.79% decrease in the level of capital gains realisations. A further implication of an elasticity point estimate that is less than 1.00 in absolute value is that any additional realisations induced by the CGT discount would be of an insufficient magnitude to compensate for the static revenue loss from the CGT rate cut.[6]

Given that there are 27 observations in the time series, Table 21 reports bootstrap-estimated results. The coefficients on all four variables in the bootstrap-estimated equations are statistically significant.



6 Where the unitary elasticity assumption holds, the required elasticity for the revenue break-even point is –1.00.

Table 21: Capital gains realisations elasticity (1988–89 to 2014–15), bootstrapping 100 replications

| | | Coefficient | Z-statistic |
|---|---|---|---|
| Constant | | –0.00<br>(0.042) | –0.00 |
| *Top marginal CGT rate* | | –2.15***<br>(0.792) | –2.17 |
| CG realisations elasticity | (at 33.9%): –0.73<br>(at 36.75%): –0.79 | | |
| *Ln(ASX 200)* | | 2.08***<br>(0.421) | 4.94 |
| *Ln(Real GDP)* | | 3.25*<br>(1.721) | 1.89 |
| *Ln(GDP deflator)* | | –3.16*<br>(0.033) | –2.13 |
| Adjusted $R^2$ | | 0.94 | |
| Wald chi² (4) | | 323.32*** | |
| Durbin–Watson<br>Number of observations | | 1.44<br>27 | |

*Notes.* Asterisks denote significance at the 1% (***), 5% (**) and 10% (*) levels. Standard errors are in parentheses.

The Durbin–Watson statistic of 1.44 in Table 20 and Table 21 is indicative of positive autocorrelation, which is a concern given there are 27 observations. This issue is addressed by way of feasible generalised least squares (FGLS) estimates, specifically Prais–Winsten estimates. In the Prais–Winsten estimate of the main equation reported in Table 22 (the main table), the transformed Durbin–Watson statistic is 1.99, and the coefficients on all four variables are statistically significant at either the 1% level—in the case of *Ln(ASX 200)* and *Ln(Real GDP)*—or 5% level—for the *Top marginal CGT rate* and *Ln(GDP deflator)*.

Table 23 reports the results of estimates for the main equation except that the CGT rate variable is in log form. Since in a log-log equation the coefficient is equal to the elasticity point estimate, the elasticity is –0.61. Notably, there are only minor differences in the coefficients and *t*statistics, in comparison to the results reported in Table 22. The results in Table 23 may allay concerns about the semi-log specification in the main equation producing results that are biased towards zero, given the similarity of the point estimates when the functional form is altered. The results for the alternative form imply that the equation is robust to changes in specification.

**Table 22: Capital gains realisations elasticity (1988–89 to 2014–15) (main table), Prais–Winsten**

| | | Coefficient | Z-statistic |
|---|---|---|---|
| Constant | | –0.00<br>(0.052) | –0.00 |
| *Top marginal CGT rate* | | –1.75**<br>(0.779) | –2.24 |
| CG realisations elasticity | (at 33.9%): –0.59<br>(at 36.75%): –0.64 | | |
| *Ln(ASX 200)* | | 1.89***<br>(0.343) | 5.53 |
| *Ln(Real GDP)* | | 4.19***<br>(1.417) | 2.96 |
| *Ln(GDP deflator)* | | –3.74**<br>(1.422) | –2.63 |
| Adjusted $R^2$ | | 0.87 | |
| *F*-statistic $F(4, 22)$ | | 45.52*** | |
| Durbin–Watson<br>Number of observations | | 1.99<br>27 | |

*Notes.* Asterisks denote significance at the 1% (***), 5% (**) and 10% (*) levels. Standard errors are in parentheses.

5

**Table 23: Capital gains realisations elasticity (1988–89 to 2014–15) for a log-log specification, Prais–Winsten**

| | Coefficient | *t*-statistic |
|---|---|---|
| Constant | –0.00<br>(0.052) | –0.02 |
| *Top marginal CGT rate* | –0.61*<br>(0.271) | –2.27 |
| CG realisations elasticity: –0.61 | | |
| *Ln(ASX 200)* | 1.89***<br>(0.342) | 5.53 |
| *Ln(Real GDP)* | 4.21***<br>(1.407) | 2.99 |
| *Ln(GDP deflator)* | –3.78**<br>(1.417) | –2.67 |
| Adjusted $R^2$ | 0.87 | |
| *F*-statistic $F(4, 22)$ | 46.02*** | |
| Durbin–Watson<br>Number of observations | 1.99<br>27 | |

*Notes.* Asterisks denote significance at the 1% (***), 5% (**) and 10% (*) levels. Standard errors are in parentheses.

## 5.3 ADDITIONAL ANALYSES—ALTERNATIVE SAMPLE PERIODS

Some of the U.S. time series studies have shown an unusually high level of sensitivity to a change in the sample period. For example, Jones (1989) confirmed the sensitivity to 1986 in U.S. studies by finding that the inclusion or non-inclusion of a dummy variable for 1986, in a 1948–86 sample period, caused the elasticity point estimates to vary from –0.89 to –0.25.

It was appropriate to test the robustness of the results for the main equation in this book. The robustness of these results was tested by two separate checks. In the first of these, the first two years were excluded from the sample period. In the second test, the last two years were excluded.

### Sub-period 1: 1990–91 to 2014–15

Table 24 reports the results for the main specification, with the years 1988–89 and 1989–90 excluded from the time series. The purpose of obtaining estimates with these two years excluded is to provide an additional robustness test. Nevertheless, the results should be interpreted with caution given the reduced number of observations. Excluding the first two tax years from the regression has the effect of decreasing the magnitude of the elasticity point estimate (in absolute terms) to –0.58 at a 33.9% tax rate and to –0.63 at a 36.75% CGT rate.[7] The coefficient on the CGT rate variable is significant at the 5% level.

**Table 24: Capital gains realisations elasticity (1990–91 to 2014–15) as per main equation, Prais–Winsten**

| | | Coefficient | *t*-statistic |
|---|---|---|---|
| Constant | | –0.01<br>(0.056) | 0.16 |
| *Top marginal CGT rate* | | –1.71**<br>(0.813) | –2.10 |
| CG realisations elasticity | (at 33.9%): –0.58<br>(at 36.75%): –0.63 | | |
| *Ln(ASX 200)* | | 1.95***<br>(0.367) | 5.31 |
| *Ln(Real GDP)* | | 4.15***<br>(1.469) | 2.83 |
| *Ln(GDP deflator)* | | –3.57**<br>(1.554) | –2.30 |
| Adjusted $R^2$ | | 0.87 | |
| *F*-statistic $F(4, 20)$ | | 39.65*** | |
| Durbin–Watson | | 1.97 | |
| Number of observations | | 25 | |

*Notes.* Asterisks denote significance at the 1% (***), 5% (**) and 10% (*) levels. Standard errors are in parentheses.

7 In comparison to the estimates from the main equation with all 27 observations.

The results reported in Table 24 indicate that the main specification is robust to changes in the years that are included in each regression. The adjusted $R^2$ for this specification is 0.87 and, as is the case for the results of the main specification, the *F*-statistic is significant at the 1% level.

### Sub-period 2: 1988–89 to 2012–13

The sensitivity analysis in this section also considers the effects of omitting two years from the end of the time series. The regression results reported in Table 25 are for the years 1988–89 to 2012–13. When the years 2013–14 and 2014–15 are omitted from the time series, the coefficient on the CGT rate variable is lower in magnitude, in absolute terms, than for the main equation (–1.37 compared with –1.75).

**Table 25: Capital gains realisations elasticity (1988–89 to 2012–13) as per main equation, Prais–Winsten**

| | | Coefficient | *t*-statistic |
|---|---|---|---|
| Constant | | 0.00<br>(0.032) | 0.02 |
| *Top marginal CGT rate* | | –1.37*<br>(0.667) | –2.06 |
| CG realisations elasticity | (at 33.9%): –0.47<br>(at 36.75%): –0.51 | | |
| *Ln(ASX 200)* | | 1.55***<br>(1.547) | 4.45 |
| *Ln(Real GDP)* | | 4.04***<br>(1.127) | 3.59 |
| *Ln(GDP deflator)* | | –0.08***<br>(0.021) | –3.59 |
| Adjusted $R^2$ | | 0.94 | |
| *F*-statistic $F(4, 20)$ | | 99.67*** | |
| Durbin–Watson | | 1.80 | |
| Number of observations | | 25 | |

*Notes.* Asterisks denote significance at the 1% (***), 5% (**) and 10% (*) levels. Standard errors are in parentheses.



## 5.4 THE CAPITAL GAINS REALISATIONS OF COMPANIES

The focus of capital gains realisations response studies has been on personal taxpayers rather than companies or other entity types. Burman and Plesko (2002) found a high degree of correlation between the capital gains realisations of individuals and companies in the United States for the years 1955 to 1999. Specifically, the correlation for the two sets of time series data (individual and corporate capital gains) was 0.97, and both sets of time series data were adjusted for inflation to remove spurious correlation. This finding is of interest given that the tax rates for personal taxpayers and companies are not the same, which implies that the similar pattern of capital gains realisations for both types of taxpayer means that tax rates may not be the most important determinant of realisations.

Plesko (2002) used time series data on the capital gains realisations of companies to test for omitted variables that were common to time series equations for the realisations of individuals and companies. As part of that study, Plesko (2002) examined the pattern of realisations of capital gains for corporations and compared this with the capital gains realisations of individuals over the same years. One of the findings was that the capital gains realisations of individuals and corporations were highly correlated even for years in which the tax rates for individuals and corporations were divergent.

This section of the book considers the capital gains realisations of companies using a similar regression specification to the main equation. This may provide a better understanding of how important (or not) the tax rate is as a determinant of capital gains realisations.

Using the same years as in the regression equations, there is a correlation of 0.91 between the capital gains realisations for Australian individuals and companies. As indicated in Figure 3, the correlation appears to be especially pronounced in the earlier and later years of the time series. The high degree of correlation is notwithstanding the fact that the 50% CGT discount for individuals, which commenced in 1999–2000, has never been available to companies.

Figure 3: Individual and company capital gains realisations, 1989–90 to 2014–15 (in millions of 2014 Australian dollars)

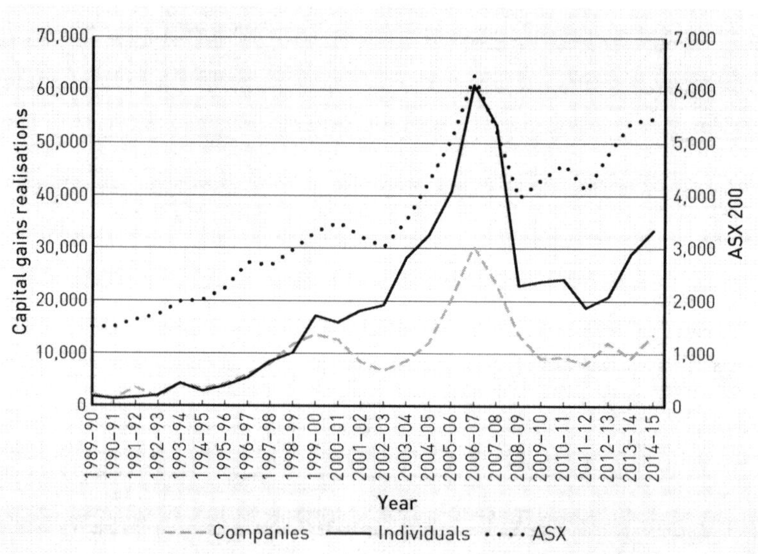


Figure 3 indicates there is a divergence in the realisations of companies and personal taxpayers that occurred around the time that the CGT discount commenced. This may reflect a short-run realisations response for the capital gains realisations of personal taxpayers that could be larger in magnitude than the long-run response. However, the long-run response is of greater interest to policy makers.

In Australia during the years 1989–90 to 2013–14, there were five different statutory tax rates for companies.[8] From 1989–90 to 1991–92, the company tax rate was 39%. In 1993–94, the rate was reduced to 33%, with same rate applying in 1994–95. The company tax rate increased to 36% in 1995–96, and it was then reduced to 34% in 1999–2000 and to 30% in 2000–01. The rate did not change from 30% in the remaining years of the time series.

As indicated in Figure 4, there is some correlation between the pattern of changes in the company tax rate and the top marginal rate of tax on capital gains for individuals. A notable difference is that for companies there is no rate preference for capital gains. If one assumes that tax rates are important to realisation decisions, it would follow that companies have less of an incentive to realise capital gains compared to individuals, in the absence of a preference for corporate capital gains. However, the correlation in the realisations of individual and corporate capital gains in Figure 3 suggests that the tax rate may not be the most important determinant of capital gains realisations.

Figure 4: Individual and company tax rates on capital gains (%), 1989–90 to 2014–15

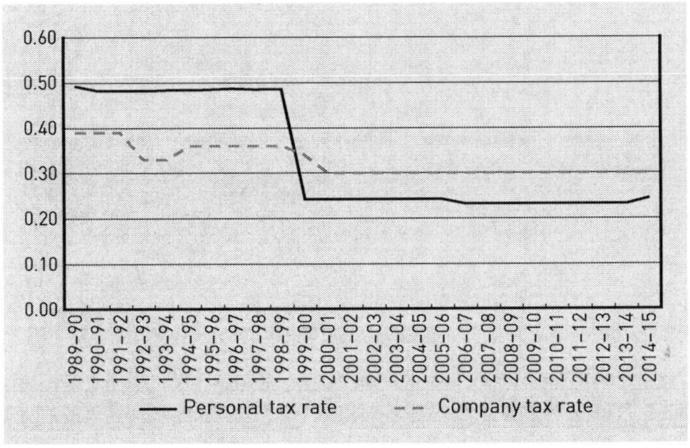


*Notes:* The tax rate for individuals is the top marginal CGT rate used in the regressions for personal taxpayers.

The pattern of capital gains realisations for individuals and companies, as per Figure 3, appears to confirm that the ASX 200 variable is an important influence on the capital gains realisations of individuals and companies. Specifically, when this index was at its highest, in 2007, the capital gains realisations of both taxpayer types were also at their highest levels, and after the index declined in subsequent years, so too did capital gains realisations.

The number of rate changes applying to companies may provide additional evidence on the capital gains realisations response. The regression equation for the capital gains realisations of companies is the same as the main equation for personal taxpayers.

Table 26 reports the results of the regression for the capital gains realisations of companies. The coefficient on the tax rate variable is not statistically significant, and it does not have the expected minus sign. It may be that, for companies, tax rates are an even less

8 In Australia, companies are taxed at a single tax rate that applies from the first dollar of taxable income.

important determinant of capital gains realisations than they are for personal taxpayers. Table 26 does not include elasticity point estimates, as it is considered that the results of the regression cannot be used to precisely estimate the capital gains realisations response of companies (Minas et al., 2018).

**Table 26: Corporate capital gains (1989–90 to 2014–15), Prais–Winsten**

| | Coefficient | *t*-statistic |
|---|---|---|
| Constant | 0.00<br>(0.038) | 0.02 |
| Company tax rate | 2.09<br>(2.412) | 0.87 |
| *Ln(ASX 200)* | 2.48***<br>(0.355) | 6.98 |
| *Ln(Real GDP)* | 4.53*<br>(2.553) | 1.77 |
| *Ln(GDP deflator)* | −1.77<br>(1.203) | −1.47 |
| Adjusted $R^2$ | 0.85 | |
| $F$-statistic $F(4, 21)$ | 36.64*** | |
| Durbin–Watson | 1.97 | |
| Number of observations | 26 | |

*Notes.* Asterisks denote significance at the 1% (***), 5% (**) and 10% (*) levels. Standard errors are in parentheses.

The coefficient on the ASX 200 variable has a positive sign, as expected. It is statistically significant at the 1% level and higher in magnitude than the coefficient on the same variable reported in the regression for individual taxpayers (Table 22).

Table 27 presents corporate capital gains regression results as per the equation for the results reported in Table 26, except that the tax rate used is the top marginal CGT rate for individuals. As for the previous equation, the ASX 200 variable is statistically significant at the 1% level. These results appear to support the estimates from the regressions for personal taxpayers. Importantly, the coefficient on the CGT rate for personal taxpayers is not statistically significant when included in the regression for companies. This statistically non-significant result for the dependent variable in the specification gives credence to the results of the regressions for personal taxpayers.

Table 27: Corporate capital gains (1989–90 to 2014–15): Corporate tax rate replaced with personal tax rate, Prais–Winsten

| | Coefficient | *t*-statistic |
|---|---|---|
| Constant | 0.00<br>(0.00) | 0.00 |
| *Top marginal CGT rate* | 0.57<br>(0.79) | 0.71 |
| *Ln(ASX 200)* | 2.43***<br>(0.35) | 6.94 |
| *Ln(Real GDP)* | 5.40*<br>(2.96) | 1.82 |
| *Ln(Real GDP deflator)* | −1.60<br>(1.17) | −1.37 |
| Adjusted $R^2$ | 0.86 | |
| *F*-statistic *F*(4, 21) | 37.93*** | |
| Durbin–Watson | 1.97 | |
| Number of observations | 26 | |

*Notes.* Asterisks denote significance at the 1% (***), 5% (**) and 10% (*) levels. Standard errors are in parentheses.

5

## 5.5 CONCLUSIONS ON THE CAPITAL GAINS REALISATIONS RESPONSE STUDY

This chapter examined the capital gains realisations response to the introduction of the 50% CGT discount for personal taxpayers in Australia and addressed hypothesis H1.[9]

The estimates from the capital gains realisations response study indicate that although the CGT rate is of some importance in the decision to realise capital gains, the realisations response for Australian personal taxpayers is moderate in magnitude. The estimates also imply that the 50% CGT discount is likely to have caused a loss of taxation revenue, as increased realisations in response to the tax rate decrease may have been insufficient in magnitude to compensate for the static revenue loss. Assumed in the analysis is that the unitary elasticity rule applies to the Australian setting.[10] The elasticity point estimates in all specifications and at all tax rates imply that only a proportion of the static revenue loss from the CGT discount has been recouped through increased realisations as a result of the CGT rate change. For example, using the estimates from the main table, the −0.59 elasticity at the 33.9% tax rate implies that 59% of the static revenue loss has been recovered by way of increased realisations.

9 The 50% CGT discount for personal taxpayers, introduced in the 1999–2000 tax year, is likely to have caused a decrease in CGT revenue over the long run.

10 This assumption would be rejected if detailed revenue forecasts demonstrated that the unitary elasticity rule did not hold.

The conclusion of the study in this chapter is that the CGT discount is of limited importance to decisions to realise capital gains. The point estimates from all specifications indicate that the elasticity is less than 1.00 in absolute value, irrespective of the tax rate at which elasticity is measured.

Although this book does not attempt to estimate a revenue-maximising tax rate, the results of this chapter imply that the revenue-maximising tax rate is higher than the rate effected by the enactment of the CGT discount.

For this study, regressions using the main equation and alternative sample periods tested the robustness of the results. The conclusion here was that for each of the two alternative sample periods—1990–91 to 2014–15 and 1988–89 to 2012–13—the tax rate coefficient was of a lower magnitude compared to the results for the full time series.

Zodrow (1992) noted the limitations of time series data and recommended caution in basing policy prescriptions on a single set of time series estimates. However, as noted in the literature review chapter, some capital gains realisations response researchers prefer time series in comparison to micro data (Eichner & Sinai, 2000). The known limitations of aggregate time series were informative to this study. Consideration was given to taking first differences of the data, and it was established this was not appropriate for the analysis. Consequently, the data were detrended to enhance the analysis and to minimise the limitations of the time series data.

Limitations common to capital gains realisations response studies also apply to this study. One example is that despite the importance of accrued gains to the realisation decisions of taxpayers, there is an absence of data on the stock of accrued capital gains.

Auten et al. (1989, p. 353) highlighted another limitation underlying estimates of realisations response, noting that 'absent a clear behavioural model, econometric analysis is as much art as science and artistic interpretations clearly vary on this subject.' Gravelle (1990) referred to the limitations of realisations response studies presenting policy makers with the challenge of using imperfect information to decide how to include a tax provision in the budgetary process. Furthermore, Burman and Randolph (1994) noted that the findings of realisations response studies are not useful in determining the effects of CGT on the cost and allocation of capital between different investment types.

A limitation of the realisations response study in this chapter is that the sample size is fairly small ($n = 27$ in most cases). Furthermore, the estimates from the realisations response study in this book are subject to the limitations that are common to all such studies. According to Krever and Brooks (1990), not much weight should be given to capital gains realisations response studies in deciding the rate at which to tax capital gains. Some of the reasons for this are that the revenue effects are unlikely to be large, and disparities in some elasticity studies may lead to the conclusion that the question of revenue effects of CGT rate changes is largely indeterminate (Krever & Brooks, 1990). Furthermore, Krever and Brooks argued that the revenue yield should not be the primary consideration in enacting a CGT and that the lock-in effect is only an important influence in a narrow range of cases. Auerbach (1988) noted that there is nothing especially important about the revenue break-even point and it may make good economic sense to reduce a distortionary tax even if this had the effect of reducing revenue.

Notwithstanding the merits of these arguments, this book argues that Australian policy makers should consider the results of a capital gains realisations response study using Australian data when determining the CGT rate. This is especially the case given the claims of positive revenue effects made by policy makers responsible for the introduction of the 50% CGT discount.[11] In the absence of empirical evidence, such claims amount to little more than assumptions, and if they continue to be untested and are in fact wrong, there is a risk that several billion dollars of CGT revenue could be lost during the years that the CGT discount is in operation.

It is apparent that nominal increases in CGT realisations are not necessarily indicative of a large realisations response. A question that realisations response studies address is: to what extent do lower tax rates cause increases in capital gains realisations? Importantly, the estimating equations in these studies typically include variables for the non-tax factors that influence capital gains realisations. Where the elasticity point estimates are low or moderate, it may be that increases in capital gains realisations relate more to non-tax determinants such as an improvement in economic conditions or in the performance of the Australian stock market, rather than the CGT rate. If it is the case that such non-tax variables are more of an influence on capital gains realisations than the CGT rate (or a change in the CGT rate), it might be the case that, in theory, a similar level of realisations would occur even if the CGT rate had remained unchanged or was moderately increased.



Certain issues appear less relevant to the capital gains realisations response in Australia than in the United States. For example, in the Australian context, there seems to be no compelling reason to include an independent variable for tax rate expectations in any of the specifications (Minas et al., 2018). This is because Australia has not had the same experience as the United States of several changes in the CGT rate over time. Furthermore, at the time of the enactment of the CGT discount in Australia, policy makers did not characterise it as a temporary CGT rate change.[12] The fact that the Henry Review recommendation to slightly reduce the rate of the CGT discount was unequivocally rejected by the then Rudd Government may add to taxpayers' expectations that the CGT rate is unlikely to change. Another institutional difference between the two jurisdictions is that Australia has not had the experience of pre-announced changes in the CGT rate, as in the United States. Thus, the transitory response to pre-announced CGT rate changes is less relevant to the analysis of capital gains realisations response in Australia. A further notable difference between the Australian and U.S. tax systems is that Australia does not have state income taxes.

The elasticity point estimates from the main table of –0.59 at a 33.9% CGT rate and –0.64 at a 36.75% CGT rate imply that the capital gains realisations response is insufficient to compensate for the static revenue loss from the introduction of the CGT discount. Although the elasticity point estimate from the main equation indicates that there is the expected inverse relationship between tax rates and realisations, it also implies

11 Policy makers deferred to the estimates of positive revenue effects contained in the Ralph Report; these are summarised in Table 1 in Chapter 2.

12 As noted earlier in the book, the CGT discount was not described as a permanent policy change either.

that the CGT discount appears to have led to lost CGT revenue. Where a CGT rate cut takes effect at a time when there is economic growth, there is a possibility that policy makers may attribute increases in CGT revenue to the rate cut rather than the economic growth.

It is indicated by Australian Treasury (2019) that the CGT discount has had a cumulative static revenue cost of several billion dollars during the time it has been in operation. For example, the Australian Treasury (2019) estimated that the forgone revenue from the 50% CGT discount for individuals and trusts in 2018–19 was $9.35 billion. Increasing the rate of CGT for individuals by removing part of the 50% CGT discount was one of the recommendations of the Henry Review,[13] and the more recent Murray Report into the financial system considered its entire removal (Murray, 2014).[14] The Henry Review recommendation and the results in this chapter indicate that reducing the CGT discount is clearly a tax policy reform worth pursuing. Removing or reducing the CGT discount would improve vertical and horizontal equity and could prove effective in the reduction of the budget deficit,[15] given the estimated realisations response of less than 1.00 in absolute value. This latter aspect may prove to be a critical consideration in any review of the Australian tax system in the near future. It is hoped that this chapter will contribute to a more informed and evidence-based debate about the implications of changes to the CGT rate. As outlined earlier, the lack of empirical evidence on the realisations response in 1999 may have impeded the quality of the debate that preceded the enactment of the 50% CGT discount. Although there have been some recent policy arguments for taxing capital gains at lower rates than other income, there appears to be no compelling policy reason for a CGT rate preference as generous as Australia's 50% CGT discount. The case for taxing capital gains at highly preferential tax rates appears to lack rigorous policy foundations. In light of this, there is no reason for governments to forgo CGT revenue unnecessarily. The results of this chapter indicate that the CGT discount is likely to have resulted in such revenue losses.

This chapter presented the results of an empirical study on the capital gains realisations response. The motivation for this study was the lack of previous empirical work in Australia on this important topic. The literature review in Chapter 2 outlined arguments for and against CGT preferences. Notably, some of the arguments in favour of CGT preferences are unsupported by sound empirical evidence. The interview study in Chapter 4 confirmed the need for an empirical quantitative study, given that several of the CGT experts interviewed identified that political considerations were a reason for CGT rate preferences in a tax system.

As outlined in the preceding chapters, the rate at which to set CGT is one of several considerations for policy makers. More broadly, policy makers should consider several

13 Recommendation 14 of the Henry Review (which was not accepted by the then Rudd Government) suggested that the CGT discount should be reduced from 50% to 40%, effectively increasing the rate at which capital gains are taxed (Henry & Australia, 2010).

14 The Murray Report notes that reducing CGT concessions would result in a more efficient allocation of funding in the economy.

15 Taxing capital gains at the same rate as other income would also reduce the complexity of the tax system.

aspects of good policy in making decisions about CGT and CGT rates. The capital gains realisations response study in this chapter has provided evidence on the likely revenue implications of a CGT rate change. The estimates imply that the CGT rate cut in 1999–2000 led to CGT revenue losses. To the extent that the main estimating equation is correctly specified, the policy justification for the CGT discount—the potential for increases in CGT revenue—is redundant.

Chapters 4 and 5 of this book suggested there is a need for CGT policy change, based upon qualitative and quantitative analysis and evidence. Chapter 6 will now examine the policy options for taxing the capital gains of individuals in Australia, and will consider a specific recommendation on how CGT for personal taxpayers in Australia might be more effectively reformed.

# CHAPTER 6

# Policy Options for Taxing Capital Gains in Australia

## 6.1 INTRODUCTION

The literature review in Chapter 2 outlined the arguments for and against a preferential rate CGT. Although there is an argument that lower tax rates may improve efficiency in a tax system, there is inefficiency by way of a distortion to investment decisions resulting from a difference in the tax rate on ordinary income and capital gains. Moreover, some of the claimed benefits of lower CGT rates have been difficult to prove empirically. For example, Burman (1999) found that numerous changes in U.S. CGT rates between 1954 and 1996 had no perceptible effect on economic growth.

Henry and Australia (2010) recommended reducing the CGT discount from its current 50% to 40%[1] and proposed that the same 40% discount rate would apply to other forms of non-labour income such as dividends and interest. However, in 2010, the then Federal Labor Government ruled out adopting this recommendation (Swan & Rudd, 2010, 2 May).[2] More recently, Murray (2014) has considered—though stopped short of recommending—the removal of the CGT discount.

Issues concerned with the appropriateness of the CGT discount continue to be raised. For example, Justice Richard Edmonds of the Federal Court questioned whether the enactment of the 50% CGT discount constituted good tax reform given that it contravened a number of important tax design principles (Edmonds, 2015). Justice Edmonds considered it surprising that the Henry Review did not recommend the removal of the 50% CGT discount: 'Indeed, Henry did not even consider its merit by reference to the tax policy criteria it advocated for the structural design of the tax system' (Edmonds, 2015, p. 402). Furthermore, Edmonds considered it important that the abolition of the

1 This effectively would result in a higher rate of CGT given that 60%, rather than 50%, of net capital gains would be included in taxable income in instances where the discount method applied.

2 This was among a list of several policies based on recommendations of the Henry Review that the then government would not implement supposedly 'in the interests of business and community certainty' (Swan & Rudd, 2010, 2 May).

existing CGT discount be 'brought to the table' for consideration and informed discussion (Edmonds, 2015, p. 403).

At around the same time, it was implied in a question posed in the Tax Discussion Paper issued by the Australian Federal Government in March 2015 that there may be a need to consider CGT policy alternatives to the CGT discount. Specifically, the discussion paper contained the following question: 'to what extent is the rationale for the CGT discount, and the size of the discount, still appropriate?' (Australia. Treasury, 2015b, p. 193). This question, on the appropriateness and magnitude of the CGT discount, is relevant to the research question in this book. However, it is arguably a biased question in that the use of the wording 'still appropriate' may be perceived as presupposing that there was a convincing rationale for the CGT discount prior to its introduction in 1999. It is the argument of this book that the enactment of the CGT discount was in the absence of a clear tax policy rationale.

Notwithstanding this point, it is important to consider whether there are other policy instruments that may be more appropriate and relevant than the CGT discount. Hence, this chapter considers various options for reforming the taxation of capital gains of personal taxpayers in Australia. The alternatives considered and the ultimate recommendations are informed by the literature review in Chapter 2, which outlined some of the arguments for and against preferential CGT rates, as well as the studies in Chapters 4 and 5. The results of the interview study in Chapter 4 revealed that many respondents were not in favour of extant (or indeed any) CGT rate preferences, and the results reported in Chapter 5 imply that the CGT discount has lost tax revenue.

The policy options considered in the remainder of this chapter are as follows: taxing capital gains at full marginal tax rates (with or without an inflation adjustment of cost base); reducing the rate of the CGT discount; taper relief; and the introduction of an annual exempt amount (AEA) for net capital gains. The first of these options (with the inflation adjustment) is the system of taxing capital gains that operated in Australia between 1985 and 1999.[3] Policy makers considered the second option as recently as the 2019 Australian federal election. The third option (taper relief) is, as will be shown, the least preferred of the alternatives. Evans et al. (2015) outlined in detail the case for the fourth option—an AEA. Although policy makers in Australia have not proposed an AEA, it is a viable alternative to the current CGT regime. This chapter outlines the case for an AEA in detail and includes estimates of the revenue implications of enacting the policy. The elasticity estimates in Chapter 5 form the basis of the revenue estimates in this chapter.

A policy option not explored in this chapter is taxing capital gains under a separate schedule. In principle, the structure of the Australian tax system is on a global, rather than schedular, basis. Taxing capital gains under a separate schedule would represent a significant departure from the current approach. Furthermore, such a change would be difficult to justify according to tax design principles. Notably, one of the American

3 Indexation of cost base was part of the Australian CGT regime as originally enacted in 1985. However, indexation applies in limited instances today. The indexation method is becoming less relevant over time as it can only apply to assets with a pre-September 1999 acquisition date. In such instances the taxpayer can compare the indexation and discount methods and choose the one that results in the lower net capital gain.

interviewees recommended that the separate schedule for the taxation of capital gains in the United States be replaced with an exclusion along the lines of that used in countries like Australia, Canada and South Africa.[4]

## 6.2 TAXING CAPITAL GAINS AT FULL MARGINAL TAX RATES

One of the main weaknesses of taxing capital gains at lower rates than other forms of income is the incentive this creates for taxpayers to characterise ordinary income as capital gains (Minas, 2011). There are efficiency costs associated with taxpayers seeking to convert ordinary income into capital gains, including the fact that governments may be required to increase the rate of other distortionary taxes in order to recoup some of the revenue lost to this activity (Auerbach, 1988). CGT has been characterised as being, essentially, an anti-avoidance measure that protects the income tax base by eliminating the incentive that would exist in its absence to convert ordinary income into capital gains (Institute for Fiscal Studies [Great Britain], 1995).

Slemrod (1992, p. 254) suggested that greater attention is paid to eliminating those parts of tax systems that 'provide rewards to taxpayers for changing the timing of transactions or for repackaging their financial claims'. Slemrod noted that taxpayers were quick to exploit such opportunities and their doing so was socially unproductive and at a cost to Treasury revenues. Notably, Slemrod saw the preferential treatment of capital gains as an activity in this category.



As outlined in Chapter 2, preferential CGT rates are counter to the good tax policy objectives of vertical and horizontal equity. According to Evans (2000), equity is the essential reason for the taxation of capital gains. A tax system with a preferential CGT rate compromises vertical equity, since the heavily skewed distribution of capital gains means that high-income taxpayers receive most of the benefit of the preference. Horizontal equity requires consistent treatment of taxpayers with the same income. A tax system where the proportion of taxable income that is capital gains influences a taxpayer's average tax rate is one that does not satisfy the policy criterion of horizontal equity. The integrity and fairness of the tax system can be improved by aligning the tax rate on capital gains and other forms of income.

Prior to the enactment of the 50% CGT discount in 1999, Australia taxed capital gains at full marginal rates with indexation of cost base. In the event that policy makers decided to abolish the CGT discount and tax capital gains at full marginal rates again, a further consideration would be whether to allow the indexation of cost base. The indexation regime ensured that the taxation of net capital gains was on real rather than nominal capital gains by allowing an inflation adjustment of the cost base of an asset. Importantly, the introduction of the indexation regime was at a time of relatively high inflation compared to the current experience with relatively low rates of inflation; for example, according to the ABS, the weighted average inflation rate increased by 7.6% between September 1984

4 Respondent A on Question Six.

and September 1985, but only by 1.0% between June 2015 and June 2016 (ABS, 2016b). The indexation of cost base does not constitute preferential treatment for capital gains; rather, it ensures that real rather than inflationary gains are subject to CGT. However, there is not a compelling need for the indexation of cost base in the current environment of low inflation.

Although there is merit in the argument that inflationary gains should not be subject to taxation, it is difficult to justify inflation adjustments to the cost base of capital gains assets and not to other parts of the tax system. Where inflation adjustments apply to net capital gains and not to other parts of the tax system, there are compromises to equity and efficiency, as well as arbitrage opportunities arising from the fact that the various parts of the tax base are subject to different inflation rules. Furthermore, the consumer price index is not a precise adjustment to the cost of living (Burman, 1999).

On balance, indexation need not be part of a regime that taxes capital gains at full marginal rates given its effect on complexity and the current environment of low inflation. Nevertheless, policy makers in Australia might view indexation as a necessary feature of a CGT regime that taxes capital gains at full marginal rates.

Chapter 2 reviewed the benefits that proponents of preferential CGT rates advanced. Several of those benefits lack empirical support. For example, there is limited empirical support for the view that a reduction in CGT rates enhances economic growth and increases savings. According to Burman (1999), a rate differential between capital gains and other income has a very small effect on the economy and it is indeterminate whether this effect is positive or negative.

The results of the study in Chapter 5 imply that, in the Australian context, increasing the CGT rate is likely to increase CGT revenue in the long run. This may allow policy makers to lower statutory tax rates. A previous example of this occurrence was in the case of the *TRA86* in the United States, which aligned the top rates of tax on capital gains and ordinary income. Essentially, the policy gave effect to an increase in the former and a decrease in the latter.

Based on the results of the qualitative and quantitative studies in this book, there is a compelling case for restoring taxation of capital gains at full marginal rates. Indeed, this is the tax policy ideal when considering the options for reform presented in this chapter. Nevertheless, this ideal may not be readily achievable in light of the effect of political considerations on CGT policy highlighted in the Chapter 4 interview study. These considerations apply to the current Australian CGT policy setting in which, despite the merits of taxing capital gains at full marginal rates, there is some reluctance from policy makers to revert to the pre-September 1999 CGT regime from the current low rates. It is possible to achieve reform of CGT that improves horizontal and vertical equity and increases tax revenue—albeit to a lesser degree than CGT at full marginal rates—by reducing the rate of the CGT discount. If this course of action is pursued it should be accompanied by a longer-term goal of restoring full-rate CGT. Reducing the rate of the CGT discount is the focus of the following section.

## 6.3 REDUCING THE RATE OF THE CGT DISCOUNT

This section considers the policy reform option of decreasing the rate of exclusion from assessable income for net capital gains.

Although a government can choose to enact the reinstatement of CGT at full marginal tax rates, the qualitative interview study in Chapter 4 highlighted the political influences on the tax reform process. Specifically, there was consensus among the interview population on the necessity of incorporating CGT rate preferences in a tax system being, at least partly, attributable to political considerations. Although the interpretation of 'political' in this context varied between respondents, some referred to political constraints and perceived difficulties in reversing a decision to introduce a preferential CGT rate. Moreover, some of the respondents based in Canada were of the view that it would be politically difficult to tax capital gains at full marginal tax rates. As outlined earlier in this chapter, similar political difficulties might also apply to the Australian context.

Given the political barriers to restoring taxation of capital gains at full marginal rates, one of several possible second-best solutions is to reduce the magnitude of the CGT discount. Although it is less than the policy ideal of taxation of capital gains at full marginal rates, it would improve vertical and horizontal equity and would be likely to result in an increase in CGT revenue. Reducing the CGT discount may be characterised as a necessary compromise to achieve an improved policy outcome. Such a reform has a high degree of political acceptability. In 2010, the then Rudd Labor Government swiftly ruled out the Henry Review recommendation to reduce the CGT discount to 40%; yet, more recently, the Labor Opposition led by Bill Shorten proposed a 25% CGT discount as one of its policies during the 2016 federal election campaign (Taylor, 2016).[5]



The case for reducing the rate of the CGT discount has been made by business and professional organisations outside the policy making process. The 2015 *Re:think Tax Discussion Paper* invited responses through a formal submission process and included the following question: 'to what extent is the rationale for the CGT discount, and the size of the discount, still appropriate?' (Australia. Treasury, 2015, p. 193). Extracts from the submissions that addressed this specific question, together with appropriate analysis, are set out in the remainder of this section.

Some submissions supported the retention of the status quo. For example, the Australian Bankers Association (2015) supported the retention of the 50% CGT discount, but suggested there was a case for like treatment of other forms of savings such as bank deposits. The National Australia Bank submission outlined the organisation's support for the retention of the 50% discount because 'any changes could negatively impact on Australia's attempts to improve productivity' (National Australia Bank, 2015, p. 14).

Other submissions called for a reduction to the rate of the CGT discount. Specifically, the KPMG (2015) submission recommended a reduction of the CGT discount to 25% and that the discount would apply to interest income and unfranked dividend income, as well as capital gains. The Westpac submission noted that a 50% discount for assets held

5 The Labor Opposition retained the policy of reducing the CGT discount from 50% to 25% during the 2019 election campaign. It was not successful in forming government in 2019.

for as little as one year did not strike the right balance between removing the impacts of inflation and 'discouraging speculative "asset flipping" behaviour' (Westpac, 2015, p. 9). The Business Council of Australia (2015) outlined the need for a review of the 50% CGT discount with the aim of achieving more neutral concessional treatment that considers other taxes and income distribution. Similarly, the Deloitte (2015) submission called for a review of the rate of the CGT discount and a consistent approach to the treatment of investment income and capital gains. The Deloitte submission also recommended a phasing-in period of several years for any future reduction to the rate of CGT discount.

Many proponents of taxing capital gains at full marginal rates would prefer a reduction in magnitude of the preference rather than maintaining the status quo in a scenario where these were the only two policy options. It follows that if policy makers had an ultimate objective of restoring CGT at full marginal rates, it does not necessarily follow that enacting a lower rate of CGT discount is an endorsement of the preference for personal capital gains. An analysis of the results of the studies in Chapters 4 and 5 of this book supports the reduction of the magnitude of the CGT discount as an overall tax policy improvement, even if one is of the view that taxation of capital gains at full marginal rates is a better option.

One of the conclusions of Chapter 5 was that the 50% CGT discount is likely to have led to a loss of tax revenue. Reducing the rate of the 50% CGT discount would serve to reduce the magnitude of future losses of CGT revenue. It is also apparent that the CGT discount does not perform well against the traditional tax policy criteria of horizontal and vertical equity, and it causes inefficiency due to the rate difference between ordinary income and capital gains. If the reduction of the 50% CGT discount is considered the most politically feasible option for reform of CGT, it is worthy of consideration. Although there are inherent problems with a rate differential between capital gains and ordinary income, a higher rate of CGT would improve vertical and horizontal equity and increase revenue.

Ultimately, a decrease in the rate of the CGT discount may be an incremental change towards a longer-term policy goal of taxing capital gains at full marginal rates. Tran-Nam, Vu and Andrew (2007) identified that an incremental approach was the most viable option for personal tax reform in Australia. However, incremental changes that are frequent may detract from the perceived stability of the tax system (Tran-Nam et al., 2006).

## 6.4 TAPER RELIEF

Under a taper relief system, there is a lowering of the CGT rate (or the amount of capital gain to be included in assessable income) according to the length of time that an asset is held prior to disposal (Minas, 2011). CGT taper relief operated in the United Kingdom for personal income taxpayers from 1998 until 2008. Australia has never had a taper relief system for CGT.

Minas (2011) noted that the introduction of a taper relief system would allow policy makers to increase the minimum holding period for the asset that is subject to the CGT event before the taxpayer can qualify for the CGT rate preference. Specifically, an increase in the minimum holding period could address concerns about access to the 50% CGT discount after a holding period of slightly more than 12 months being overly generous (Minas, 2011). It may be that in the current regime there is an incentive for some taxpayers to time the realisation of capital gains to be as close as possible to when they qualify for the CGT discount. Notwithstanding the benefits of deferral, such timing may ensure the taxpayer receives the maximum benefit of the CGT discount (Minas, 2011).

There are several disadvantages associated with taper relief. First, taper relief reduces the efficiency of a tax system to the extent that it distorts the capital gains realisation decisions of taxpayers. Second, the fact that a taper relief system typically increases the magnitude of the CGT rate preference according to the time the taxpayer has held the asset is counter to the benefits of deferral (Minas, 2011). Taylor (2008) explained there are opportunity advantages arising from CGT being on a realisation basis that justify an additional compensatory tax for the benefits of deferral. Third, a taper relief system has inherent complexity since there are several different rates that apply to capital gains (Minas, 2011). According to Evans (2002), the former U.K. taper relief system introduced in 1998 was inefficient, caused more tax system distortion and imposed additional compliance burdens.

In summary, taper relief is the least preferred of the options for reforming the taxation of capital gains for personal taxpayers in Australia.

## 6.5 ANNUAL EXEMPT AMOUNT



The remainder of this chapter sets out the case for the removal of the CGT discount and its replacement with an AEA. An AEA is a non-cumulative exempt amount for net capital gains that applies in each year of income. The United Kingdom and South Africa are examples of tax jurisdictions that have used an AEA.[6] The South African CGT regime, introduced in 2001, was based upon the U.K., Canadian and Australian regimes, though arguably with significant improvements in design gleaned from careful analysis of the history of the operation of all three other regimes (Evans et al., 2015).

Evans et al. (2015) noted that the United Kingdom has the most pronounced example of an AEA in operation, with an AEA of £11,100 (approximately A$19,604 at May 2019 conversion rates) in the fiscal year ending on 5 April 2016. South Africa also has an AEA, which is referred to as an annual exclusion. For the year ending 29 February 2016, the AEA in South Africa was set at R30,000 (approximately A$2,856 at May 2019 conversion rates). A distinguishing feature of the AEA in South Africa is that the threshold increases in a taxpayer's year of death; this increased threshold for the year ending 29 February 2016 was R300,000. The United Kingdom taxes the capital gains of personal taxpayers under a separate rate schedule, whereas South Africa taxes capital gains by way of a 25% inclusion rate.

In Australia, there is a disproportionate amount of time and effort spent on ensuring that the relatively large proportion of personal taxpayers with small capital gains amounts pay tax on these gains (Evans, 2003). The inherent complexity in the current CGT system is a characteristic that the proposed AEA would address. The AEA would ensure enhanced

6 Both the United Kingdom and South Africa operated an AEA at the time of writing.

simplicity through the removal of a large proportion of taxpayers from the CGT net. It would also improve vertical and horizontal equity by imposing a per-taxpayer limit on the amount of net capital gains that are eligible for the preference. Specifically, the preference would be limited to the amount of the AEA threshold for each taxpayer.

The proposed AEA is a type of CGT preference, although it is not a traditional CGT rate preference.[7] The AEA is distinct from the CGT discount, which is a rate preference that applies to the net discount capital gains of personal taxpayers. Although the AEA gives effect to a zero tax rate for net capital gains up to the amount of the threshold, all net capital gains over the threshold amount are subject to tax at the taxpayer's marginal tax rate. The important distinction between the two preferences is that the AEA imposes a per-taxpayer limit on the amount of the preference, whereas the CGT discount does not.

The AEA would restore equity to the CGT system, as the preference for capital gains it gives effect to is progressive in its impact. In terms of the percentage by which the AEA reduces the taxpayer's real tax rate on capital gains, it is directed more towards lower-income taxpayers with capital gains,[8] rather than being heavily skewed towards higher-income taxpayers, as is the case with the CGT discount. Essentially, the current Australian regime ensures that the more taxable capital gains a taxpayer has, the higher the proportion of their assessable income that will be taxed at preferential rates. By contrast, the AEA limits the amount of capital gains per taxpayer that can be taxed at a preferential rate.

The proposed AEA would allow personal taxpayers to qualify for a complete exemption from any CGT liability by meeting one of the following two criteria:

1. the net capital gain for the income year is equal to or less than the AEA[9]; or
2. the total capital proceeds from all relevant CGT events for the personal taxpayer in the income year are equal to or less than an amount which is twice the AEA.

The AEA would still operate as a CGT-free threshold for those taxpayers with a net capital gain in excess of the threshold. Its purpose is not only to exempt from CGT those taxpayers who meet one of the above criteria, but also to allow taxpayers with net capital gains above the AEA threshold to apply the AEA to reduce their taxable net capital gain by the amount of the AEA. Like the tax-free threshold for income tax, the AEA is non-cumulative: to the extent that a personal taxpayer is unable to use part or all of the AEA in a given tax year, it is not available to be carried forwards or backwards to other tax years.

If an AEA were to be introduced in Australia, the operation of the capital loss and AEA provisions would be on a similar basis to the equivalent provisions in the United Kingdom. In the first instance, the taxpayer would be required to apply all current year capital losses to their capital gains. If the resultant amount was less than the AEA, the taxpayer would have no CGT liability. If, however, the amount was more than the AEA and the taxpayer had capital losses from previous years, they could apply so much of these

7 Typically, CGT rate preferences are achieved through a separate rate schedule, although the 50% CGT discount is, in effect, a rate preference.

8 Given that lower-income taxpayers typically have smaller amounts of taxable net capital gains.

9 In this chapter, the fiscal implications for two possible AEA thresholds, respectively $10,000 or $1,000, are estimated.

capital losses to their capital gains that would reduce them to the AEA threshold amount. If the capital losses from prior years did not reduce capital gains to an amount within the AEA threshold, the taxpayer would be liable for CGT on the remaining capital gain after applying current and prior year capital losses and the AEA.

The removal of the CGT discount and the introduction of an AEA are designed to enhance the equity, efficiency and simplicity of the regime for taxing personal capital gains in Australia. The main simplicity benefit is the removal of up to 71% of existing personal taxpayers currently exposed to the compliance burden of the CGT regime from their obligations without loss of revenue to the government.

## Estimating the tax revenue impact of the reform

This section estimates the static revenue the government would have forgone in 2013–14 if it had removed the CGT discount and enacted an AEA. It is also concerned with the dynamic revenue effect of removing the CGT discount and takes into account the possible behavioural responses of taxpayers to what would effectively be an increased rate of tax on capital gains. These second-round effects are notoriously difficult to predict (U.S. CBO, 1988),[10] and they depend upon estimates of the capital gains realisations response.

### Estimating the static revenue effect of removing the CGT discount

*Taxation Statistics* contains information on selected items reported in tax returns and CGT schedules by taxpayers, including the amount of the CGT discount applied by taxpayers. In 2013–14, the total amount of the CGT discount applied by taxable individuals was $14.23 billion (Australian Taxation Office, 2016).

6

In estimating the revenue forgone from the CGT discount for individuals in 2013–14, an average tax rate on capital gains is applied to the additional taxable capital gains that would have been taxable in the absence of the discount. According to *Taxation Statistics* (Australian Taxation Office, 2016), the average tax rate on net capital gains in 2013–14 was approximately 33.1%.[11] Using this ATO-reported[12] average tax rate on capital gains for taxable individuals, the static revenue cost from the operation of the CGT discount for personal taxpayers in 2013–14 is estimated to be $4.76 billion.[13]

### Estimating the dynamic revenue effect of removing the CGT discount

An elasticity point estimate of –0.64 at a 36.75% tax rate—from the main equation in Chapter 5—is the basis for the dynamic revenue effect estimates in this section. An elasticity point estimate of –0.64 implies that for every 1% increase in the CGT rate,

10 This is, in part, because the revenue estimates depend on the estimates of realisations response. The uncertainty surrounding capital gains revenue estimates is compounded by the fact that taxpayers have discretion over the timing of their capital gains realisations.

11 *Taxation Statistics*, 'Individuals - selected items, for income years 1978–79 to 2013–14' reports total net capital gains for taxable individuals of $14.38 billion, with tax payable on these capital gains of $4.76 billion. This implies an ATO-calculated tax rate on net capital gains of 33.1%.

12 The rate is described as ATO-reported as its calculation is dependent on the amounts of net capital gains and tax on these capital gains as reported in *Taxation Statistics*.

13 33.1% of $14.38 billion.

capital gains realisations would decrease by 0.64%. The 36.75% tax rate is appropriate for the elasticity point estimate used for the dynamic revenue estimates, as this rate is the midpoint between the top marginal tax rate and half of the top marginal tax rate[14].

The change in revenue from the behavioural response to the abolition of the CGT discount was estimated by multiplying the elasticity estimate of –0.64 by the revenue from discount capital gains in 2013–14 (i.e. $4.76 billion) and multiplying the result by the change in the tax rate over the 2013–14 tax rate (1 in this case[15] ). The result is an estimated 64% decrease in revenue from discount capital gains from $4.76 billion to $1.71 billion.

## Estimating the static revenue effect of introducing the AEA

The introduction of an AEA for all personal taxpayers would clearly impose an annual cost to government revenue. The revenue cost of an AEA set at $10,000, based on *Taxation Statistics* for 2013–14, would be approximately $699,000,000. This calculation is based on the number of personal taxpayers with taxable capital gains of $10,000 or more in 2013–14 (149,994) multiplied by the $10,000 AEA, multiplied by the average tax rate on capital gains in that year (33.1%). For taxpayers with capital gains under $10,000, the amount of capital gains reported in *Taxation Statistics* is multiplied by the average tax rate and this is aggregated with the amount calculated in the previous step.

In the event that the AEA was set at $1,000, the revenue cost based on the same year would be approximately $114,000,000. This calculation is based on the number of individuals with taxable gains of $1,000 or more in 2013–14 (294,792) multiplied by the $1,000 AEA, multiplied by the 33.1% average tax rate on capital gains in that year. For taxpayers with capital gains under $1,000, the amount of capital gains reported in *Taxation Statistics* is multiplied by the average tax rate and this is aggregated with the amount calculated in the previous step.

Table 28 sets out the estimated static revenue cost of introducing an AEA and the percentage of taxpayers that an AEA would remove from the CGT net. The estimate of the proportion of taxpayers who would be removed from the CGT net is derived from data in *Taxation Statistics* 2013–14 (Australian Taxation Office, 2016) on the number of personal taxpayers with net capital gains between certain ranges.[16]

**Table 28: Static revenue cost of introducing an AEA and percentage of taxpayers removed from the CGT net (2013–14)**

| | | |
|---|---|---|
| Annual exempt amount ($) | 10,000 | 1,000 |
| Revenue cost ($billion) | (0.699) | (0.114) |
| Percentage of taxpayers removed from the CGT net | 69% | 39% |

*Notes.* All dollar amounts are in Australian dollars.

14 Half of the top marginal tax rate is the 'tax rate' on discount capital gains before the application of the 50% discount.

15 The change in the tax rate compares the current real tax rate with the real tax rate if the CGT discount were abolished.

16 The ranges of net capital gains used in the ATO data are $1 to $9; $10 to $99; $100 to $999; $1,000 to $9,999; $10,000 to $99,999; $100,000 to $999,999 and $1,000,000 or more.

In addition to the information in Table 28, estimates of the revenue cost and percentage of taxpayers removed from the CGT net for 2010–11, 2011–12 and 2012–13 were prepared to provide assurance that 2013–14 was not an unrepresentative year. These estimates are set out in Table 29.

**Table 29: Static revenue cost of introducing an AEA and percentage of taxpayers removed from the CGT net (2010–11, 2011–12, 2012–13)**

| | 2010–11 | | 2011–12 | | 2012–13 | |
|---|---|---|---|---|---|---|
| AEA ($) | 10,000 | 1,000 | 10,000 | 1,000 | 10,000 | 1,000 |
| Revenue cost ($billion) | (0.637) | (0.109) | (0.496) | (0.081) | (0.578) | (0.093) |
| Percentage of taxpayers removed from the CGT net | 70% | 37% | 68% | 38% | 71% | 43% |

*Notes.* All dollar amounts are in Australian dollars.

The estimates of the revenue effects of introducing an AEA only capture the static effects of this particular policy change. The estimates do not consider the possible behavioural effects of the proposed AEA. For example, there is the possibility that the introduction of the AEA may encourage realisations of capital gains that some personal taxpayers would have chosen not to make in the absence of the provision, effectively unlocking capital gains that would not have been realised under the existing regime. Such a behavioural effect would not be problematic from a simplicity perspective, since a taxpayer realising capital gains up to the AEA would not incur a CGT liability. Another possible effect of the AEA is that some taxpayers may choose to realise capital gains of an amount that is in excess of the AEA threshold, given that their overall CGT rate would be lower than in the absence of an AEA. Moreover, if a taxpayer who would otherwise not have realised any capital gains decides to realise an amount of capital gains up to the AEA threshold, the government will not have lost any CGT revenue in comparison to 2013–14, the latest benchmark year (Evans et al., 2015).

Although data limitations constrain the ability to estimate the dynamic revenue effects of introducing an AEA,[17] it is unlikely that such revenue costs would exceed the net revenue benefits to the government derived as estimated in this chapter. Moreover, when contrasted with the simplicity dividend that can be achieved as a result of being able to take more than two-thirds of existing personal taxpayers out of the CGT regime on an ongoing basis, any such revenue cost of the AEA is likely to 'pale into insignificance' (Evans et al., 2015, p. 758).

The net increase in revenue from static and behavioural responses is set out in Table 30. This conservative estimate, assuming a moderate behavioural response, is an overall revenue gain in 2013–14 of $1.011 billion where the AEA is set at $10,000 and an overall revenue gain of $1.596 billion where the AEA is set at $1,000. This confirms that

17 The fact that there has not been an AEA in Australia and that, consequently, the behavioural response that it may induce is unknown is, in itself, an impediment to estimating the dynamic revenue effects.

replacing the CGT discount with an AEA results in an overall revenue gain. Given that the revenue cost of the AEA is a fraction of that of the CGT discount, the proposed reform is clearly more fiscally sustainable than the current CGT regime (Evans et al., 2015).

**Table 30: Summary of the net revenue effects of the AEA proposal in 2013–14**

| | Annual exempt amount ($) | |
|---|---|---|
| | 10,000 | 1,000 |
| Government revenue benefit of removing the CGT discount ($billion) (static): (1) | 4.76 | 4.76 |
| Government revenue benefit of removing the CGT discount ($billion) (dynamic): (2) | 1.71 | 1.71 |
| Government revenue cost of introducing an AEA ($billion) (static): (3) | (0.699) | (0.114) |
| Net increase in government revenue ($billion) (static): (1) – (3) | 4.061 | 4.646 |
| Net increase in government revenue ($billion) (dynamic estimate of the benefit of removing the CGT discount, less the static estimate of the cost of the AEA introduction): (2) – (3) | 1.011 | 1.596 |

*Notes.* All dollar amounts are in Australian dollars.

In comparing these estimates of forgone revenue from the operation of an AEA with the revenue benefit of abolishing the 50% CGT discount, it is evident that removing the CGT discount and introducing an AEA (whether set at $10,000 or $1,000) would result in a net revenue gain. The CGT discount is an expensive policy measure (from the perspective of the government) compared to the AEA, which has a revenue cost that is a fraction of the revenue cost of the CGT discount. Even if the number of taxpayers who realised capital gains as a result of the AEA increased substantially, the revenue cost would still be substantially less than that of the CGT discount (Evans et al., 2015).

As noted above, it is estimated that the proposed revenue package would contribute between $1.011 billion and $1.596 billion to Treasury coffers, depending upon whether a $10,000 or $1,000 AEA were adopted and assuming there would be a moderate behavioural response in the form of reduced capital gains realisations to the removal of the CGT discount. Clark (2014, p. 51) explained that 'over the thirty years since its inception, CGT has become a significant stream of Australian Government revenue.' Typically, CGT comprises between 2% and 6% of total tax yield (Cooper & Evans, 2014). The additional revenue generated by the proposed reform would provide welcome relief to a government facing revenue deficits and financial constraints.

There are certain limitations to the analysis in this chapter. In particular, it was not possible to furnish definitive estimates of the overall revenue impact of the reform package, partly because the estimates have been prepared using aggregate taxpayer data. Moreover, the analysis does not include an estimate of the dynamic response to the introduction of the AEA, as it requires data on the marginal tax rate on capital gains for a sample of taxpayers in the population. Specifically, in a tax system with an AEA, personal taxpayers will face a different marginal tax rate on capital gains in comparison to their tax rate on ordinary income. There is no information on net capital gains and other assessable income at the individual personal taxpayer level in the aggregate taxpayer data in *Taxation Statistics* (Australian Taxation Office, 2016).

Nevertheless, it can be concluded from the analysis that the revenue outcome for the government would be at least revenue neutral and would far more likely be positive, even when factoring the behavioural responses to the introduction of the AEA into the estimates.

The AEA may constitute a feature of the tax system that influences taxpayer behaviour.[18] There is an argument that, to the extent that this is correct, it can cause inefficiency. However, the abolition of the CGT discount overall would result in increased efficiency, given it would address the distortions that exist in the current tax system because of the discount. The equity arguments in favour of the proposed reform are strong, as are the simplicity outcomes.

The reform proposed in this chapter would enhance equity and efficiency in the tax system, reduce complexity for a majority of affected taxpayers and increase revenue collected. In a 2015 interview, Jane Gravelle characterised tax reform as a change that enhances at least one of efficiency, equity and simplicity, without making the other criteria much worse; she distinguished such tax reform from a mere tax law change (Cummings & Swirski, 2015). The policy proposal in this chapter meets this threshold for being a true tax reform, given the resultant improvements to efficiency, equity and simplicity.



## 6.6 SUMMARY

This chapter has considered a number of reforms to the taxation of capital gains for personal taxpayers in Australia. The taxation of capital gains at the prevailing marginal income tax rates would constitute a significant improvement in the taxation of personal capital gains. If policy makers reinstated the taxation of capital gains at full marginal rates, such a regime would be likely to include the indexation of cost base. Although indexation ensures that inflationary gains are not subject to tax, it is necessarily complex. For example, a taxpayer who expends amounts to be included in the cost base of an asset at several points in time after its acquisition is likely to have a different indexation rate for each of these expenditures. In this case, the compliance costs associated with a CGT regime with indexation may outweigh its benefits for some taxpayers.

If policy makers prefer to retain a preference for capital gains, the preferred policy option—of those presented in this chapter—is to abolish the 50% CGT discount and introduce an AEA. Although the taxation of capital gains at full marginal tax rates may be the ideal, there are political barriers that may impede its reintroduction. One of the main benefits of the AEA is in its pronounced effects on simplicity. An improvement to simplicity will have occurred to the extent that it removes a large proportion of personal

18 For example, some taxpayers may choose to realise capital gains up to the amount of the AEA threshold in each tax year in order to maximise the amount of capital gains that are not subject to tax. However, this type of planning is not available to all taxpayers with capital gains given that the amount of capital gains available for realisation for an individual asset may exceed the AEA threshold.

taxpayers from the CGT net. It is also the case that under the proposed change, net capital gains in excess of the AEA would be subject to tax at full marginal rates. By imposing a per-taxpayer limit on the amount of net capital gains that receive preferential treatment by way of the AEA, there is less of an incentive for taxpayers to receive income in the form of capital gains.

The possible influence of political barriers on an AEA is worthy of consideration. It may be that if policy makers enact an AEA, some taxpayer groups would argue for regular and/or sizable increases to the AEA threshold. Ultimately, any adjustment to the threshold would be a decision for governments. It would be important to preserve the simplicity benefits of the policy by avoiding any temptation to introduce new CGT preferences in addition to the AEA threshold.

This chapter considered the policy alternatives to the existing CGT 50% discount. Chapter 7 now sets out the conclusions of the book; it also sets out the opportunities for future research and the limitations of the studies in Chapters 4 and 5.

# CHAPTER 7

# Conclusions

## 7.1 SUMMARY AND KEY FINDINGS

This book considered policy issues related to capital gains and CGT preferences and the 50% CGT discount for personal taxpayers in Australia. The debate about how to tax capital gains gives rise to the research question identified in this book: are CGT rate preferences a necessary feature of CGT systems? This question originated from the literature review in Chapter 2. One of the conclusions of the literature review is that much of the tax literature considers a CGT regime without rate preferences a better alternative to the preferential CGT regimes that operate in several countries, including Australia.

This book developed a model for estimating the capital gains realisations response of personal taxpayers in Australia and advanced the knowledge in this area of research by providing estimates of the same.

This book recommends the abolition of the 50% CGT discount and its replacement with a $10,000 non-cumulative AEA, as outlined in Chapter 6. This recommendation is based upon, and informed by, the analysis developed in a series of chapters as follows: First, a literature review focused on capital gains preferences and the capital gains realisations response (as detailed in Chapter 2). Second, a mixed methods approach was adopted for the book (as detailed in Chapter 3). Third, interviews were conducted with CGT experts in Australia, Canada and the United States. The interview data were scrutinised and themes identified on the taxation of capital gains and possible areas for reform of CGT policy (as detailed in Chapter 4). Fourth, the capital gains realisations response was estimated using time series data (as detailed in Chapter 5). Finally, the results of the mixed methods study informed the consideration of a number of options for CGT policy in Australia and the ultimate recommendation of an AEA with the abolition of the 50% CGT discount (as detailed in Chapter 6).

The topic of CGT preferences was analysed by way of the qualitative interview study in Chapter 4. Chapter 5 was concerned with the more specific question of how responsive personal taxpayers are to a reduction in the CGT rate. The results of the qualitative study in Chapter 4 broadly informed the study in Chapter 5. One of the main motivations for the capital gains realisations response study was the lack of research in this area in Australia.

Chapter 4 set out the results of a qualitative interview study with CGT experts. Although the views of the respondents were not unanimous, there were several respondents who were critical of CGT rate preferences and did not agree with the arguments advanced by proponents of preferences. Some of the objections raised to CGT rate preferences included unfairness and inefficiency and the incentive created for characterising income as capital gains. Nevertheless, there was a view that a CGT rate preference may reduce the lock-in effect, especially where individual income tax rates are high. The study also highlighted the importance of political considerations in CGT policy, with most of the interviewees agreeing that such considerations were at least part of the reason for the retention of CGT rate preferences.

The quantitative study in Chapter 5 confirmed an inverse relationship between the CGT rate and capital gains realisations. However, the estimates implied that the importance of the CGT rate in taxpayers' realisation decisions was moderate. More specifically, the elasticity point estimates from the main equation are –0.59 at a 33.9% tax rate and –0.64 at a 36.75% tax rate. These estimates imply that any additional realisations induced by a lower tax rate are of an insufficient magnitude to compensate for the static revenue loss from the tax rate cut. The main estimating equation also indicated there was a strong correlation between GDP and capital gains realisations. This may imply that economic conditions are a better predictor of capital gains realisations than the tax rate.

Chapter 6 considered a number of policy approaches to the taxation of capital gains and recommended the abolition of the CGT discount and the introduction of a non-cumulative AEA for capital gains. This recommendation would see the retention of a preference for capital gains, but one of a significantly lower revenue cost than the current 50% CGT discount. Critically, this proposal would dramatically simplify CGT by removing up to 70% of personal taxpayers from the CGT net at little revenue cost. It would also improve equity in relation to the taxation of capital gains given that the AEA amount would be the same for all taxpayers, rather than the current preference, which increases in magnitude according to the amount of capital gains that are realised.

An alternative to the AEA proposal, which would still constitute an improvement to the current taxation of capital gains, would be to decrease the magnitude of the CGT discount. Although this would constitute the retention of a rate preference and not produce the simplification dividend afforded by the AEA proposal, it would nonetheless reduce vertical and horizontal inequity and might also reduce the magnitude of the inefficiency caused by the different tax rates applying to capital gains and other forms of assessable income.

## 7.2 CONTRIBUTION

This book has contributed to the body of knowledge on CGT rate preferences and the capital gains realisations response for personal taxpayers in Australia. It is the first known book to estimate the capital gains realisations response for Australian personal taxpayers. The study in Chapter 5, and the elasticity point estimates reported, provide useful information—which may be of interest to policy makers—on the revenue implications of a past CGT rate change. These estimates, although not predictive, can inform future decisions on the CGT rate.

A second major contribution of this book is that it has added to the literature on CGT rate preferences and the capital gains realisations response. The qualitative and quantitative studies in Chapter 4 and 5 respectively, as well as the critique of various CGT policy options in Chapter 6, are part of this contribution.

A third contribution of this book is that it used a mixed methods approach to examine CGT preferences and, more specifically, the 50% CGT discount for personal taxpayers in Australia. This book made an original contribution to the tax literature in combining a qualitative interview study and an empirical study on the capital gains realisations response. The choice of methodology and the use of qualitative and quantitative methods for the research enhanced the originality of the contributions to the literature on CGT. Furthermore, this book recognises that revenue considerations are one of several issues in CGT policy. Previous research on the capital gains realisations response has focused on estimating the elasticity of capital gains realisations. Given that the research in this book includes a qualitative study that is not limited in its scope to the capital gains realisations response, it has extended the approach used in some previous studies. This book integrates and combines the two phases of the mixed methods research by using the results of each to make specific CGT policy recommendations in Chapter 6. As outlined in previous chapters, notwithstanding the importance of the revenue effects of CGT rate changes, there are several other issues related to CGT for policy makers to consider.

A further contribution of the work in this book is that it may provide a platform for future research on the important topic of the capital gains realisations response. The anticipated enduring contribution of the book is to provide the empirical foundations for a better-informed policy discussion in Australia on how to improve the current taxation of personal capital gains. Such a discussion, and particularly one that considers the alternatives, is especially important in light of the privileged status of the status quo in taxation law, as detailed in Chapter 2.



## 7.3 LIMITATIONS

As with most research, the qualitative and quantitative studies in this book are subject to several limitations. This section acknowledges and outlines the limitations of each of these studies.

### Qualitative research

Chapter 4 detailed the results of a comprehensive qualitative interview study. The semi-structured in-depth interviews sought to discover the views of CGT experts in Australia, Canada and the United States on the taxation of capital gains. A particular focus of the study was on the rate preferences that are a feature of the three jurisdictions. The interviews provided a rich data set that allowed for analysis and comparison of the views of the experts. The results of the Chapter 4 study were informative to the quantitative study that was the subject of Chapter 5 and to the policy recommendations in Chapter 6. It is acknowledged, however, that there are certain limitations attached to this approach.

First, the required anonymity of the interview population is a limitation of the qualitative study. Although Chapter 4 outlined the process used to identify CGT experts, it may be that readers of the book would prefer to know who the interviewees were. While this point is recognised, each individual interviewee contributed to the study on the understanding that their interview data will always remain anonymous, and it is therefore not possible to identify any of the interview population. Nevertheless, the anonymity requirement does not detract from fundamental outcomes of the qualitative study.

Second, while the interviews sought the views of the experts on how to best reform the CGT system in each country, they did not seek the respondents' views on the best means of achieving these reforms or, more specifically, address whether the suggested reforms were likely to be achievable in practice. Nevertheless, several of the interviewees made specific reference to potential political impediments to their suggested CGT reforms.

Third, a qualification to the research findings in Chapter 4 is that the interviewee sample is unbalanced due to its composition.[1] Specifically, there were no interviews conducted in Australia or Canada with tax economists and no interviews conducted in the United States with experts from academia. In addition, restricting the sample to the three countries may constitute a form of selection bias. There may have been suitably credentialed CGT experts outside of Australia, Canada and the United States. However, the composition of the interviewee sample is not a significant limitation given that the research is qualitative rather than quantitative (Minas & Lim, 2013). Furthermore, according to McKerchar (2010), where interview-based qualitative research is undertaken, statistical conclusions should not be generalised to broader populations, and no attempt at extrapolation has been made in this book.

## Quantitative research

Chapter 5 presented the results of the quantitative research. As described in Chapter 2, there is a considerable volume of literature—predominantly from the United States—reporting the results of econometric studies on the capital gains realisations response. Gravelle (1994) outlined the limitations of estimating realisations response using an econometric approach and highlighted the fact that the specifications used in these studies are essentially a type of reduced form model.

The fact that the quantitative study in Chapter 5 used aggregate taxpayer data is arguably one of its limitations. The literature review in Chapter 2 detailed some of the limitations of time series studies. According to Zodrow (1992), time series may have the problem of being quite sensitive to the choice of sample period.

First, the use of time series data may cause aggregation bias and, according to Auerbach (1988), there may be inference problems associated with the time series properties of aggregate data. Furthermore, the absence of data on individual personal taxpayers means it is not possible to observe timing responses. As explained in the literature review, timing responses are distinct from the permanent capital gains realisations response. Micro data

1 The budgetary constraints influenced the number of interviews that could be conducted and this, in turn, was an influence on the composition of the interview sample.

are required to observe the realisation behaviour of taxpayers whose marginal tax rate changes over time. The timing effect for such taxpayers is their deciding to realise capital gains in tax years when their tax rate is atypically low. This is distinct from the response of taxpayers to the prevailing statutory tax rate.

A second limitation of aggregate taxpayer data is that it does not allow the researcher to estimate the different elasticities that may apply to taxpayers within a sample. By contrast, using a panel of taxpayer data allowed Dowd et al. (2012) to estimate that 75% of taxpayers in their sample always had elasticities that were less than 1.00 in absolute value, whereas the remaining 25% of the sample had elasticities in excess of 1.00 in absolute value.

The third potential limitation of the Chapter 5 study is that the results were limited to OLS estimates. Notwithstanding the use of OLS in previous realisations response studies, according to Zodrow (1992), simultaneity problems are common in capital gains regression equations, irrespective of the data type used. In the event that an equation was known to be simultaneous, some of the literature suggests that OLS estimates are less than ideal.[2] Nevertheless, Jones (1989) found, in his research on the capital gains realisations response, that the OLS estimates were less problematic than the instrumental variables (IV) estimates. This was because of collinearity problems that resulted from the use of IV estimates for tax rates (Jones, 1989).

A fourth limitation of the Chapter 5 study is that it does not attempt to estimate what Zodrow (1995, p. 29) identified as 'important feedback effects on other components of income tax revenues'. These feedback effects include changes in dividend payouts and the incidence of tax avoidance strategies (Zodrow, 1995).[3]

A fifth limitation of the Chapter 5 study is that the sample size is fairly small ($n$ = 27 in most cases). A potential limitation of a small sample size is that it may affect the extent to which the quantitative results are generalisable.

Due to the prevailing tax rates in the years of the time series, the focus of the quantitative study is necessarily limited to one major tax rate change: that effected by the enactment of the 50% CGT discount in the 1999–2000 tax year.[4] This policy setting is quite distinct from that in the United States, where there have been several CGT rate changes. Although there are some advantages of a data set with one significant tax rate change, the ideal setting for estimating the capital gains realisations response is one in which there have been two or more significant tax rate changes. To the extent that this argument is correct, a change to the CGT rate in the future would allow for improved estimates of the capital gains realisations response. However, it is more likely that increasing the number of observations would improve the estimates, whether or not the additional years of data included another tax rate change.

Although there are limitations of econometric studies per se, their results provide useful information for policy makers. Triest (1998) cautioned that it is important not to

2 The equation is simultaneous when the value of the dependent variable affects one or more of the independent variables.

3 Zodrow (1995) noted that there have been mixed results from attempts to estimate the importance of these factors.

4 This is notwithstanding that there were some minor changes in statutory tax rates in several years of the study.

become overly cynical about the limitations of econometric studies, one reason being that estimates from econometric analysis of how taxation affects taxpayer behaviour have led to a more informed debate on tax policy.

Notwithstanding the methodological limitations associated with the quantitative study in Chapter 5, the results are still useful and relevant. The estimates are in the range of credible estimates for an aggregate time series study and the elasticity point estimates are similar to those reported by Dowd et al. (2015) in their recent U.S. study on capital gains realisations response.

The study in Chapter 5 remains an important contribution to the knowledge on the capital gains realisations response, and it paves the way for further research on this overlooked tax policy question in the Australian context. The following section briefly outlines some opportunities for future research.

## 7.4 OPPORTUNITIES FOR FUTURE RESEARCH

First, the study in Chapter 4 offers an original contribution to the literature on the taxation of capital gains given its use of an underutilised methodology for the topic. The study focused on some themes relating to CGT that were relevant to the research questions in this book. There were other themes explored in the interview data that could be utilised in future research. CGT preferences other than rate preferences could be a focus of further research based on the interview data. The main residence exemption in Australia is a prominent example of a CGT preference in this category, and there are similar provisions that ensure the preferential CGT treatment of owner-occupied housing in Canada and the United States (Minas & Lim, 2013).

Second, another possible area for future qualitative research is a larger-scale interview project that seeks the opinions of experts about tax policy more broadly, similar to the work undertaken by Professor Joel Slemrod in the United States (Slemrod, 1995b).

Third, with respect to quantitative research, future studies on capital gains realisations response could extend the time series to include more years of data, as these become available. Increasing the number of observations in a capital gains realisations response study can provide more confidence in the results.

Fourth, another possible opportunity for future quantitative research is a panel data study. This is dependent on the development of a suitable panel data set in Australia. Panel data would allow researchers to track the changes in taxable income for individual personal taxpayers over a number of years. With this information, one could control for realisations in years when a taxpayer's taxable income is unusually low.[5] As noted in Chapter 2, Jacob (2011) found that there was an increased propensity for taxpayers to realise capital gains when their income in a particular year was less than their average income. Panel data would also counter the problem of aggregation bias and provide information on demographic variables that may influence realisations, such as the age of the taxpayer.

5 The rationale for doing so is that such realisations are better explained as a timing response rather than a long-run response to the prevailing CGT rate.

A second-best alternative to a panel data study may be a time series study with an increased number of observations within the constraints of the available time series data. For example, treating taxpayer income brackets as separate observations could increase the number of observations. The results of such a study may provide insight into how the realisations response varies according to taxpayer income. Of particular interest would be the realisations response of taxpayers in the higher income group, as this demographic realises a high proportion of capital gains. A comparison of the estimates from a future study using taxpayer income groups with the estimates from the main equation in Chapter 5 would also be of interest.

Another opportunity for future research in relation to the quantitative study is to undertake a comparative study that estimates the capital gains realisations response in several similar tax jurisdictions that offer preferential CGT rates. The results of a comparative study might provide a better understanding of the capital gains realisations response and provide insight into the role of institutional factors that are specific to particular jurisdictions.

## 7.5 FINAL COMMENTS

The overarching conclusion of the book is that the CGT discount should not persist in its current form. This point was recognised by the last major tax system review in Australia—the Henry Review—and the findings and recommendations of this book will hopefully give policy makers cause to revisit the issue of the CGT discount as an area of tax policy that is in particular need of reform. Importantly, the estimates of the capital gains realisations response are moderate and imply that the CGT discount is likely to have caused a loss of tax revenue. The claim that such rate preferences can increase tax revenue collections is a claim that is—in the context of capital gains realised by Australian personal taxpayers—not substantiated by the evidence.

CGT rate preferences are inequitable. This is the case whether evaluated from the perspective of vertical equity or horizontal equity. CGT rate preferences are a cause of vertical inequity since capital gains accrue to, and are realised by, a disproportionately large number of high-income taxpayers. It follows that there is a skewing of the benefits of the preference towards these taxpayers. Horizontal inequity is a consequence of CGT rate preferences, as taxpayers with the same economic income bear different tax burdens—as a proportion of income—depending on the proportion of their total taxable income that is capital gains. The rate disparity between ordinary income and capital gains also creates inefficiencies, and it compromises the integrity of the tax system as some personal taxpayers seek to re-characterise ordinary income as capital gains, given the incentive to do so created by the lower tax rate on the latter.

If lower tax rates are a priority of policy makers, a better and more equitable way to pursue this goal is to reduce the overall tax rate, rather than create a rate differential between two types of income. Lowering the overall tax rate is more likely to be a viable tax policy option for government when there has been a reduction in the number of tax expenditures, such as the CGT discount. Although Australia operates a global tax system,[6]

6 One in which a tax is applied to a taxpayer's total income, whatever its nature or source.

the CGT discount has contributed to a type of de facto schedular system, where the tax rate is dependent on the type or category of income that the taxpayer is in receipt of. The arguments in favour of a CGT rate preference are not persuasive. Specifically, claims that a rate preference will increase investment in riskier assets or create incentives for entrepreneurship are built on weak empirical foundations. It is clear that a rate preference, such as the CGT discount, creates a bias in favour of old rather than new capital. This is counter to creating incentives for new investment, and there is no compelling policy reason for creating such a bias.

The preferred option for reform is to abolish the CGT discount and introduce an AEA.[7] If policy makers consider a CGT rate preference to be necessary, there is a compelling case to decrease the CGT discount percentage from its current 50%. Minarik (1992) argued that the burden of proof rests with those who advocate CGT rate preferences to demonstrate how they are appropriate. It is difficult to argue that policy makers in Australia have proven the appropriateness of the CGT discount for personal taxpayers. Minas (2011) noted that although there was debate on the effects of a rate preference for capital gains, there was a lack of justification from policy makers on why the 50% CGT discount rate was considered appropriate. The fact that revenue raising was cited by the Ralph Review as a key justification for the policy in 1999–2000 should cause policy makers to revisit the issue of the appropriateness, or otherwise, of the CGT discount. This is especially the case given that the estimates from the empirical study in Chapter 5 indicate that the CGT discount is unlikely to have provided an increase in revenue for the government.

In conclusion, based on the research in this book, there is a tax policy imperative to explore alternative ways of taxing personal capital gains. The taxation of capital gains at the same rate as other forms of assessable income can be characterised as the tax policy ideal, as it would improve vertical and horizontal equity and efficiency and would be likely to lead to an increase in tax revenue. Such an increase in revenue may allow for a reduction in the overall tax rate. The analysis in this book has recognised that, in the short term, policy makers are unlikely to restore the taxation of capital gains at the same rate as ordinary income. Given the political barriers to implementing the policy ideal, the preferred policy option is the abolition of the CGT discount, accompanied by the introduction of an AEA of $10,000.

7 As outlined in Chapter 6.

# REFERENCES

Aberbach, J.D. & Rockman, B.A. (2002). Conducting and coding elite interviews. *PS: Political Science and Politics*, *35*(4), 673–6. https://doi.org/10.1017/s1049096502001142

Auerbach, A.J. (1988). Capital gains taxation in the United States: Realisations, revenue, and rhetoric. *Brookings Papers on Economic Activity*, 595–637. https://doi.org/10.2307/2534537

Auerbach, A.J. (1989). Capital gains taxation and reform. *National Tax Journal*, *42*(3), 391.

Auerbach, A.J. (1991). Retrospective capital gains taxation. *The American Economic Review*, *81*(1), 167–78.

Auerbach, A.J. (1999, 11 November). Testimony. In Senate Finances and Public Administration References Committee, *Inquiry into Business Taxation Reform*. Canberra: Senate Printing Unit.

Auerbach, A.J. & Siegel, J. (2000). Capital-gains realisations of the rich and sophisticated. *The American Economic Review*, *90*(2), 276–82. https://doi.org/10.1257/aer.90.2.276

Auerbach, A.J. (2010). Directions in tax and transfer theory. In Melbourne Institute, *Australia's Future Tax and Transfer Policy Conference*, 65–71. Melbourne, Australia. Retrieved from http://taxreview.treasury.gov.au/content/html/conference/downloads/afts_tax_and_transfer_policy_conference.pdf

Auerbach, A.J. (2012). Reforming capital gains taxation. *Tax Notes*, *135*(11), 1399–400.

Ault, H.J. & Arnold, B.J. (2010). *Comparative Income Taxation – A Structural Analysis* (3rd edn). Alphen aan den Rijn: Kluwer Law International.

Australia. Review of Business Taxation & Ralph, J. (1999). *A Tax System Redesigned: More Certain, Equitable and Durable: Report*. Canberra: Treasury. Retrieved from http://rbt.treasury.gov.au/publications/paper4/

Australia. Senate Finances and Public Administration References Committee. (1999). *Inquiry into Business Taxation Reform*. Canberra: Senate Printing Unit.

Australia. Treasury. (1985). *Reform of the Australian Tax System: Draft White Paper*. Canberra: Australian Government Publishing Service.

Australia. Treasury. (2015). *Re:think: Tax Discussion Paper: Better Tax System, Better Australia*. Canberra, Australia: The Treasury. Retrieved from https://treasury.gov.au/sites/default/files/2019-03/c2015-rethink-dp-TWP_combined-online.pdf

Australia. Treasury (2019). *Tax Benchmarks and Variations Statement*. Retrieved from https://treasury.gov.au/publication/p2019-357183

Australian Bankers Association. (2015). *Response to Federal Government Tax Discussion Paper*. Retrieved from https://treasury.gov.au/consultation/c2015-tax-white-paper-dp

Australian Bureau of Statistics. (2012). *Australian Economic Indicators Jul 2012*. (Cat. no. 1350.0). Retrieved from http://www.abs.gov.au/ausstats/abs@.nsf/mf/1350.0/

Australian Bureau of Statistics. (2016a). *Australian System of National Accounts 2015-16.* (Cat. no. 5206.0). Canberra, Australia: ABS. Retrieved from http://www.abs.gov.au/ausstats/abs@.nsf/mf/5206.0

Australian Bureau of Statistics. (2016b). *Consumer Price Index, Australia, 2015-16.* (Cat. no. 6401.0). Canberra, Australia: ABS. Retrieved from http://www.abs.gov.au/ausstats/abs@.nsf/mf/6401.0

Australian Taxation Office. (1999). *Taxation Statistics 1996-1997.* Canberra: Australian Government Publishing Office. Retrieved from https://www.ato.gov.au/About-ATO/Research-and-statistics/In-detail/Taxation-statistics/

Australian Taxation Office. (2016). *Taxation Statistics 2013-2014.* Retrieved from https://www.ato.gov.au/About-ATO/Research-and-statistics/In-detail/Taxation-statistics/

Auten, G.E. & Clotfelter, C.T. (1982). Permanent versus transitory tax effects and the realisation of capital gains. *The Quarterly Journal of Economics, 97*, 613–32. https://doi.org/10.2307/1885102

Auten, G.E., Burman, L.E., & Randolph, W.C. (1989). Estimation and interpretation of capital gains realization behaviour: Evidence from panel data. *National Tax Journal, 42*, 353–74.

Auten, G.E. & Cordes, J.J. (1991). Policy watch: Cutting capital gains taxes. *The Journal of Economic Perspectives, 5*(1), 181–92. https://doi.org/10.1257/jep.5.1.181

Auten, G.E. (2005). Capital gains taxation. In J.J. Cordes, R.D. Ebel, & J.G. Gravelle (eds), *The Encyclopedia of Taxation & Tax Policy* (2nd edn) (pp. 46–50). Washington, D.C.: The Urban Institute Press.

Avi-Yonah, R.S., Sartori, N., & Marian, O. (2011). *Global Perspectives on Income Taxation Law.* Oxford, England; New York, NY: Oxford University Press.

Avi-Yonah, R.S. & Zelik, D. (2015). Are we trapped by our capital gains? *University of Michigan Public Law Research Paper No. 476.* Retrieved from http://ssrn.com/abstract=2642860

Bartlett, B. (1985). The case for ending the capital gains tax. *Financial Analysts Journal, 41*(3), 23–30. https://doi.org/10.2469/faj.v41.n3.23

Baum, C.F. (2006). *An Introduction to Modern Econometrics Using Stata.* College Station, TX: Stata Press.

Benge, M. (1997). Capital gains and reform of the tax base. In R. Krever & J. Head (eds), *Taxation Towards 2000* (pp. 354–5). Sydney, Australia: Australian Tax Research Foundation.

Bentley, D. (1996). Does a capital gains tax work? The Australian experience eleven years on. *Journal of Malaysian and Comparative Law, 23*, 13–36.

Blum, W. (1957, April). A handy summary of the capital gains arguments. *Taxes – The Tax Magazine*, 247–66.

Bogart, W.T. & Gentry, W.M. (1995). Capital gains taxes and realisations: Evidence from interstate comparisons. *The Review of Economics and Statistics, 77*(2), 267–82. https://doi.org/10.2307/2109864

Bosworth, B. (1984). *Tax Incentives and Economic Growth.* Washington, D.C.: The Brookings Institution.

Bracewell-Milnes, B. (1992). Capital gains tax: Reform through abolition. In B. Bracewell-Milnes (ed.). *A Discredited Tax: The Capital Gains Tax Problem and Its Solution* (pp. 1–14). London: Institute of Economic Affairs.
Bradford, D.F. (1986). *Untangling the Income Tax*, Cambridge, MA: Harvard University Press.
Brannon, G.M. (1986). Tax loopholes as original sin: Lessons from tax history. *Villanova Law Review*, *31*, 1,763–85.
Burman, L.E., Clausing, K.A., & O'Hare, J.F. (1994). Tax reform and realizations of capital gains in 1986. *National Tax Journal*, *47*, 1–18.
Burman, L.E. & Randolph, W.C. (1994). Measuring permanent responses to capital-gains tax changes in panel data. *American Economic Review*, *84*, 794–809.
Burman, L.E. (1999). *The Labyrinth of Capital Gains Tax Policy: A Guide for the Perplexed.* Washington, D.C.: The Brookings Institution Press.
Burman, L.E. & Plesko, G.A. (2002). Individual and corporate capital gains are highly correlated. *Tax Notes*, *28 October*, 553.
Burman, L.E. (2009). Taxing capital gains in Australia: Assessment and recommendations. In C. Evans & R. Krever (eds), *Australian Business Tax Reform in Retrospect and Prospect* (pp. 124–5). Sydney, Australia: Thomson Reuters (Professional) Australia Limited.
Business Council of Australia. (2015). *The Future of Tax: Tax White Paper Initial Submission.* Retrieved from https://www.bca.com.au/initial-submission-to-the-australias-future-tax-system-review
Canada & Carter, K. (1966). *Report of the Royal Commission of Taxation.* Ottawa, Canada: Queen's Printer.
Canada Revenue Agency. (2017). *Canadian Income Tax Rates for Individuals – Current and Previous Years.* Retrieved from http://www.cra-arc.gc.ca/tx/ndvdls/fq/txrts-eng.html
Chamley, C. (1986). Optimal taxation of capital income in general equilibrium with infinite lives. *Econometrica, 54*(3), 607–22. https://doi.org/10.2307/1911310
Clark, J. (2014). Capital gains tax: Historical trends and forecasting frameworks. *Australian Treasury Economic Roundup, 2*, 35–51. Retrieved from https://treasury.gov.au/publication/economic-roundup-issue-2-2014
Clark, S.W. & Organisation for Economic Co-operation and Development. (2006). *Taxation of Capital Gains of Individuals: Policy Considerations and Approaches.* Paris, France: Organisation for Economic Co-operation and Development. https://doi.org/10.1787/9789264029507-en
Clarke, K.A. (2005). The phantom menace: Omitted variable bias in econometric research. *Conflict Management and Peace Science, 22*, 341–52. https://doi.org/10.1080/07388940500339183
Commonwealth of Australia. Senate. (1999). *Parliamentary Debates (Official Hansard).* Retrieved from http://www.aph.gov.au/binaries/hansard/senate/dailys/ds291199.pdf
Commonwealth Taxation Review Committee & Asprey, K. (1975). *Full Report, 31 January 1975.* Canberra: Australian Government Publishing Service. Retrieved from http://adc.library.usyd.edu.au/view?docId=law/xml-main-texts/p00087.xml;database=;collection=;brand=ozfed;

Constantinides, G.M. (1983). Capital market equilibrium with personal tax. *Econometrica, 51*, 611–36. https://doi.org/10.2307/1912150

Cook, E.W. & O'Hare, J.F. (1987). Issues relating to the taxation of capital gains. *National Tax Journal, 40(3)*, 473–88.

Cooper, G. & Evans, C. (2014). *The CGT Handbook.* Sydney, Australia: Thomson Reuters.

Cordes, J.J., Klamer, A., & Leonard, T.C. (1993). Academic rhetoric in the policy arena: The case of capital gains taxation. *Eastern Economic Journal, 19*(4), 459–79.

Cresswell, J.W. (2009). *Research Design, Qualitative, Quantitative and Mixed Methods Approaches* (3rd edn). Thousand Oaks, CA: Sage Publications Inc.

Cummings, J.L. Jr. & Swirski, A.J.J. (2015). Dr. Jane G. Gravelle. (Library of Congress Congressional Research Service Senior Specialist in Economic Policy) (Interview). In *News Quarterly, 34*(3), 4–7.

Cunningham, N.B. & Schenk D.H. (1993). The case for a capital gains preference. *Tax Law Review, 48*, 319–80.

Cunningham, N.B. (1996). Taxation of capital income and the choice of tax base. *Tax Law Review, 52*, 17–44.

Deloitte. (2015). *Submission to the Tax White Paper Task Force.* Retrieved from https://www2.deloitte.com/content/dam/Deloitte/au/Documents/tax/deloitte-au-tax-submission-for-tax-discussion-white-paper-190615.pdf

Dowd, T., McClelland, R., & Muthitacharoen, A. (2012). Heterogeneity in the tax responses of personal capital gains realizations. *National Tax Journal, 65*(4), 827–40. http://dx.doi.org/10.17310/ntj.2012.4.05

Dowd, T., McClelland R., & Muthitacharoen, A. (2015). New evidence on the tax elasticity of capital gains. *National Tax Journal, 68*(3), 511–44. http://dx.doi.org/10.17310/ntj.2015.3.02

Edmonds, R. (2015). Structural tax reform: What should be brought to the table? *Australian Tax Forum, 30*(1), 393–409.

Eichner, M. & Sinai T. (2000). Capital gains tax realizations and tax rates: New evidence from time series. *National Tax Journal, 53*(3), 663–82. http://dx.doi.org/10.17310/ntj.2000.3S.03

Eilbott, P. (1985). The revenue effects of a lower capital gains tax. *National Tax Journal, 38*(4), 553–9.

Evans, C. (1998). The Australian capital gains tax: Rationale, review and reform. *Australian Tax Forum, 14*(3), 287–323.

Evans, C. (2000). Curing Affluenza?: A critique of recent changes to the taxation of capital gains in Australia. *University of New South Wales Law Journal, 23*(2), 299–308.

Evans, C. (2002). Taxing capital gains: One step forwards or two steps back? *Journal of Australian Taxation, 5*(1), 114–35.

Evans, C. (2003). *Taxing Personal Capital Gains: Operating Cost Implications.* Sydney, Australia: Australian Tax Research Foundation.

Evans, C., Minas, J., & Lim, Y. (2015). Taxing personal capital gains in Australia: An alternative way forward. *Australian Tax Forum, 30*(4), 735–61.

Fane, G. & Richardson, M. (2005). Negative gearing and the taxation of capital gains in Australia. *The Economic Record, 81*(254), 249–61. https://dx.doi.org/10.1111/j.1475-4932.2005.00259.x

Feldstein, M. (1976). On the theory of tax reform. *Journal of Public Economics, 86*, 77–104. http://dx.doi.org/10.1016/0047-2727(76)90042-6

Feldstein, M. & Yitzhaki, S. (1978). The effects of the capital gains tax on the selling and switching of common stock. *Journal of Public Economics, 9*(1), 17–36. https://doi.org/10.1016/0047-2727(78)90024-5

Feldstein, M., Slemrod, J.B., & Yitzhaki, S. (1980). The effects of taxation on the selling of corporate stock and the realization of capital gains. *Quarterly Journal of Economics, 94*(4), 777–91. https://doi.org/10.2307/1885668

Feldstein, M., Slemrod, J.B., & Yitzhaki, S. (1984). The effects of taxation on the selling of corporate stock and the realization of capital gains: Reply. *Quarterly Journal of Economics, 99*(1), 111–20. https://doi.org/10.2307/1885723

Freebairn, J.W. (2005). Income tax reform: Base broadening to fund lower rates. In P. Dawkins & M. Stutchberry (eds), *Sustaining Prosperity*. Melbourne, Australia: Melbourne University Press.

Gillingham, R., Greenlees, J.S., & Zieschang, K.D. (1989). *New Estimates of Capital Gains Realisation Behaviour: Evidence from Pooled Cross-section Data*, U.S. Department of Treasury, OTA Paper 66.

Gillingham, R. & Greenlees, J.S. (1992). The effect of marginal tax rates on capital gains revenue: Another look at the evidence. *National Tax Journal, 45*(2), 167–77.

Graetz, M.J. (1977). Legal transitions: The case of retroactivity in income tax revision. *University of Pennsylvania Law Review, 126*(1), 47–87. https://doi.org/10.2307/3311758

Gravelle, J.G. (1990). Can a capital gains tax cut pay for itself? *Tax Notes*, July 9, 209–91.

Gravelle, J.G. (1991). Limits to capital gains feedback effects. *CRS Report for Congress*, 15 March, 91–250. Washington, D.C. (Reprinted in *Tax Notes*, 22 April, 363–71).

Gravelle, J.G. (1994). *The Economic Effects of Taxing Capital Income*. Cambridge, MA; London, England: The MIT Press.

Gravelle, J.G. (1995). Prepared statement of Jane G. Gravelle to the *Tax Treatment on Capital Gains Hearing before the Committee on Finance, United States Senate, One Hundred Fourth Congress, First Session*. 15 February 1995. Washington, D.C.: U.S. Government Printing Office.

Gravelle, J.G. (1999, 11 November). Testimony. In Senate Finances and Public Administration References Committee, *Inquiry into Business Taxation Reform*. Canberra, Australia: Senate Printing Unit.

Gravelle, J.G. (2010). Capital gains tax options: Behavioral responses and revenues, *CRS Report for Congress*, 1–18. 10 August. Washington, D.C.

Greene, J.C., Caracelli, V.J., & Graham, W.F. (1989). Toward a conceptual framework for mixed-method evaluation designs. *Educational Evaluation and Policy Analysis, 11*(3), 255–74. https://doi.org/10.2307/1163620

Grindsted, A. (2005). Interactive resources used in semi-structured research interviewing. *Journal of Pragmatics, 37*(7), 1,015–35. https://doi.org/10.1016/j.pragma.2005.02.011

Grote, M. & Fletcher, K. (2000). Capital gains tax in South Africa. *South African Journal of Economics*, *68*(4), 343–7. https://doi.org/10.1111/j.1813-6982.2000.tb01277.x

Grubel, H. (2000). *Unlocking Canadian Capital: The Case for Capital Gains Tax Reform.* Vancouver, Canada: Fraser Institute.

Gujarati, D.N. (2003). *Basic Econometrics.* Boston, MA: McGraw-Hill Inc.

Halperin, D. (1993). Commentary: A capital gains preference is not EVEN a second-best solution. *Tax Law Review*, *48*, 381–91.

Head, J. (1987). Capital gains tax and capital income taxation. *Australian Tax Forum*, *4*(1), 35–62.

Henry, K.R. & Australia. (2010). Treasury and Australia's future tax system review panel. *Australia's Future Tax System: Final Report.* Canberra, Australia: The Treasury. Retrieved from https://taxreview.treasury.gov.au/content/Content.aspx?doc=html/pubs_reports.htm

Hesse-Biber, S.N. & Leavy, P. (2011). *The Practice of Qualitative Research* (2nd edn). Thousand Oaks, CA: Sage Publications Inc.

Holt, C.C. & Shelton, J.P. (1962). The lock-in effect of the capital gains tax. *National Tax Journal*, *15*(4), 337–52.

Hungerford, T.L. (2010). The economic effects of capital gains taxation. *CRS Report for Congress*. Washington, D.C.

*Income Tax Act*, RSC 1985, c. 1 (5th Supp.) (Canada). Retrieved from http://laws-lois.justice.gc.ca/eng/acts/I-3.3/

*Income Tax Assessment Act 1936* (Cth). Retrieved from https://www.legislation.gov.au/Details/C2019C00228

*Income Tax Assessment Act 1997* (Cth). Retrieved from https://www.legislation.gov.au/Details/C2017C00136

*Income Tax Assessment Amendment (Capital Gains) Bill 1986* (Cth). Retrieved from https://www.aph.gov.au/binaries/library/pubs/bd/1986/1986bd127.pdf

Ingles, D. (2015). *Should Capital Income Be Taxed? And If So, How?* (TTPI-Working Paper 4/2015). Canberra, Australia: Tax and Transfer Policy Institute, Australian National University. Retrieved from https://taxpolicy.crawford.anu.edu.au/publication/ttpi-working-papers/7564/should-capital-income-be-taxed-and-if-so-how

Institute for Fiscal Studies (Great Britain). (1995). *Budget Briefing: The IFS 'Green Budget'.* London, England: The Institute for Fiscal Studies.

*Internal Revenue Code* (United States). Retrieved from https://www.law.cornell.edu/uscode/text/26

Ivankova, N.V., Creswell, J.W., & Stick, S.L. (2006). Using mixed-methods sequential explanatory design: From theory to practice. *Field Methods*, *18*(1), 3–20. https://doi.org/10.1177/1525822x05282260

Jacob, M. (2011). *Tax Regimes and Capital Gains Realisations* (Working Paper 2011:9). Uppsala, Sweden: Uppsala Center for Fiscal Studies.

Johnson, C.H. (2008). Taxing the consumption of capital gains. *Virginia Tax Review*, *28*(3), 477–529.

Johnson, R.B. & Onwuegbuzie, A.J. (2004). Mixed methods research: A research paradigm whose time has come. *Educational Researcher*, *33*(7), 14–26. https://doi.org/10.3102/0013189x033007014

Jones, J. (1989). An analysis of aggregate time series capital gains equations. *OTA Paper 65*, Washington, D.C.: Office of Tax Analysis.

Judd, K.L. (1985). Redistributive taxation in a simple perfect foresight model. *Journal of Public Economics, 28*(1), 59–83. https://doi.org/10.1016/0047-2727(85)90020-9

Keany, F. (2016, 13 February). Labor leader Bill Shorten to announce capital gains tax, negative gearing election strategy. *ABC News*. Retrieved from http://www.abc.net.au/news/2016-02-13/bill-shorten-negative-gearing-capital-gains-tax-plans/7165462

Kenny, P.L. (2005). Australia's capital gains tax discount: More certain, equitable and durable? *Journal of the Australasian Tax Teachers Association, 1*(2), 38–109.

Kesselman, J. (2005). Capital gains taxation: Augmenting the advisory panel's reform report. *Tax Notes, December 26*, 1,687–90.

KPMG. (2015). Response to Federal Government tax discussion paper. Retrieved from https://treasury.gov.au/consultation/c2015-tax-white-paper-dp

Krever, R. & Brooks, N. (1990). *A Capital Gains Tax for New Zealand*. Wellington, New Zealand: Victoria University Press for the Institute of Policy Studies.

Leech, B. (2002). Asking questions: Techniques for semistructured interviews. *PS: Political Science and Politics, 35*(4), 665–8. https://doi.org/10.1017/S1049096502001129

Liamputtong P. & Ezzy, D. (2005). *Qualitative Research Methods* (2nd edn). Melbourne, Australia: Oxford University Press.

Lindsey, L. (1987a). Capital gains taxes under the Tax Reform Act of 1986: Revenue estimates under various assumptions. *National Tax Journal, 40*(3), 489–504.

Lindsey, L. (1987b). Rates, realisations and revenues of capital gains. In M. Feldstein (ed.), *Taxes and Capital Formation*, (pp. 17–26). Chicago, IL: University of Chicago Press.

Lochan, F. (2002). Should inflation be a factor in computing taxable capital gains in Canada? *Canadian Tax Journal, 50*(5), 1,833–67.

McCarten, W. (1988). *Capital Gains Realizations and Personal Income Taxation in Canada*. (Doctoral dissertation, Duke University, Durham, NC).

McKerchar, M. (2010). *Design and Conduct of Research in Tax Law and Accounting*. Sydney, Australia: Thomson Reuters.

Mcnaughton, A. (2014). Current tax reading [Peer commentary on the paper "Taxing capital gains – views from Australia, Canada and the United States" by J. Minas & Y. Lim]. *Canadian Tax Journal, 62*(3), 924.

Maddala, G. (2001). *Introduction to Econometrics* (3rd edn). Chichester, NY: John Wiley.

Mariger, R. (1995). Taxes, capital gains realisations and revenues: A critical review and some new results. *National Tax Journal, 48*(3), 447–62.

Mather, J. (2017, 9 March). Chris Cuffe says CGT discount is 'no longer appropriate'. *The Australian Financial Review*. Retrieved from http://www.afr.com/news/policy/tax/chris-cuffe-says-cgt-discount-is-no-longer-appropriate-20170309-guujoq

Mayhall, V. (1980–81). Capital gains taxation – the first one hundred years. *Louisiana Law Review, 41*(1), 81–100. Retrieved from http://digitalcommons.law.lsu.edu/cgi/viewcontent.cgi?article=4530&context=lalrev

Mehrota, A.K. & Ott, J.C. (2016). The curious beginnings of the capital gains tax preference. *Fordham Law Review, 84*(6), 2,517–36.

Miller, M.H. & Scholes, M.S. (1978). Dividends and taxes. *Journal of Finance, 6*, 333–64. https://doi.org/10.1016/0304-405x(78)90009-0

Minarik, J.J. (1984). The effects of taxation on the selling of corporate stock and the realization of capital gains: Comment. *The Quarterly Journal of Economics*, *99*, 93–110. https://doi.org/10.2307/1885722

Minarik, J.J. (1992). Capital gains taxation, growth, and fairness. *Contemporary Policy Issues*, *10*, 16–25. https://doi.org/10.1111/j.1465-7287.1992.tb00232.x

Minas, J. (2011). Taxing personal capital gains in Australia – is the discount ready for reform? *Journal of the Australasian Tax Teachers Association*, *6*(1), 59–67. Retrieved from http://classic.austlii.edu.au/au/journals/JlATaxTA/2011/5.html

Minas, J. & Lim, Y. (2013). Taxing capital gains – views from Australia, Canada and the United States. *e-Journal of Tax Research*, *11*(2), 191–215. Retrieved from http://www.austlii.edu.au/au/journals/eJTR/2013/11.pdf

Minas, J. (2014). Data choice in capital gains realisation response studies – a review. *Journal of the Australasian Tax Teachers Association*, *9*(1), 157–79. Retrieved from http://classic.austlii.edu.au/au/journals/JlATaxTA/2014/9.html

Minas, J., Lim, Y., & Evans, C. (2018). The impact of tax rate changes on capital gains realisations: Evidence from Australia. *Australian Tax Forum*, *33*(4), 635–66.

Minichiello, V., Aroni, R., & Hays, T. (2008). *In Depth Interviewing: Principles, Techniques, Analysis* (3rd edn). Sydney, Australia: Pearson Education.

Morgan, D. (2014). *Integrating Qualitative & Quantitative Methods: A Pragmatic Approach.* Thousand Oak, CA: Sage Publications Inc.

Murphy, K. & Hutchens, G. (2017, 16 February). Malcolm Turnbull rules out changes to capital gains tax or negative gearing. *The Guardian.* Retrieved from https://www.theguardian.com/australia-news/2017/feb/16/malcolm-turnbull-rules-out-changes-to-capital-gains-tax-or-negative-gearing

Murray, D. (2014). *Financial System Enquiry: Final Report.* Parkes, Australia: The Treasury. Retrieved from http://fsi.gov.au/publications/final-report/

Musgrave, R.A. (1968). The Carter Commission report. *The Canadian Journal of Economics*, *1*(1), 159–82. https://doi.org/10.2307/133829

National Australia Bank. (2015). *Response to Federal Government Tax Discussion Paper.* Retrieved from https://treasury.gov.au/consultation/c2015-tax-white-paper-dp

Patton, M. (2002). *Qualitative Research and Evaluation Methods* (3rd edn). Thousand Oaks, CA: Sage Publications Inc.

Pechman, J.A. (1987). Tax reform: Theory and practice. *The Journal of Economic Perspectives*, *1*(1), 11–28. https://doi.org/10.1257/jep.1.1.11

Pederick, W. (1984). Fair and square taxation for Australia. *Taxation in Australia, 19(6),* 575–81.

Plesko, G.A. (2002). *Omitted Variable Bias in Time Series Estimates of Capital Gains Realisations.* https://doi.org/10.2139/ssrn.356780

Poterba, J.M. (1989). Capital gains tax policy towards entrepreneurship. *National Tax Journal*, *42*(3), 375–89.

*Revenue Act 1978* (United States).

Reynolds, A. (1999, July). *Capital Gains Tax: Analysis of Reform Options for Australia.* A study commissioned by the Australian Stock Exchange Ltd for the Review of Business Taxation.

Richardson, G. (2006). Determinants of tax evasion: A cross-country investigation. *Journal of International Accounting, Auditing and Taxation, 15*(2), 150–69. http://dx.doi.org/10.1016/j.intaccaudtax.2006.08.005

Sandford, C. & Evans, C. (1999). Capital gains tax – the unprincipled tax. *British Tax Review, 5*, 387–405.

Sandford, C. (2000). *Why Tax Systems Differ: A Comparative Study of the Political Economy of Taxation.* Bath, England: Fiscal Publications.

Saunders, M., Lewis, P., & Thornhill, A. (2003). *Research Methods for Business Students* (3rd edn). Harlow, England: Financial Times Prentice Hall, an imprint of Pearson Education.

Schenk, D.H. (2004). A positive account of the realization rule. *Tax Law Review, 57*(3), 355–96.

Seltzer, L. (1951). *The Nature and Tax Treatment of Capital Gains and Losses.* New York, NY: National Bureau of Economic Research.

Shaviro, D.N. (1993). Commentary: Uneasiness and capital gains. *Tax Law Review, 48*, 393–418.

Shobe, W.M. (1991). *The Effects of Taxation on Capital Gains Realisations: Theory and Evidence.* (Doctoral dissertation, University of Minnesota).

Shumway, R.H. & Stoffer, D.S. (2011). *Time Series Analysis and Its Applications.* New York, NY: Springer-Verlag.

Simons, H. (1938). *Personal Income Taxation: The Definition of Income as a Problem of Fiscal Policy.* Chicago, IL: University of Chicago.

Slemrod, J.B. & Shobe, W.M. (1990). The use of panel data in the analysis of the behavioral response to taxation. In J. K. Brunner & H. G. Peterson (eds), *Simulation Models in Tax and Transfer Policy: Proceeding of an International Symposium.* (pp. 447–60). Frankfurt, Germany.

Slemrod, J.B. (1992). Do taxes matter? Lessons from the 1980's. *The American Economic Review, 82*(2), 250–6.

Slemrod, J.B. (1995a). Income creation or income shifting, behavioural responses to the Tax Reform Act of 1986. *The American Economic Review, 85*(2), 175–80.

Slemrod, J.B. (1995b). Professional opinions about tax policy: 1994 and 1934. *National Tax Journal, 48*(1), 121–47.

Slemrod, J.B. (2003). The truth about taxes and economic growth. *Challenge, 46*(1), 5–14.

Slemrod, J.B. & Bakija, J. (2008). *Taxing Ourselves* (4th edn). Cambridge, MA; London, England: The MIT Press.

Stiglitz, J. (1969). The effects of income, wealth, and capital gains taxation on risk-taking. *The Quarterly Journal of Economics, 83*(2), 263–83. https://doi.org/10.2307/1883083

Stiglitz, J. (1983). Some aspects of the taxation of capital gains. *Journal of Public Economics, 21*(2), 257–94. https://doi.org/10.3386/w1094

Swan, W. & Rudd, K. (2010, 2 May). *Stronger, Fairer, Simpler: A Tax Plan for Our Future* [Press release]. Retrieved from https://parlinfo.aph.gov.au/parlInfo/search/display/display.w3p;query=Id%3A%22media%2Fpressrel%2FKSQW6%22

Taylor, C.J. (2008). CGT reform and the reduction of tax law complexity. *Australian Tax Forum, 23*, 427–56.

Taylor, L. (2016, 13 February). Labor promises to cut negative gearing and capital gains tax concessions. *The Guardian*. Retrieved from https://www.theguardian.com/australia-news/2016/feb/13/labor-promises-to-cut-negative-gearing-and-capital-gains-tax-concessions

Thomas, R. M. (2003). *Blending Qualitative & Quantitative Research Methods in Theses and Dissertations*. Thousand Oaks, CA: Corwin Press Inc.

Tran-Nam, B., Addison, G., Andrew, B., Drum, P., & Evans, C. (2006). Personal income tax in Australia: The way forward. *Australian Tax Forum, 21,* 441–64.

Tran-Nam, B., Vu, L., & Andrew, B. (2007). Personal income tax in Australia: A specific proposal. *Economic Analysis and Policy, 37*(2), 163–83.

Triest, R. (1998). Econometric issues in estimating the behavioral response to taxation: A nontechnical introduction. *National Tax Journal, 51*(4), 761–72.

U.S. Congress. Joint Committee on Taxation. (1990). *Explanation of Methodology Used to Estimate Proposals Affecting the Taxation of Income from Capital Gains.* Washington, D.C.: U.S. Government Printing Office.

U.S. Congressional Budget Office. (1988). *How Capital Gains Tax Rates Affect Revenues: The Historical Evidence.* Washington, D.C.

U.S. Congressional Budget Office. (1990). *The Effects of Lower Capital Gains Taxes on Economic Growth.* Washington, D.C.

U.S. Congressional Budget Office. (1997). *Perspectives on the Ownership of Capital Assets and the Realization of Capital Gains.* Washington, D.C. Retrieved from https://www.cbo.gov/publication/10597

U.S. Department of Treasury, Office of the Secretary of the Treasury, Office of Tax Analysis. (September 1985). *Report to Congress on Capital Gains Tax Reductions of 1978.* Washington, D.C.

U.S. Department of Treasury, Office of the Secretary of the Treasury, Office of Tax Analysis. (May 2016). *Taxes Paid on Long-term Capital Gains 1977–2014.* Washington, D.C. Retrieved from https://www.treasury.gov/resource-center/tax-policy/tax-analysis/Documents/Taxes-Paid-on-Long-Term-Capital-Gains.pdf

Westpac. (2015). *Response to Federal Government Tax Discussion Paper.* Retrieved from https://treasury.gov.au/consultation/c2015-tax-white-paper-dp

White, D.I. (2015). *Personal Capital Gains or Rate of Return Taxation? A Survey of Theory in Reform Proposals* (Working Papers in Public Finance 05/2015). Wellington, New Zealand: Victoria University Wellington.

Wooldridge, J. (2016). *Introductory Econometrics: A Modern Approach* (6th edn). Boston, MA: Cengage Learning.

Zodrow, G.R. (1992). Economic analyses of capital gains taxation: Realisations, revenues, efficiency and equity. *Tax Law Review, 48*(3), 419–527.

Zodrow, G.R. (1995). Economic issues in the taxation of capital gains. *Canadian Public Policy, 21,* Supplement: The Canadian experience of the lifetime capital gains exemption, S27–S57.

# Appendix: Interview Questions Used in the Chapter 4 Qualitative Study

The following is a complete list of interview questions used for the qualitative study in Chapter 4. Funding for the interview study was awarded under the New Appointee Research Grant Scheme (NARGS) at the University of Tasmania. The NARGS project was entitled 'A comparative analysis of the role of exclusions and discounts in the personal taxation of capital gains in common law jurisdictions.' Prior to contacting interviewees and conducting the interviews, ethics approval for the project was granted (University of Tasmania Ethics Reference Number: H0011499).

- What do you consider to be the main benefits and disadvantages of CGT preferences?
- On what basis have previous changes to the taxation of individual capital gains in (Australia/Canada/the United States) been justified by policy makers? In your view, what are the merits or otherwise of these justifications?
- Given the benefits of deferral that apply to capital gains and the ability of the taxpayer to effectively choose when and if they will realise a capital gain, are preferential rates for capital gains considered appropriate?
- Is there an incidence of capital gains tax (effective) rate competition between tax jurisdictions that applies to the taxation of individual taxpayers? If so, is the mobility of capital an appropriate justification for capital gains tax preferences for individuals?
- The literature identifies a theory of 'home bias' which holds that investors in public company shares demonstrate a preference for domestic investment. If home bias does exist, how can it be reconciled with the greater mobility of capital arguments that are used as a justification for individual capital gains tax preferences?
- Is a capital gains tax indexation system that adjusts the 'cost base' or 'basis' of an asset for the effects of inflation preferable to one which offers capital gains tax exclusions or discounts? Can a capital gains tax exemption or discount be considered a suitable substitute for an inflation adjustment?
- How does the preferential treatment of capital gains affect economic efficiency? Is the overall effect on economic efficiency positive or negative?
- There have been a number of empirical studies that have been undertaken on the elasticity of capital gains realisations which have disagreed on the importance of transitory effects and which have given significantly different estimates of elasticity. In your view, does a lower effective rate of capital gains tax induce a higher volume of asset realisations than would be the case if capital gains were taxed at full rates? What level of importance should be ascribed to transitory responses to capital gains tax rate changes?
- How successful do you think CGT rate preferences have been in achieving the economic objectives that they were intended to? For example, can they be considered

to have enhanced capital mobility and encouraged investment in capital that wouldn't have otherwise occurred?

- Does a lower effective rate of capital gains tax lessen the extent of the lock-in effect?
- Does a preferential rate of capital gains tax result in a loss of capital gains tax revenue or an increase in capital gains tax revenue through a higher level of capital gains realisations?
- To your knowledge, is there any evidence of taxpayers re-characterising ordinary income as capital in order to reduce their tax liability? If so, have there been any instances of the revenue authority using specific anti-avoidance provisions to counteract this behaviour? Are there any examples of methods of the avoidance technique of re-characterising ordinary income as capital which revenue authorities have difficulty detecting or counteracting?
- Is the reform of capital gains tax considered to be an issue of any importance amongst taxpayers in (Australia/Canada/the United States)?
- Should taxpayers be allowed full deductibility of capital losses against ordinary income as a way of lessening the lock-in effect? If full deductibility is not considered appropriate, how can a tax system best provide for the offset or deduction of capital losses?
- Should tax jurisdictions consider using an accrual-based capital gains tax system for liquid assets that can be easily valued, whilst retaining a realisation-based capital gains tax for illiquid assets?
- Is an annual capital gains tax-free threshold an appropriate way of reducing the lock-in effect? If such a threshold was introduced would it justify decreasing the level of capital gains tax preferences? What would be an appropriate income level at which to set a CGT-exempt threshold?
- Is comprehensive income an appropriate concept to apply to the taxation of capital gains? If so, how can the tax system, with particular reference to capital gains, be reformed so that it is more in accord with comprehensive income concepts? If not, what is the economic justification for taxing non-labour income or income from capital at preferential rates?
- In a number of tax jurisdictions, taxpayers are able to deduct, in full, the amount of interest on borrowings relating to a capital asset that will be taxed on a deferred basis and only if the gain is realised. Given the opportunities that the taxpayer is presented with here, should they only be allowed to deduct a reduced amount of interest expense as a way of achieving a more symmetrical treatment of taxable gains and deductible expenses?
- Where a CGT preference exists in a tax system, should it be accompanied by a minimum asset holding period in order to qualify for the preference? If so, on what basis is such a minimum holding period justified? What are the economic efficiency arguments for and against a minimum holding period for capital gains assets?

- Is the case for retaining capital gains preferences due mostly to economic efficiency considerations, political considerations or a combination of both?
- Is international competitiveness in relation to attracting capital best achieved through a lower rate of capital gains tax or a lower overall tax rate?
- How do you think that the capital gains tax system in (Australia/Canada/the United States) can best be reformed?